FLAT/WHITE

D1596879

TED BOTHA

FLAT/WHITE

THE **STRANGE CASE** OF A **NEW IMMIGRANT**
IN AN **OLD BUILDING** AND **THINGS GOING BADLY**

TED BOTHA

ABOUT THE AUTHOR

Ted Botha grew up in Pretoria, for the most part. He worked as a journalist in South Africa before travelling through Africa, which resulted in the book *Apartheid In My Rucksack*. His other books, published in the United States, include *Mongo: Adventures In Trash*, *The Girl With The Crooked Nose* and a novel, *The Animal Lover*, a romance set in 1940s West Africa. He lives in New York, where he is an editor at Reuters.

Published by Mercury
an imprint of Burnet Media

•

Burnet Media is the publisher of Mercury and Two Dogs books
info@burnetmedia.co.za   www.burnetmedia.co.za
Facebook: Two Dogs / Mercury Books
Twitter: @TwoDogs_Mercury
PO Box 53557, Kenilworth, 7745, South Africa

•

First published 2014
1 3 5 7 9 8 6 4 2

•

Publication © 2014 Burnet Media
Text and cover illustration © Ted Botha

•

•

Distributed by Jacana Media
www.jacana.co.za

•

Printed and bound by Mega Digital
www.megadigital.co.za

•

ISBN 9780987043771

To the cat in the window, who was always there.

CHAPTER 1
METROPOLIS

I moved to New York from South Africa with no profound reason. To be honest, I felt like a bit of a fraud.

Other South Africans emigrating at the time were making an earth-shattering, life-changing move. They were selling their homes, uprooting their families, packing their bags forever, leaving South Africa never to return because life was too dangerous and violent or because of affirmative action and they couldn't get a job. The most undesirable species on the market was a white adult male. So, lots of families were preparing to adopt a new country, a new nationality, a new life. And the countries of choice were places where they knew the language: Australia, New Zealand, England, Canada or, as a last resort, America. Moving abroad for them wasn't *adieu*, it was goodbye.

My motivation was a lot less exciting. I wasn't really emigrating; I was going to have a look-see. I was a single male freelance journalist without a family or obligations, and I was bored.

The new millennium was approaching. Nelson Mandela was president, apartheid was over, things were changing, and life in South Africa was actually pretty darn good. But I wanted something new, something big, something better. Not for me life on the edge of the world in some forgotten colony, thank you very much.

I had written articles for magazines and newspapers in South Africa and England, and I'd had a book published in South Africa (about the misadventures of trying to travel through Africa during the apartheid years with a surname that was a synonym for bad politics). At this point there was only one market left to tackle for an artist with ambitions: the USA. I would move from what many people regarded as the least desirable metropolis on earth, Johannesburg, to the most desirable, New York. For any writer, nowhere was bigger, better, brighter.

I wanted to work at the best magazines in the world, like *Vanity Fair* and *Esquire*. I wanted to get a book published in the same city as my heroes, authors such as F. Scott Fitzgerald and John Irving. I had read E.B. White's *Here Is New York* a dozen times, and the

image I had etched into my brain was o.
to the city from the cornfields of the Midwest
tucked under his arm and a gleam in his eye.

New York, for many of us, was the pinnacle.

White lie

So it was that I landed in the pinnacle, at John F. Kennedy Airport, in the middle of an almighty blizzard. I had no job, no work papers and virtually no money, only a place to stay. A South African friend let me use her couch – or, as I would come to learn in the constantly overworked and ever-expanding English/ American dictionary that many immigrants carry around in their heads at all times, her *sofa* – indefinitely.

After several months I found a job as a copy editor – or what seemed to be what we called a subeditor in English, more or less – at *Time Out New York*.

I knew about *Time Out New York* from another South African, who I'd met on a visit to the city a few years earlier. She had been friendly with Tony Elliott, the founder of *Time Out* in London, and was doing almost all the legwork to launch the first American edition of the British magazine. By the time I got to New York, she was long gone (as was any overt connection to Britain or anything British), but I used her name to get my foot in the door and then made up a white lie to stay there.

I told the managing editor I had work papers, even though I didn't – at least not yet – but I could possibly get them. Through a twist of fate, I had been born in New York, when my parents were working there, but we had left when I was nine months old. Until now, even though I sometimes joked that I too was an African-American, I had never actually tried to become legal.

"Bring the papers to me later," the managing editor said, a bit carelessly, I thought, before she promptly put me to work.

A few days later, with my stomach firmly in my throat, I went to an office of the Department of Immigration, certain that an alert

,cial would immediately notice something dubious about a man
ί thirty-five suddenly applying for a passport and documentation
that would make him American. But no-one did. I had been born
in the USA, and September 11 was still only a random date that
meant nothing to anyone. Nobody was as vigilant and suspicious
of outsiders as they would soon become.

Within a few months of arriving in New York, I had not only
a passport but a social security number – nine priceless digits that
open doors into a whole new world – and I was commuting on
the subway several times a week to a freelance job at a hip new
magazine. I wasn't earning much – $15 an hour; about R75 at the
time – but I had a bit of money, I was legal, and I had a couch/sofa.

My new immigrant life had begun.

"Now that you've arrived, get out!"

One of the first things I noticed about New York was the
magazines. Other people noticed the huge servings of food, the
outsized cars, the incessant noise, but for me it was the magazines.
In Johannesburg, they always looked a bit sad and in need of
replenishment, spread sparingly across the walls of the news
agency, which here they called a newsagent.

In New York, by contrast, hundreds of titles – possibly thousands
– were piled thick, overlapped one another, clamoured for space,
which they had barely received before they were displaced by
newer editions that were already lying in plastic-wrapped piles on
the floor waiting to be unloosed on the ravenous public.

Time Out New York was a relative newcomer to this ocean of titles,
but a cheeky one, a magazine that clearly wanted to be noticed.

"Now that you've gotten to New York," ran one of its first ads,
exhorting people to explore, "get out!"

Everyone in the office was, like me, from somewhere else, albeit
from somewhere else in America: Idaho, Kentucky, Wisconsin
– states that I for some reason pictured covered in golden wheat
fields and peopled by strong farmers with a suntan. And each

one of them was like those youngsters I had read about in E.B. White: young, bright-eyed and eager to make their mark on the publishing capital of the world.

In those first weeks at the magazine, I would sometimes look up from the copy-editing desk and see fifty or sixty people milling about. The office was a large open-plan area with high-tech lights and desks, although the exposed brick and wood floor reminded you it probably began life as a factory space. The scene was exactly what I had pictured a New York magazine to be like: the old office with just enough modern touches, the people energetic and hungry for success, the smell of coffee on the air. Even the view out of the large windows seemed perfect: old water towers with their hat-like peaks atop buildings and, if you cast your eyes down, cars and taxis coursing nonstop along Broadway.

It might not have been *Vanity Fair* or *Esquire* and I was just a lowly copy editor, but I was now part of the pinnacle.

The Queen's English
The copy-editing desk was located in a far corner of the office, set off to one side, not exactly part of the hurly-burly but close enough to get a whiff of it. There were three or four of us on duty at a time, and our job was to pick up the spelling, punctuation and language mistakes made by the writers. We were essentially the last grammatical buffer zone before going to print.

The focus of *Time Out New York* was all things in the city that were new, fashionable, hot: clubs, clothes, theatre, restaurants, bars, music, books, art, the gay life. Each section ended with page upon page of listings, row upon row of tiny print that was the magazine's lifeblood. Where to go, when, how much it cost to get inside, what week some famous performer was coming to town, which avant-garde movie was playing where, who sold the best daiquiris, the most delicious hot dogs, the most desirable earrings, anything you could think of.

Having grown up in a country where books came in two versions, the British or American kind – and you weren't always paying attention to which one you were reading – some words and spellings were not entirely unfamiliar. Colour was *color*, realise *realize*, no-one (or noone) *no one*, dustbin *trash can*, rubbish *garbage*, and a flat was an *apartment*. Other words caught me off-guard daily: antique store became *antiques store*, chips *fries*, crisps *chips*, single *one-way*, cotton wool *cotton balls*, candy floss *cotton candy*, university *college*, mail *post*, white coffee *coffee with cream*, while a theatre doubled as both a *theater* and a *theatre*.

Like many other South Africans, I had been warned not to call a traffic light a robot, although no-one/no one had warned me of the raised eyebrows and childish titters that would meet you if you used the words pot plant instead of the accepted *potted plant*.

A city, meanwhile, could also be called a town, whereas for me a town was definitely never a city. England and English, meanwhile, were interchangeable with Britain and British. As for gerunds, you didn't double up on letters – so it was *traveling*, never travelling – except in those cases where you could, although it wasn't clear when that rule applied.

Thinking in duplicate, therefore, quickly became habit. Every word had a possible trap. *Obligate*, for instance, sounded wrong, but it wasn't. *Colonial*, which we jokingly called ourselves back home – South Africa being a former colony and all – in America referred not to people at all but to the original thirteen colonies. For the most part, the word seemed to be used in conjunction with buildings and furniture from the colonial period. And *expatriate*, a word that South Africans used unthinkingly, since everyone seemed to know one, was a concept quite unthinkable to everyone around me. Give up your country? Forever? So impossible and traitorous was the idea, in fact, that it often got spelled – a word that I wrote "spelt" before quickly ditching it with many other words I was familiar with – *ex-patriot*.

Idioms and expressions, meanwhile, were a minefield all of their own. *Close but no cigar*? Maybe. *Cut the mustard*? Possibly.

But when *Jump the shark* first appeared, I found myself looking awkwardly around the copy desk for an answer. I tried to limit my questions to the other copy editors, convinced that I was at *Time Out New York* on borrowed time, the only non-American at a magazine where being familiar with hip, up-to-date American expressions was crucial. Ask one question too many about jump-the-shark-type idioms, and the holiday/vacation might be over. So it wasn't unusual, when confronted by a strange expression that could just as easily have been a mistake, that I read it and moved on, assuming it to be a widely accepted turn of phrase. So, right or wrong, jump the shark it would have to be.

One day, though, I carelessly circled a headline that said something about a new clothing designer or chef or club owner *giving it the whole nine yards*. Give something yards? I'd forgotten what a yard was anyway. More than a metre/meter? Less? I tried to figure out what it could mean. I changed the words to metric. Give something nine metres? Did we have a saying anything like that in English? If so, it escaped me for the moment. After several cautious minutes I decided it had to be wrong. Noticing my red mark on the final print-out, the managing editor, who was at least ten years my junior, beckoned me over.

"Giving something the whole nine yards?" she said with a smirk. I felt like the new child at school, just arrived from the bundu/boondocks. "You don't know what that expression means?"

A bit exhausted after five hours of reading minuscule print giving the directions to a club on Delancey Street, a thoroughfare I'd never been to, via subway lines I still hadn't figured out, and correcting the spelling of *steak frites* in a write-up (or was it a writeup?) of a new restaurant I couldn't afford, I felt like telling her off.

"American," I wanted to say, with just the right touch of colonial arrogance, "is actually my third language, after English – and that would be the proper English, the Queen's English, even though we don't really care for the Queen in South Africa, which you might think we do – and Afrikaans, if you know what that is. I even had to relearn yards and feet and pounds and inches for you, having unlearnt/unlearned them in grade school, which we call junior school, when South Africa went metric, a feat we managed to achieve while Americans and even the British/English gave up trying. So, while I am juggling various dictionaries and measuring systems and thesauruses in my head, you have to deal with exactly one of each."

That's what I wanted to say. But I was a new employee, a new citizen with new papers I wasn't entirely confident about, finding my way around a new city, sleeping on a couch everyone else called a sofa, and I didn't want to risk getting fired for insubordination. So nodding at the managing editor – "Ah, of course, the whole nine yards. I get it! What was I thinking?" – I obediently slunk back across to the far end of the office and joined my colleagues at the copy desk.

A geography lesson
The office of *Time Out New York* couldn't have been better situated, smack bang / smack dab as it was at the crossroads of two famous arteries, Broadway and Houston Street. To one side of us lay the West Village, to the other the East Village. Half a block away was SoHo, which stood for South of Houston. In the patchwork of streets around us were the clubs we wrote about and the shops where fabulous new designers showed their wares. Offbeat galleries displayed Andy Warhol-type art made of garbage that people paid thousands of dollars to own.

For any new immigrant who knew little about the city, *Time Out New York* was, it struck me, the perfect place to get a crash course in things and places New York. Not only were all the subjects we wrote about hot, but so was our location. We fell into an area known as Downtown.

Broadly speaking, New York City has three distinctive zones – Downtown, Midtown and Uptown. The only place to be, to be seen, to eat, to shop, to live – at least, it seemed, for people working at the magazine – was Downtown. It wasn't downtown as I had come to know the word, meaning a business district, but downtown as in trendy, hip, cool.

Midtown, meanwhile, was the real downtown, the office zone, with lots of skyscrapers and hotels, where it was about as likely for people to live as they might in the centre/center of Johannesburg and which people evacuated en masse at dusk.

Uptown, the third and final zone, was more vast than the other two and had numerous neighbourhoods. The word "uptown" had also, like downtown, gained its own meaning: older people, families, and one step closer to suburbia, except without the houses and the gardens. Once you'd moved Uptown, you had settled, and the excitement of Downtown publicised weekly by *Time Out New York* was pretty much over for you.

Uptown, too, was exactly where my South African friend's couch and flat were, in an area called the Upper East Side.

Curb your dog

A pleasant area, at least to start out with, the Upper East Side was also very wealthy. It was the kind of wealthy that was described as rarified, written as *rarefied* in these parts, which somehow made it even more so. Movie stars had homes here, and so did diplomats and billionaires. If New York was the pinnacle, the Upper East Side was where many of the pinnacle's pinnacle lived.

The streets were lined with large old trees, the buildings had freshly planted flowers and trimmed hedges surrounding them, and signs just big enough not to be obtrusive urged pet owners to CURB YOUR DOG – a pun that made more sense to Americans, who spelt kerb *curb* – or be fined $200. And, for the most part, people obeyed.

Just one block west of my friend's building was that world-renowned rectangle of green, the 341 hectares / 843 acres of Central Park. A short walk down Fifth Avenue took you to the Guggenheim and the Metropolitan museums. Hidden on side streets you found three- and four-storey/story buildings done in sandstone the colour of a chocolate, which gave the edifices their popular moniker: brownstones. A single brownstone could make up an entire home.

Intersecting the streets were the broader, more renowned avenues – Park, Madison and Fifth. They stretched into other sections of the city, but it was on the Upper East Side that they acquired their sheen and million-dollar value. Apartment buildings rose fifteen floors and were known as prewar and postwar. Which war that was exactly I didn't know – I assumed World War II – although the term seemed to be less to define age than pedigree.

"It's prewar."

"Ah. Nice."

Or this: "You live in a prewar? How lucky you are."

Sharecropper
My South African friend's flat was in a prewar.

It was a small flat, about fifty square metres/meters in all. The non-metric version of that, five hundred square feet, sounded more generous, but it was still small, the smallest flat, in fact, in the entire prewar, which had about sixty flats in all. Hers had been part of a bigger flat that someone had partitioned off long ago and sold, which made my friend something of a sharecropper – or what in Afrikaans is known as a *bywoner*, a modest tenant farmer – someone living there by the charity of a richer neighbour/ neighbor. As for me, I was much further down the chain, living on a *bywoner*'s couch.

My friend called her flat a studio – which meant it had only one room – except she had turned her wide hallway into a sort of second, L-shaped living space. The large room was an amalgam of sorts – living room, TV room, dining room, library and breakfast nook – and it also housed the couch. In one corner was a window seat that you couldn't sit on for long because below it was hidden a radiator that was fired up almost all the time now that it was winter. Within five minutes the seat of your pants would be burning up.

In the L-shaped room next door, my friend had constructed a

captain's bed (a kind of bunk bed with no lower bunk) about two metres above the ground, where she slept, with storage cupboards below. The longer wall she used for an easel where she did her work as an illustrator.

Her kitchen was big enough to accommodate no more than two people standing, neither of whom could move once they were lodged between the stove and the cupboards. My friend cooked a lot, but she told me this was not common in New York. People ordered takeaways/takeout or went out to eat. My friend also regularly had people over to dinner, and they never failed to comment on how unusual an event this was. They were more used to choosing a mutually acceptable restaurant to eat at and then splitting the bill/ check afterwards.

The bathroom in the studio, though cramped, had a spacious shower with a big window overlooking the rooftop of a store that daily emitted the aroma of fresh bagels. Beyond it, directly across Madison Avenue, there was a flat where, my friend told me, you could on occasion see the occupant, a very large lady, walking around without her clothes on.

I never caught a glimpse of the naked woman, and even if I had, it would have taken binoculars to see her with any definition. It was for this reason, I suppose, that some people had binoculars and even telescopes at the ready, often set up quite conspicuously in front of a window. Here you viewed not animals on the veld/veldt or constellations in the sky but neighbours in adjacent buildings. I smiled a little at the whole idea of people-watching binoculars, but I shouldn't have because prying was in my future too, but of a very different kind.

As strange and new as all of this was to me in the beginning – the binoculars, the takeaway meals, the dogs their owners paid someone else to walk, the beds in couches and accepted it all as the manner of my new used to the men standing sentry at our fron

Four men, three uniforms

A big green awning ran from the front door of my friend's building to the edge of the pavement/sidewalk. Under it you could always find one of the four doormen: Frank, Jaroslav, Lazlo and Phil. They worked in shifts, and all of them had been there long enough to have witnessed residents' children grow up, go to school and graduate from university/college.

Much of what I knew about New York before arriving came from movies: Central Park, Times Square and, of course, uniformed, behatted doormen who blew their whistles for yellow taxis/cabs to stop for them.

The doorman's exact purpose, I now saw on a daily basis, was to serve a number of functions: security guard, taxi hailer, butler, policeman, parcel collector, public relations agent, major-domo. They allowed or denied entry to visitors, announced any stranger's arrival to a resident, whistled for a taxi to come fetch you, made pleasant conversation about the weather, held an umbrella for you when it rained, took your bags from you as soon as you approached the front door, walked your dog if you asked them to.

A fifth person who sometimes hung out at the front door was Francisco, the superintendent, who lived in the basement, didn't wear a uniform, and was responsible for looking after the small, everyday problems that might occur in the building, whether it was a broken pipe or a lock that got jammed. Every big residential building had a live-in super, as they called them here, a 24-hour Mr Fixit.

Entering or leaving the building, I always stopped for a few minutes to talk to the doorman on duty, usually Frank, who worked the day shift. He came from Puerto Rico, the others from Krakow and Louisiana. They all lived out in Queens and New Jersey, far away across the Hudson or East rivers, so they had long commutes to get to work and home. Frank, who had saved enough money to buy himself a summer home in Florida, told me that most doormen were either Puerto Rican, like him, or Eastern European. Not too

20

long ago they had been Irish-American, although those men were now in construction. Few doormen, he added, were black.

Our fourth doorman, Phil, was black. He didn't wear a uniform like the other three and he had the worst hours, the midnight-to-dawn shift, when the front door was locked, hardly anyone entered or left the building, and he spent most of the time cleaning the upper floors and sorting out the garbage.

I tried not to read too much into this – no uniform, worst hours, oldest in years, the only black doorman – but something in me, the country that I came from, wouldn't let it go.

The tic

Call it a voice, a tic, a kneejerk reaction, but it turned out to be a totally unexpected and inescapable part of being a new immigrant. You noticed things that other people didn't, not only because they were new and unlike anything you were familiar with, but also because they were more familiar than you could have imagined.

Maybe all immigrants had a tic: the Bangladeshis agog at the roads without potholes; the Chinese perplexed by the taste for body piercings and torn clothing that cost a lot of money; the British sensitive to voices so loud they addressed an entire subway car; the French appalled by the plethora of bad shoes in this Mecca of fashion.

For me, though, it was other things.

I picked up on the barbed wire threaded across the second floor of buildings in certain neighbourhoods to deter intruders. I wondered what made doormen standing in front of buildings any different from the security guards protecting houses in Johannesburg. I homed in on articles in the newspapers – mostly the tabloids like the *Post* and the *Daily News*, rarely the broadsheets like *The New York Times* – about violent crime, shootings, rapes. I noticed too that the bad things often took place in low-income areas like Harlem and the Bronx.

Most of all, though, I fixated on the racial quirks. After realising that Phil was the only black doorman in the building, and a lesser doorman at that, I noticed that there were no black residents in the building either. Nor, for that matter, did there seem to be any in the neighbourhood. People of other races, who invariably seemed to be nannies or labourers making up part of a contracting crew or delivering pizza, left after dark like once upon a time they might have quit a white suburb in Johannesburg. Even at work, which I had at first thought to be my ideal of a New York workplace, I started counting. Out of a staff of sixty there were exactly two people who were not white like me.

Every time the tic occurred I felt like rapping myself over the knuckles. I had brought a South African radar with me that I needed to quickly decommission. I felt stupid, naïve and politically very incorrect. Even as I write this years later, I feel the same way, because I still do it. I don't do it as often and the radar's ping is fainter, but I realised at some point that to live in New York you had to accept it for what it was. I had my reasons for seeing certain things, and the city had its reasons for not seeing them.

A view of ankles

Every now and then my friend went away for a few months, so I had her flat in the prewar to myself. Before she left, I received strict instructions that I was to lie on her behalf. If anyone asked me, I was her "cousin", and I was to utter not a word about paying her rent. Her neighbours wouldn't be happy if they found out.

My friend owned her flat, as did everyone else in her building, and she paid a monthly fee called maintenance, which we called a levy back home. Despite being an owner, she was forbidden from renting her flat to someone of her own choosing because her building was a "co-op", short for cooperative. A co-op was a very peculiar piece of New York real estate with very peculiar rules. It was also a place, I would soon learn, where co-operation was probably the last thing on anyone's mind.

So, in order to keep my friend's neighbours happy, and to keep my cheap couch, I lied.

The doormen, of course, cottoned on to us, and Frank always smirked when he overheard me using the word "cousin". But, as they did countless times a day when they heard or saw something they shouldn't have – whether it was skimpy Victoria's Secret lingerie being delivered to the plump woman on the twelfth floor or a surfeit of empty wine bottles weekly in the garbage of the man on the fourth – the doormen didn't say a thing. Our secrets were theirs.

Whenever my friend got back to town, I carried on using her couch or shuttled around to other places. Two or three times I got a short-term rental through kind friends of hers. For a few months I lived in a basement across from a synagogue on the Upper West Side, which was also Uptown but not as rarified as the Upper East Side. On Friday evenings, after shul, I could see the legs of young couples in conservative clothes pass by as they walked down the street to the Hudson River two by two.

Other than the novelty of living under street level, with a view through my one window of people's ankles, the basement flat was dark and unmemorable. An open spiral staircase led to the ground floor – which they called the first floor – and let in even the most discreet sound made by my landlord upstairs.

After living there for three months, my friend let me use her couch one more time, but then she informed me the holiday was over. I would have to find a place of my own.

The great search begins

At *Time Out New York* two topics of conversation regularly drifted over to the secluded corner where the copy desk was. One of them was about food.

Come lunch hour, people talked about what they were planning to eat today (a particularly sought-after item at the time was *arugula*, which I quickly had to learn was the salad leaf we called rocket), what someone else was eating and whether it was worth getting too, and what choices were good at, say, the new dosa shop that had opened in SoHo.

Maybe it was the magazine's focus on new stores that had opened, but I had never been in a place where the subject of food and the eating of it took up such a large portion of daily conversation. For quite a few hours every day, there could have been nothing more important in the whole world.

The second topic was accommodation, which, like *antiques store*, they attached an *s* to, so it became *accommodations*. The newsroom was often abuzz: someone had just returned from seeing a vacancy, was going out early to get a jump on the queue/line for a place that had been advertised, or, more rarely, had just landed a flat of their very own. As excited as they sounded, what they described in breathless terms sounded to me small, undesirable and extremely overpriced.

Foremost amongst their considerations was never How Much or How Big or How Cosy but Where. Your neighbourhood/neighborhood was your identity. Elsie lived on the top floor of a small building that had a bar downstairs, as a result of which she seldom got to sleep before 4am. Jessica lived in a studio with a communal bathroom down the hallway, which she shared with five other people. Ben had a bathtub in his kitchen. Julie had to climb over a homeless man in her doorway every morning and night. And Steve had four roommates in a two-bedroom flat, with the living room doubling as a sleeping place.

But none of these things mattered because their flats were, most critically, Downtown. It was as if the other two-thirds of the island – not to mention Brooklyn, Queens and New Jersey, across the East and Hudson rivers – didn't exist.

So, long before I had to start looking for a place of my own – and I knew that time was fast approaching – I made a mental note: when looking for a flat, make sure it's not small and terribly overpriced. This meant I would be staying far away from Downtown.

A glitzy honcho boasting

I had now been in the city for eighteen months. Even though I hadn't found a full-time residence, I had got a fair amount of part-time work three or four days a week at two other magazines. And one of them happened to be the publication that I had set my sights on long before I'd arrived in New York: *Vanity Fair.*

Getting copy-editing jobs, I discovered, was pretty simple. Once you had learnt/learned the standard quirks at each magazine – such as whether they used a serial comma, who allowed "fuck" to be written out in full rather than with one asterisk or two, if not deleted altogether, or when they stopped writing out numbers (at ten, twelve, twenty, or ninety-nine) – it was fairly smooth sailing.

Vanity Fair had, in addition, a list of words writers weren't allowed to use, such as "boast". No-one could ever boast, joke or chuckle in a story, and they mostly had to "say" something. "Honcho" and "eatery" (neither of which were part of a South African's vocabulary anyway) were verboten, another word that was probably not allowed. No "plethora" or "glitzy" either.

I didn't know what to make of this arbitrary list of censored words at such a venerated magazine, although it seemed quite silly. But clearly the editor-in-chief had his reasons, which I, as a new part-time employee at the pinnacle of publishing in New York, couldn't begin to fathom. I was simply grateful to be there, even if it wasn't as a writer but, once again, as a lowly, little-seen copy editor, a job that at *Vanity Fair* was even lowlier and less visible than usual. We were stuck away in a back room that no-one ever passed, and our job was severely limited. You didn't circle anything in red unless you had a darn good reason, and even then it would probably be overruled by the copy chief.

One day I pointed out to him that suddenly, after five or six thousand words, a story about a Las Vegas mobster mentioned a character we were supposed to know but hadn't yet met. The article was an excerpt from an upcoming book by some writer famous to Americans, and clearly this Mr X had been introduced in a previous chapter, but his name would be unknown to anyone reading the excerpt.

The copy chief, after contemplating whether this omission was worth taking up the chain of authority, finally said I should approach the editor in charge of the article, a man whose name was high up on the masthead, somewhere just below the editor-in-chief.

On my way from the copy-editing room to his office, I walked through the dimly lit warren of cubicles, excited to be there but also struck by the sense of anxious quiet, as if people were convinced they too, like newly arrived immigrants without the right papers, might be here on borrowed time.

The office was quite unlike the frenetic, exciting scene that met you at *Time Out New York*, except for one thing – voice, tic, kneejerk – there were no black people. At first convinced that this couldn't be true – not at *Vanity Fair* surely? – I sometimes took five minutes off during my lunch break to wander between the cubicles acting as if I was lost but in fact trying to find evidence to the contrary about the makeup of the staff. Maybe I didn't look long or hard enough, but I never found it.

With the Las Vegas article in hand, I finally reached the office of the editor, whom I had never met before but assumed, this being *Vanity Fair*, must be especially talented to have reached this highly sought-after position in publishing. A bit starstruck, and suddenly aware of how odd words like "Nevada" and "mafia" sounded coming out of my African mouth, I nervously explained the problem of Mr X having arrived in the story totally without introduction. I waited for him to come up with a fantastic solution, as I was sure he would, because this was the pinnacle and you didn't get this far without some brilliance.

He waited a moment before answering.

"Don't worry," he said finally. "No-one will read that far in the story anyway."

A fantastic deal

In between *Vanity Fair* and *Time Out New York*, I started working at another lifestyle magazine, which produced laborious and glossy ten-page articles on very rare edible mushrooms and the joy of drinking tea. At all three publications I picked up from the other copy editors and editors (together with a growing English/American vocabulary) lots of valuable domestic information: where they lived, in what circumstances, and how they had managed to find their living quarters in the first place.

Besides the few real-estate words I already knew – brownstone, studio, co-op – I was introduced to numerous others: *loft, terrace apartment, alcove, L-shaped apartment, walk-up building, junior 1 and junior 4* (neither of which I understood, nor why there was no 2 or 3), *condominium,* and finally, *tenement.* Some of these words referred to flats you rented, some to flats you bought, and some to both, although most people – by far – rented.

In order to get a rental property you made use of a *realtor* (or what I knew as a real-estate agent), who charged something called a *broker's fee* (a concept that I didn't know). This was, in effect, the equivalent of one or two months' rent in advance, which you never got back again, even though the people doing the looking – Ben, Julie, Elsie, Jessica – had, as far as I could tell, done all the legwork themselves. Some people even forked over a non-refundable payment to have their names put on a list, which didn't even guarantee them a flat. But such was the insatiable demand for a place to live in New York City that no-one seemed to question the broker's fee or the fact that they'd never get their deposit back.

The words most prized in the real-estate lexicon were "rent-controlled" and "rent-stabilised". If these were attached to your flat, you were guaranteed – because of some city ordinance that no-one could explain the details of, even if they benefited from it – a below-average rent for life. Anyone with such a place held on to it, even after they moved out, renting it to someone else, who, once they were done with it, would rent it to someone else again.

Bizarre-sounding scenarios were quite common. Someone would be renting out a place they had no title to and hadn't lived in for a decade. Another person, quite possibly a millionaire who could afford a splendid penthouse all his own, wouldn't think of buying because his rent was too incredible to ever give up. A lone artist with a meagre income, meanwhile, would be renting a four-bedroom flat that could fetch ten or twenty times the price each month, but he'd got the place when the area was known for muggings, graffiti and drug-dealing neighbours. Now that he'd lived through the bad years, he was savouring the good – and could afford them because his rent was frozen in a previous decade.

Such fantastic deals, however, I could only dream of ever finding.

Zigzagging

So my focus on the city changed. I went from being a visitor, a bed hopper, a carefree itinerant, to being someone desperately seeking a place of my own. I had until now been wandering the city every chance I got – this was New York, after all, the Big Apple, and I worked at two magazines that had, as they said here, the inside scoop on everything new – but it had been to see the sights. Now it was to see the real estate/realty.

The layout of New York was straightforward enough. The wide avenues ran north-south, the narrower streets east-west, with even-numbered streets going east, odd numbers west. The first numbered street, 1st Street, started not at the southern tip of the island but just above Houston Street – right at the *Time Out New York* offices, in fact – and ended some two hundred blocks later, near the top of Manhattan, a distance of about ten miles or sixteen kilometres. To gauge how far you had travelled/traveled, the city's layout provided a simple calculation: one avenue block or ten street blocks equalled about half a mile or eight-tenths of a kilometre.

Every chance I got, I explored. I walked, more or less, from the southern tip of Manhattan, where the very first immigrants arrived and there were still a few cobbled streets from the olden days, and

28

gradually made my way north. I walked from west to east, from Hudson River to East River, and then east to west, zigzagging my way up the island.

In spite of a 42-kilometre shoreline, flats close to the water were rare. On the rivers one found mostly industrial properties, warehouses, sanitation depots, power stations, railway yards and a ribbon of highways that almost circled the island. It was an oversight that, curiously, brought my old and new cities closer together, made New York a bit more imperfect, but in a good way. The custom of building closer to the centre of the island, away from the waterside views, reminded me of Johannesburg, where architects had for a long time built houses with their broad porches facing not the view but the traffic.

Almost the only apartment buildings near the river were ugly brown blocks about a dozen floors high and positioned in clumps of at least six or seven at a time, like tree stumps for a giant to sit on. Each building was perforated with windows too small to enjoy the river view, which, in any case, was interrupted by the ribbon of highways on their doorstep.

No-one I worked with or ever met in the city mentioned these brown buildings as a potential place to live. They were for low-income people, and the word used for them was one more to add to my real-estate lexicon: *projects*.

Dark foyers, telephone poles
After several months of searching, I felt like I had been everywhere.

I had walked through Midtown, Uptown and Downtown – which, I discovered, had quite a few not-so-trendy sections that didn't get a mention at *Time Out New York* and certainly didn't deserve the sought-after adjective "downtown".

I crossed the East River into Brooklyn and Queens. I went from Washington Heights, where lots of signs were in Spanish, to Chinatown, where, I had read in the newspaper, immigrants lived in abhorrent conditions, ten to a room, sleeping in shifts in the same beds, like they might in a dormitory on a Witwatersrand gold mine.

In Hell's Kitchen I found a simulacrum of the New York City I had come to expect from the books I'd read – sullied, aged buildings full of character closer to the Hudson River but with no view of it, one or two even with stables in them for horses that were used to pull carriages in Central Park. The West Village, too, was perfect: leafy, unpredictable roads speckled with coffee shops frequented by people who dressed like artists.

On the Lower East Side I stood in line to see places with aspiring Australian actors, young brokers starting on Wall Street and students looking for something they could share.

But in each place I had no luck.

I trekked out to areas that no-one was talking about, like Bedford Stuyvesant and Crown Heights. I went to parts of Harlem, a vast area where the people hanging out on the front stairs of buildings looked as though they could just as easily live there as not. In Williamsburg, where I found myself on many a Sunday, I regularly passed one particular corner where a dozen Hasidim in round black felt hats stood sentry-like on their own, not communicating, while behind them young boys rode bicycles with yarmulkes and long ringlets in their hair.

In each neighbourhood I knocked on doors and left notes in dark foyers. I followed up on notices posted on telephone poles and in dusty doorways that said APARTMENT TO RENT, only to find out they had expired so long ago that the phone numbers no longer worked.

Back at *Time Out New York* I kept hearing more alarming tales of rents that were much higher than anything I could afford for hovels too small to conceive living in. And the longer I didn't find a place, the more desperate the stories sounded. Flats were either taken before I got there or went to another applicant. As a freelance copy editor, I didn't earn enough or wasn't stable enough to even come into consideration.

My options were quickly running out.

You say trash, I say garbage

During my search for a place to live, I found myself unintentionally sidetracked by a second search for something completely different.

It began one evening right outside my friend's building on the Upper East Side. It was there that I noticed a perfectly good leather armchair sitting in between the garbage that was waiting to be removed the following morning. At first I thought someone had mistakenly left it there – not that I could imagine who would have purposely misplaced a fine piece of furniture like that – and I was sure they would come and fetch it later on. I nevertheless circled it greedily, ready to pounce, like a hungry lion might a lone impala at sunset.

"Hees trash," Andrew the doorman said, smiling at me.

He saw my surprise.

"We don't throw this kind of thing away where I come from," I said, although it sounded like I was boasting.

Andrew nodded sympathetically, as if he pitied me for giving garbage a second thought.

"And in Poland?" I asked. "You surely wouldn't throw this away, would you?"

He scratched his head trying to remember. It had been a long time since he'd last been in Krakow.

Even though I didn't take the armchair, it unlocked something in me. I suddenly started noticing more chairs and couches and countless other perfectly good free offerings on the pavements, especially during my search for a flat. Each neighbourhood I went to had its own garbage-collecting days and times and kinds of garbage, so there was always something interesting tossed out somewhere. Even the less wealthy neighbourhoods, like Harlem and Crown Heights, threw out very good things, sometimes even better than the wealthy areas. Maybe the act of discarding valuable items was a way of showing that you were moving up.

Often I would go out looking for a flat only to come home with a side table or a vase under my arm. The two activities became so intertwined that I soon set myself a challenge: should I ever get my own place in the city, I would furnish it entirely from what I found on the street.

Frank the doorman let me store my discoveries in the basement of my friend's building. Within a short time – much to Frank's growing dismay – I had accumulated a faux leather chair, a sofa with three almost unnoticeable coffee stains, a mattress, a dish rack, some cutlery, numerous plates, a pile of old *New Yorker* magazines, two side tables, several not-too-objectionable paintings, a vase and four rattan window shades, which here they called blinds.

Lesotho on Park Avenue

As much luck as I had finding things on the pavement, though, I still had none finding a home of my own to put them in. One day, in desperation, I ventured into an area I had never even vaguely considered. Bizarrely enough, it also lay right under my nose, barely a few blocks from my friend's flat. But it was an area that got mentioned very rarely in conversation and in the press, and when it did it was in the most unflattering terms. So I had unthinkingly dismissed it, the same way people with their sights set on Downtown would dismiss anywhere other than Downtown.

If New York had such a thing as a list of Most Undesirable Places to Live, this area would have landed near the top. It was a part of Harlem that Harlem itself seemed to have disowned. Not in the central or western sections – the famous Harlem, the jazz Harlem, the Harlem that tourists went to for the Apollo Theatre and a taste of soul food – it lay to the east, a polyp of land skirted by the less visited East River. It was known for crime, a disproportionately high incidence of asthma and diabetes, and the largest concentration of low-income projects and pollution-causing bus depots. Through its heart like a dirty arrow ran a blackened viaduct carrying trains north out of the city.

What made the enclave appear even darker and less approachable was that its gateway was the bucolic, very neat Upper East Side, an area that couldn't have been more dissimilar. The dividing line between them was 96th Street – almost halfway up the city's two hundred numbered streets – although the thoroughfare might as well have been a border between two very different countries. Depending on the time of day you crossed over – nighttime was worst – it could be a split, a chasm or a cliff, taking you headlong into another zone.

All across New York neighbourhoods overlapped, but they faded one into another almost imperceptibly. Barely noticeable was where Little Italy ended and Chinatown began; NoHo borrowed its name from SoHo, the two areas divided by a street no-one paid attention to, boutiques on one side and cafés on the other; and Tribeca was a district Downtown you wouldn't realise you had strayed into unless someone told you so.

But here, between the Upper East Side and the east side of Harlem, there was no gradual change. Within the space of just one street, vast, unimaginable wealth – in fact, some said it was the greatest concentration of wealth in America – tumbled into the grime and chaos of a marginal district, First World into Third World (which here, for some reason, they called the Developing World, as if the other name suggested we were somehow coming last in the race).

To the south of the Split, the Chasm, the Cliff were carefully cultivated lawns down the centre/median of Park Avenue, pavements punctually hosed down to remove bits of chewing gum and unsightly pools of dog pee, functioning traffic lights on every block, yellow taxis by the hundreds, expensive Italianate buildings designed by men now celebrated in history books, chic stores where they sold designer clothes for children and extravagantly priced gourmet sandwiches, nail parlours staffed by bevies of Korean women, organic dry cleaners, immense cathedrals and synagogues, restaurants that served *prix-fixe* dinners until 7pm.

To the north, meanwhile, was a quartet of railway tracks that carried the traffic out of Grand Central Station. The trains ran invisible and almost inaudible under the grassy strip of Park Avenue, only to be expunged at the Split, where the viaduct began, rending the leafy thoroughfare into two darker, narrower one-way lanes. These were the famous Park Avenue's unfortunate and unmentioned relatives Every few minutes engines and carriages clattered up or down the open railway tracks bearing their cargo into and out of the city.

All around the railway tracks and in the streets beyond were broken streetlamps; pavements filled with garbage and dog poo that no-one cleaned up; small buildings no-one wrote books about and which were fronted by rusted fire escapes; tiny churches with names like Providence Baptist and Fountain of Living Waters Ministries and Iglesias Liberacion y Sanidad; hair-braiding salons; and McDonald's. As for yellow taxis, there weren't any, either because no-one could afford them or because the drivers didn't want to risk crossing the Split.

It was a world I recognised instantly, more broken and haphazard than the perfect, sanitised, all-white Upper East Side; a world closer to Africa. It was West Germany going into the East, Hungary into Romania, Sandton into Alexandra, South Africa into Lesotho. Even the ubiquitous Western Union outlets called to mind the informal *spaza* shops in the townships, where people could make calls to relatives back home, cash cheques or have money wired to the wives, sons and daughters they had left behind in other, poorer countries. It was an area for people from elsewhere, immigrants.

And it felt, to me, a lot like home.

Five grenades

I spent a week crisscrossing the eastern section of Harlem, although I quickly learnt that there was very little to see. Many buildings that looked habitable were, on closer inspection, abandoned and their windows bricked up. Landlords had, for some reason, closed the front doors and thrown away the keys.

One wintry day, after going through my usual routine – leaving notes in dirty foyers, ringing bells that never got answered, taking down phone numbers I was sure had long been disconnected – I had some very good luck. At a small building that faced the viaduct, its upper two floors overlooking the railway tracks, a sweet old woman came to the door and told me that she and her sister were the owners. Hearing her accent, I asked where she was from.

Jamaica, she said.

I played up the fact that I, too, was a new immigrant and from Africa. She liked that, and I liked her. She also had a vacant flat that was not only cheap and clean but bigger than anything I'd seen, and it was on one of the floors overlooking the tracks. Other people might not have liked that view, but, being a lover of trains, I did. I also for some reason took it as a good sign,

After several return visits and lots of haggling – or, rather, me supplicating the sisters quite pathetically – they gave the flat to a single mother who worked as a nurse at a nearby hospital.

Leaving the sisters' building for the final time – my best hope in the last few months dashed – I felt dismal. Nothing was going my way, and the ambience/ambiance did little to lighten my spirit: a blackened wall dividing this lonely side of Park Avenue from the railway tracks was topped with a lethal-looking palisade. It was, I suspected, meant to stop you from scaling the wall and, perhaps depressed at how things weren't working out the way you'd planned, hurling yourself into the path of an oncoming train.

At that moment a noisy locomotive shot out of the tunnel to the south, emitting a plaintive cry. The trees to my left were leafless and the sky grey. Or was it gray? Even the choice of spellings suddenly seemed to be working against me.

"What a godforsaken area this is!" I reflected gloomily. "Johannesburg in the dead of winter, covered in smog, the veld blackened, couldn't look as bad. What a horrible place this would be to live. I'd never want a flat here anyway."

As I walked in line with the viaduct, I chanced to look up and spy, on the fifth floor of a small old building, two windows without curtains. I'm not sure why my eyes fell on those random windows or why I made the deduction that I did, but I immediately had a thrilling thought.

"Vacancy!"

I stopped and had been looking at the two windows for a few moments when I heard five grenades go off.

"Hang jew! Wash ooh wong!"

Two men were leaning against a fence. One of them was sucking a cigarette, had a heavy growth of beard and, with his thick pitch of mussed black hair, looked as if he had just woken up. He looked not unlike a bandit out of an old movie. Shorter by at least a head, the other man stood close by and talked constantly, like someone trying, not entirely successfully, to appease his companion. The shorter man was the one who'd shouted at me, while his friend languorously scanned the street.

Facing them were three tenements, narrow buildings maybe eight metres across, five storeys high, two windows on the first floor, four windows on each floor above that, their fronts latticed with fire escapes corroded by the weather and old age. The tenement on the left and the one next to it, which had the vacant windows, looked like a set of twins, both with mud-coloured steps leading up to their entrances. The third tenement, the one on the right, was a bit shorter and squatter.

A fourth tenement, standing to the right on its own and separated by an alley, stretched to the corner closest to the railway tracks. Unlike its three neighbours, it was built sideways, so instead of being narrow and deep, it was shallow and perhaps twenty-five metres wide, with eight windows across each floor.

Taking up the rest of the block down to our left, at least two-thirds of it, was a massive open lot covered in scrub. Old plastic bags whipped up by frigid bursts of wind got tangled in the surrounding chain-link fence, and I saw at least one feral cat dash anxiously into the dry veld-like grass.

The first two tenements next to the lot, the ones with the mud-coloured steps, were cared for by the tall bandit-looking man, and the third tenement, the squat one, quite appropriately, by his short friend. They were the superintendents. After I explained that I was looking for a place to rent, the shorter man said something I couldn't understand to his friend.

Turning away from us disinterestedly, the taller swarthy man snapped a string of words – in Spanish, I think – that joined the cigarette smoke from his mouth. It sounded like another rejection.

"What?! An affordable apartment for rent in *this* market? And he doesn't want to pay a broker's fee? He's crazy!"

But the words the shorter man translated were, more or less, the following: the curtainless apartment – or rather, the *pockmong* – was indeed uninhabited and available to rent.

I was given a telephone number, which I immediately called. The woman who answered said I was more than welcome to view the place. I should tell the tall man to let me in, she said, and then hung up.

It all happened so quickly, so effortlessly, I was sure there had to be a catch.

The shotgun

Jangling a set of keys to what could easily have been a hundred doors, the swarthy man led the way across the street to the middle tenement, one of the two with mud-coloured steps.

The lock on the front door was broken, as was one on a second inner door, and there was a tiny vestibule in between them. In front of us lay a narrow hallway, with a door halfway down on either side and a third door at the far end under the stairs. The walls, which were warped in places, were painted two shades of brown: shit-brown from eye level down and vomit-brown from eye level up. The floor, covered in cigarette butts and food wrappers, had been another shade of brown once upon a time. Above us burnt long fluorescent tubes, and the air was heavy with stale smoke and second-day beer. Graffiti was scratched into the paint with sharp objects along the ground/first floor but diminished as you went up the stairs, and then ended, inexplicably, by the third floor (the American one, that is).

Each storey consisted of three flats and a small landing allowing access to them. We climbed up to the fifth floor, the top one, with the swarthy man leading the way. A growing heaviness in both his step and his sighs made it sound like he was sorry now that he had said anything about the vacancy.

As soon as he unlocked the door to the flat, there was a sudden fluttering and thrashing on the other side. Dozens of pigeons flew about chaotically in a rush to escape through any opening they could find. Bird shit lay in thumb-deep piles on the floor and streaked the cupboards, the ancient stove, the corroded fridge, the bath, the window panes and sills, and basically anything the birds could get to.

The flat had the traditional layout of a tenement – straight, long, and less than four metres across at its widest. The rooms, four of them, lay one behind the other and were boxy in shape, and the doors between them were placed in a row. As a result, you could see from one end of the flat to the other, which is how it had earned its nickname, "a railroad" or "a shotgun", since a moving train or a just-fired bullet could easily travel from one end to the other without touching a perimeter wall.

The windows throughout the flat, seven of them in all, had broken sashes or didn't close properly. One of the two in front that faced the street had bars across it to stop people climbing in from the fire escape, and the bathroom window had been reduced in size so no-one could climb in from the public hallway window.

The floors, coated in the same forgettable tiles as the public hallways, slanted severely to one side, suggesting that the old building might be sinking in the middle. The toilet jutted out unevenly, and the walls, like those in the hallways, were warped.

So little was there to like about the tenement, the flat and the street that I felt disheartened. I had seen some pretty awful places so far, but this one was possibly the worst. For a moment I even had the crazy notion of carrying on my search for a new home somewhere else, but then I heard how much the flat cost.

The swarthy man, not relying on his companion any longer to translate for him, gave the figure with an accent so heavy that at first I thought I'd heard wrong. The lowest rent I had come across in the city so far – and this was for a tiny studio with a toilet down the public hallway or a bathtub in the kitchen – was $750 a month (the equivalent of R3,750 at the time). These four rooms I had just seen, which I could have all to myself, were going for $600.

I wasn't the only person startled by the price.

"Queng?!" exclaimed the small guy.

I wasn't sure what he meant, but it was evident from his surprise that the flat was a deal in a million.

Not wasting a moment, I rushed off to call the woman I'd spoken to on the phone earlier to tell her that I definitely wanted the flat, but she was no longer there. It took about a month of repeated calls, and increasing pessimism on my part, to get hold of her. I was convinced she wasn't answering because a thousand other people had been in line for that fantastic deal, and she'd given it to one of them.

When I finally got through to her, though, she expressed shock that I had left so many messages for her, and assured me she had received not a single one of them.

"My name is Shoshanna," she said. "Come and see me tomorrow."

Above the pizza place
Shoshanna's office was on the second floor of a small, nondescript building in Midtown. On the street level, in between a cluttered hardware store and a pizza outlet that here they called a parlour/parlor, was an inconspicuous doorway where the agency's name was handwritten on a tiny piece of paper taped to a dented buzzer. The staircase sagged, the carpeting was stained and every step you

took felt like it might be your last before the wood underneath gave way.

I was anxious to make a good impression on Shoshanna. Real estate agents, it was no secret, could make your future or end it. Who got a vacancy and who didn't was entirely up to them, and for those few moments that an applicant stood before them they were gods.

After five minutes a pretty, matronly woman in her thirties with thick, plainly cut brown hair came out and greeted me. She wore dark colours, a long heavy skirt that ended below her knees and a long-sleeved shirt.

"I am Shoshanna," she said.

Holding her one arm across the front of her body as if it were somehow damaged, she led us down a short hallway to a small office that, even with only two chairs and her desk inside, already felt cramped.

The rent for the flat, Shoshanna confirmed, was truly as low as tall dark man had said, and that's because it was intended for low-income people. There were very strict guidelines that needed to be followed in order to qualify as a renter, she continued, and the most important of these – she paused here – was that I could earn no more than a certain amount every month.

I was overcome in equal parts by excitement and confusion. Me low-income? I had never thought of myself that way before, but maybe I was, at least on paper. It wasn't something to brag about, but I did earn hardly anything. What had been my biggest drawback at the other flats I'd seen – earning too little, not having a full-time job, being an undesirable risk who might flee in the night owing thousands of dollars in rent – was here my shiniest asset. Shoshanna actually *wanted* me to be poor.

Before she even told me what the minimum salary requirement was, I knew it could never be lower than what I earned. My dream had actually come true: I'd found one of those flats that everyone else wanted but no-one could get, a flat that defied comparison and was in a class of its own, one of New York City's fantastic deals.

At that point, Shoshanna asked me what kind of work I did, and I said that I was a freelance copy editor at several magazines around the city. A bit too eagerly, I mentioned *Vanity Fair*. Instead of going for *Time Out New York,* the lesser, grungier title that was more in keeping with the flavour of the tenement, I went for the glossy one.

She was immediately suspicious.

"*Vanity Fair?*"

"Yes."

She instinctively pulled her arm closer to her waist.

"How can you earn so little at a place like that?"

It was a very stupid mistake. Linking myself and the low-income building to an upmarket magazine full of stories about Hollywood and the Riviera and rich people with nothing better to do than murder each other might have just cost me the fifth-floor, bird-shit-splattered flat.

"But it's true," I said. I could hear myself pleading. "It really is possible. Freelance copy editors don't earn much. We shouldn't be called editors at all. We are very low down on the ladder. Really we are."

Unconvinced, Shoshanna told me that I would in any case have to provide her with my latest tax return, which would prove how paltry my salary was.

"And one last thing," she added before I stood up to leave.

By now I was familiar with the sound of bad news approaching, and I was sure this was one of those times.

"Yes?" I said anxiously.

"You couldn't bring me a few copies of the magazine, could you?"

I didn't say it, but I thought it: "You bet I can!"

The next day I dropped by her office above the pizza parlour with not only my latest tax return but also a full year's supply of *Vanity Fair.* Twenty-four hours later Shoshanna called to tell me the news: the flat was mine.

CHAPTER 2
THE FLAT

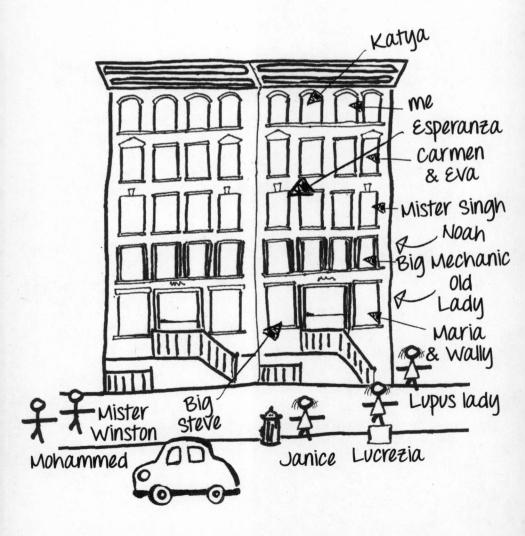

A mystery landlord

Before I could move in, the curtainless flat had to be cleaned up, the birds vanquished, the bird shit scraped off everything, the walls painted and the dirty ugly floor tiles replaced by clean ugly ones. The tall swarthy man I had met on the pavement who had shown me the flat was in charge of doing the work.

His name, I had learned on that first day I'd seen him, was Noah, and his short talkative friend was Floyd. I don't know why, but those two names immediately struck me as so ill-fitting they could have been randomly plucked from the air, like aliases they'd chosen because they were trying to hide something or because New Yorkers would never be able to pronounce their real names. (I knew how they felt, for my own name Americans found impossible to say, turning it into Bother, Bow-ta, Butta, Botta — never what it should have been.) Maybe, I thought, they were really Arcimboldo and Gustavius; they certainly didn't look like a Noah and a Floyd.

Noah, besides being the superintendent of the old building, was also the in-house contractor, although he seemed in no particular rush to finish the job.

Over the next few weeks, I occasionally wandered down the sad, wind-blown street to see if there was any progress, but through the open windows on the fifth floor I could hear no sound of hammering or sawing. I kept asking myself who owned the old building. What kind of a landlord would leave a flat empty for so long in a city clamouring for accommodation and then, after he had found a willing tenant, still let it languish? Who was this mystery person?

When the flat was finally ready, a few friends helped me move in. Up the mud-coloured front stairs we carried the odd pieces of furniture and bric-a-brac that I had collected off the street and stored in my friend's basement waiting for this moment.

As we slowly made our way up the five tight-cornered floors, I suddenly felt a bit embarrassed about bringing people I knew into the old building, like it reflected badly on me. It seemed grungier and more graffiti-coated than usual. But when I looked at them, it wasn't disgust I saw in their faces but total horror and even a touch of fear.

Of the many qualities I'd seen in the old building so far, danger certainly wasn't one of them. How could a building in New York run by sweet Shoshanna, where you had to pay monthly rent, be dangerous?

"It's cheap," I reminded them.

"But there are projects," one of them said with a low voice, in case someone behind one of the closed doors might be listening and take offence/offense.

He meant the two large brown twelve-storey buildings across the street, built in the same thoughtless style as the countless other low-income projects I had seen around the city. They were identical in design, each shaped like the letter X, with a front door so small and inconspicuous the architect might not have intended you to ever find it.

"But there are projects everywhere," I replied. "All over the city."

They wouldn't be dissuaded, and smiled at me sympathetically, as if I didn't realise what I was in for.

"Hey, you!" a voice boomed down from above, interrupting us.

A woman leant/leaned over the railing on the fourth floor, her breasts like melons that might at any moment burst through the thin blue fabric of her tight shirt.

"You moving in?!" she shouted.

I nodded.

"I hope you don't make no noise!" she carried on at the top of her voice.

Instead of thinking how odd it was for someone to be demanding silence with a voice that could wake up the entire building, I immediately felt like pointing out to my friends that there was clearly some kind of order in the place. Here was a nice woman telling us to be mindful of her and the other neighbours.

"There's babies living here!" the woman carried on. It was a voice you didn't argue with. "Me, I got a baby!"

Carrying my mattress up the next flight of stairs, not daring to say another word, I squeezed past her and mumbled a greeting. The woman was barefoot and her toenails were freshly painted a luscious red, like she had done them especially for her outing onto the fourth-floor landing.

"Hi, honey," she said and smiled. For once she wasn't shouting. "I'm Carmen."

Outing in a Cadillac

At about eleven every Tuesday morning, Carmen went shopping. She lived directly below me with her teenage daughter Eva and her young son, who rode a plastic scooter up and down their flat for long stretches every day. The boy, who was already three years old, was whom Carmen had been referring to as her "baby".

Some days when I didn't have to copy-edit, I stayed at home and tried to write. Sitting behind my desk at my front window, with a view down onto the street, I could hear Carmen getting ready to leave. Shopping day was one of the rare occasions that she left the building, so she made sure to get the most out of it. Their preparations reached me in stereo – through my windows and my floor.

Carmen shouted at Eva, who shouted back even louder. Eva was about seventeen and beautiful, with long lustrous dark hair and a body engineered for very tight jeans. Sometimes mother and daughter shouted in unison. In between, the boy rode his scooter faster and faster, building up to a mad frenzy of spinning plastic wheels on old vinyl tiles, calling out Carmen's name.

"What's it, baby?" she replied.

The scooter ground to a halt but the boy's voice was too weak to make it up to my flat. He didn't speak in public either, and for some reason I thought he seemed damaged.

"Sure, baby," his mom said. "Take it with you."

Then the scooter started up again, working its way into another crescendo, before Carmen, who couldn't take the noise any more,

45

brought it to a stop.

"Shut! The! Fuck! Up!"

Instantly the boy started crying, setting off even more protests from his mother. Then Eva broke in.

"Where you? Fuck!"

Carmen's flat had exactly the same configuration as mine, where you could see from one end to the other with a single step to the left or the right no matter where you stood, so it was mystifying how they repeatedly managed to lose one another in such a confined space.

"Where you, ma?!"

"Here, baby! Fucking shoes won't go on! Come help me!"

"Fuck!"

A friend of Carmen's always joined them on shopping day. In her early thirties, she was skinny, flat-chested, cut her hair in a severe style, and always wore loose-fitting short pants. Without fail, she never missed a chance to mention the fact that she had lupus. I didn't know what lupus was, but she made it sound very serious and the prime reason why she found it so hard to climb the stairs to Carmen's place more than once a week.

Chaperoning them all was a man who drove a white Cadillac and wouldn't have looked out of place in one of those '70s movies about gangsters in Harlem. He wore a full-length cream-coloured coat with a sliver of fur at the neck, a fedora, heavy jewellery/jewelry and dark glasses, and he double-parked outside the tenement so Carmen didn't have far to walk once she exited the front door. She wore a short dress that quickly bunched up around her thighs, and her high heels either didn't fit properly or were strapless, so that she clattered down each step, flight after flight.

Halfway down, she remembered something.

"Eeeee-Vuhhhh!"

Silence.

"Eeeee-Vuhhhh!"

Nothing.

"Eeeee-Vuhhhh!"

If it was possible for a door to slam open, instead of closed, it did.

"Fuck's it, ma? Fuck!"

"Bring my cigarettes!" Carmen hollered, then added, "Thanks, baby."

But Eva had already – with fury – shut the door.

The man in the fedora, never saying a word, carried the little boy's pram/stroller, his coat fanning out behind him as if on a breeze. The lupus lady came somewhere in between, descending as feebly as someone fifty years her senior. After a lot more shouting back and forth, Eva swearing, heels clickety-clacking, people losing one another, reuniting seconds later, doors opening and slamming, the group finally left.

Immediately an unusual silence fell over the place, like you'd imagine the quiet that might follow a massive explosion. Carmen so filled the building when she was there, even when you couldn't hear her or see her, that when she was gone you could actually sense her absence.

Eva's trail

By early Tuesday evening, Carmen's group had returned, loaded down with more than a dozen shopping bags bursting with groceries. One bag in each hand, Carmen tackled the four flights of stairs as if they were a mountain.

"I'm getting too old for this shit," she wheezed before coming to a halt somewhere between the second and third floors.

Carmen was probably in her thirties, although she looked a lot older, especially when the unflattering fluorescent lights in the hallway ceilings picked up the scars in her face left by acne. She had an inviting smile and it wasn't hard to imagine that she had looked like her daughter Eva not too long ago. Indeed, she told me many months later when I passed her on the landing – the only place where we ever really saw each other – that she had once been an airline stewardess.

"I gotta give up smoking!" Carmen huffed, putting the two shopping bags in one hand and gripping the banister with the other as she took on the next stage of her own Everest.

After the Cadillac had left – the man in the fedora never stayed for dinner – cooking pans started banging the stovetop in Carmen's kitchen, and the hallways were soon filled with the aroma of fried chicken and spices. If anyone joined them for dinner, they would be gone promptly by nine o'clock.

The next morning the evidence of the dinner was lying at Carmen's front door: a large black garbage bag.

Carmen's garbage had a life of its own, occupying a special place in the public hallways, a constantly changing character, barely moving but almost always present. The bag sat there for several days, during which time it was joined by other bags, all of which steadily began changing shape and splitting, their contents of chicken bones and leftover portions of spiced rice, avocado skins and ear buds / Q-Tips spilling onto the floor.

When the bags were finally removed, the task fell to Eva, who did it with little enthusiasm and even less stamina. She took away one bag at a time, talking on her cellphone and smoking a cigarette as she went. Behind her she left a trail all the way to the front door and down the stairs outside. Sometimes a guy who lived on the first floor – large, in his late twenties, usually with some stubble on his ruddy cheeks – was standing outside the front door with three or four friends, so Eva stopped to talk and maybe share a zol/joint with them.

Our garbage cans were located about ten metres away from the mud-coloured front steps, in front of the chain-link fence beyond the second tenement. Needless to say, Eva ran out of strength well before reaching her target and most of the garbage ended up on the pavement.

Noah should have cleaned up but didn't, so the trail of spillage lay around, both inside and out, until little by little it got trampled into the hallway floor or the pavement. The area outside Carmen's flat remained empty for a day or two, but on Tuesday she and the others went shopping again and by the following morning you could count on the first black bag of the week making its appearance.

Toast and cigarettes

Very early every weekday morning, someone far below me started yelling like a banshee, trying to raise the old building from slumber.

"Wah-hee! Waaaah-heeeee!"

The voice originated on the first floor, travelling without any hindrance through the air shaft that ran up the side of the building, in between the left side of Floyd's tenement and mine.

"Wah-hee! Wake the fuck uuupp!"

The air shaft was, after the one-room-after-another layout of the flats, the most distinctive architectural feature – if you could call it that – of the tenement. When tenements were first built in the 1880s for the hundreds of thousands of immigrants coming through Ellis Island, the narrow long buildings were erected quickly and with little forethought. They had no toilets and there were windows only in the front and the very back, nothing in between. The combination of no ventilation, no light, lots of wood and indoor fires was disastrous.

After several decades and countless tragedies, the design was changed to include the air shaft. Today if you look at a row of tenements from above, they would not be dissimilar to numerous hourglasses placed side by side.

Onto my air shaft faced three of my seven windows and three of my four boxy rooms. Without much difficulty, I could reach out and touch the outstretched arm of my neighbour across the way in Floyd's tenement, who also had three windows. He and I, however, were as close as we were distant. I knew his daily rituals – the time he woke, the hour his friends left, the number of times his fax went off every day, the sound of his footfall – but not his name. His blinds always drawn, I saw him through the window maybe once

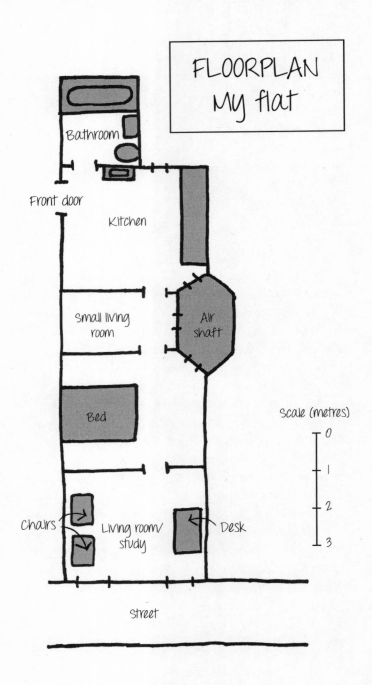

FLOORPLAN
My flat

Bathroom

Front door

Kitchen

Small living
room

Air
shaft

Bed

Scale (metres)

0

1

2

3

Chairs

Living room/
study

Desk

Street

before the day he moved, two years later.

Unlike the olden days when the air shaft had a function – allowing air and light into the inner rooms – it had long stopped playing a role. Electricity had brought alternatives: light bulbs, fans and air conditioners. Now the windows onto the air shaft served only as a reminder that they led nowhere and provided no view. They served as home to flocks of pigeons, which nested on the windowsills, rising and falling in waves all day long, clucking and cooing in spurts through the night.

Being on the top floor, I got some natural light from the air shaft, but looking down into its dark well I couldn't see how my lower neighbours benefited. The air shaft these days served almost uniquely as an ear trumpet or a hearing aid, carrying the sound of radios, televisions, fights, doorbells, telephone conversations, clanking pans and fat frying. Sometimes it also acted as a funnel for smells.

At seven o'clock on weekday mornings, an hour after "Wah-hee" (who, it turned out, was in fact a six-year-old named Wally) got his wake-up screeches, an alarm clock went off. It came from the flat on my other side, which was lived in by a young Polish schoolteacher. Sometimes she heard it, but more often she didn't.

The smell of toast, cigarettes and sometimes marijuana was on the air, drifting up the stairwell or the air shaft. Doors opened and shut, echoing up the stairwell and through the closed front door.

Out my back window, meanwhile, sounds bounced off the walls from half a block away. Someone, inexplicably, had a rooster that crowed at strange hours, and two parrots often engaged in enthusiastic conversation. Gathered on a rear fire escape that I could glimpse across a patchwork of unused back yards were four or five cats. Their owner, a woman in her fifties with heavily painted red lips who sometimes pushed an empty pram along the viaduct, would every now and then remember she actually had the pets and stick her head out of her window to offer them food. At night, going by the sounds of it, they were perpetually in heat.

By 7.30am, the now-woken Wally and his mother headed out the front door, with her holding his hand so tightly you would have thought someone was about to steal him. Across the street, Noah and Floyd were leaning against the fence, Floyd chattering senselessly as Noah dragged on his cigarette, scanning the street lethargically.

At some point after nine, an old man would arrive and climb the mud-coloured front stairs at the building next door, where he wouldn't go in but instead leaned on his cane and swayed his head to a beat only he could hear.

The day had begun.

Our man from Yemen

Like a new boy at school, I made sure to always be on my best behaviour/behavior in the old building. I had been given a fantastic deal and I didn't want to screw it up. So I made sure to smile and say hello to everyone.

When Eva was on the stairs, having a cigarette or painting her nails, I greeted her as I stepped over her splayed-out body. Further down I might bump into Esperanza, coming in after taking her Chihuahua Tiny for a short walk around the block. If she said hello she made sure to cover her mouth the way people do who have just received a set of braces.

Out on the street I chatted with the postman and the sanitation guy. Mister Winston and Mohammed were there too – as they were during most daylight hours – tending to their vehicles, parking them, re-parking them (the limit on a parking space, it seemed, was two days), cleaning them, but for the most part just sitting in them.

Mister Winston, who lived in the sideways tenement on the corner near us, was never without his cowboy hat, while Mohammed, who lived in the second tenement with mud-colored steps, had a distinctive beard not unlike Osama bin Laden's.

Other car owners came and went – some with a more specific

purpose than others, as I would come to see – but these two men were always on the street, part of its lifeblood. Any day without them there would have seemed odd, Mister Winston checking the buff on his green van and Mohammed sitting behind the wheel of his Toyota coupé. Mohammed's window was usually rolled up, whether or not he was smoking, and if he opened it even a crack for you, it was a sign of approval. He must like you.

When Mohammed found out I was from South Africa, he casually told me that he too was African.

"You are?" I asked, excited to have found a fellow African on my street. "Where are you from?"

"Yemen," he said.

"But that's not Africa," I said, sorry I'd replied so quickly to correct him.

Mohammed smiled, and I couldn't tell if he was playing with me or if he really didn't come from Africa but had randomly chosen a country's name to make it sound like he did. Either way, his grin and his choice of Yemen, a nation whose name rarely got mentioned, made me like him instantly.

Joining Mohammed and Mister Winston in the row of parked cars occasionally – but never talking to them – was an enormous man from my building. He must have weighed at least 140 kilograms and had greasy thinning hair he configured into a rat's tail. A mechanic of sorts, his focus was never one car but two, and he moved between the bonnet/hood of one to the stereo in the boot/trunk of the other over the course of several hours. To power his tools he ran an electric cord through one of the front windows on the second floor.

By afternoon a small group of men was scattered around his workspace. The stereo he was fixing got switched on and off repeatedly, the volume turned up so loud that the vibrations shook the building's front wall. I could feel my desk throb under my hands. Some of the men leaned against the railings of the tenement, and the smell of oil and marijuana drifted through my open window.

At dusk the mechanic finished off his work. He climbed up to his flat on the second floor and pulled the black electric cord into his front window. The only evidence that he had been outside were patches of oil, some rags and a bright assortment of twisted wires.

Ruddy cheeks

Besides the mechanic, there lived on the second floor a musician you seldom saw because he played the jazz clubs Downtown late at night and slept by day. Noah the superintendent lived in the flat at the back.

On each floor were three flats, set in a U-shape. Two long ones like mine were in front and faced the street, and the third was in the back, which meant they probably got the full-on acoustics of the rooster, the two parrots and the five howling cats every morning.

Below me and Carmen lived a tall Indian man in his fifties, Mister Singh, who occasionally got visited by an older, larger woman with a moustache/mustache whose name was Guadelupe. He didn't seem to know her very well, even though they were married and she called him "honey" in a loud voice, like she wanted to make sure everyone heard her. No-one said anything, but we all knew there must be some kind of arrangement.

Next floor down was the 140-kilo mechanic, who seldom appeared unless he had cars to work on.

Last in the line below me was the woman who screamed for Wally at six every weekday morning. She was Maria, a plump woman in her forties with a pretty face that you couldn't believe was responsible for unleashing the obscenities that filled the air shaft several times a day.

In the back on my floor lived a family of three, their son a year or two older than Carmen's boy. The mother was beautiful, with dark brown eyes, her husband plain-looking next to her. Whenever they went out, they looked dressed for church. Their front door, which they left open longer than they needed to, was right next to the stairs, so you could look in. The front room was dark, and things were piled precariously high on top of a computer monitor. From the look of it, they were preparing to move out.

On the fourth floor, below them, was a woman with a very loud laugh. The word bellicose didn't even begin to describe it – not exactly a sputtering car engine or an insistent horn, but a bit of both. Her teenage son shuttled between her flat and the mechanic's two floors down.

Between the bellicose woman on Four and Noah on Two was a flat I never saw anyone go into or out of, so I assumed it was empty.

Under Noah, on the first floor, was an old lady whose face, no matter how hard I tried, I could never remember. I knew her only by the little cart she trailed behind her whenever she left the building to go grocery shopping. Unlike Carmen, she was very quiet and never said a word, even if you greeted her.

Across from me, in a railroad-style flat that was the mirror image of mine, lived Katya, the schoolteacher from Warsaw. Under her was a shy young woman who, from 4pm to midnight, worked as a paralegal Downtown. She climbed over Carmen's garbage bags whenever she came or went, saying nothing and keeping her head down. On Three was Esperanza, who lived with her Chihuahua and a daughter who sometimes smoked on the stairs with Eva, although as soon as Esperanza found out she screamed bloody murder and told her to get the hell back downstairs. Below them was the jazz musician.

On the first floor, opposite Maria and Wally, lived a large man in his twenties with ruddy cheeks who sometimes hung out on the front steps with his friends. He too owned a car, although you never saw him parking it or standing with Mohammed and Mister Winston. His front window, meanwhile, was always covered on the inside with a sheet of black plastic, so you couldn't see in.

I always made sure to smile at the ruddy-cheeked man when I passed through his cordon of friends, who were drinking out of brown paper bags and sometimes sharing a joint. Never saying anything, he merely nodded, and after a while I noticed that as much as the others smoked and drank, he never touched either. In spite of that, he was clearly the one in charge, and you got the feeling that the others would do anything he asked.

I didn't know his name yet, but I would soon learn it well: Big Steve.

On the prowl

Late at night there was often someone entering or leaving Big Steve's flat. It was never the same person, but he was usually young, wore sunglasses despite the late hour, and would always be in a hurry.

I noticed this because it was always late at night that I would go out looking for street finds for my flat. That was the best time to forage, when doormen and porters had put out the garbage for the next morning, the streets were less busy, and New York was, more or less, yours for the taking.

My usual route led me across the Split and into the wealthy Upper East Side, where the offerings were possibly the best in the city. That was one place where they always had great garbage.

Other collectors were out too. For the most part, they were men who, going by their rumpled oversized clothing, looked like they lived and slept on the street. A year earlier I would have quite unthinkingly used the word "hoboes", which I had always imagined quite romantically to be free-spirited men crossing America by hopping trains. They had no cares. But now, having been told that this was for some reason a derogatory term, I called them "homeless people".

The nighttime quest of these collectors was mostly empty cooldrink / soda cans. By dawn the more industrious of them would have filled huge bags, which they slung over their shoulders or loaded into shopping wagons, before heading northward up the island in a kind of pilgrimage, to a place where they exchanged the cans for five cents / a nickel apiece.

Out of curiosity, I tried to talk to them – Did they like particular areas for collecting? Were there some hours better than others? How many cans could they collect at once? – but they didn't respond or seemed frightened. Some even turned tail and fled. It seemed wisest then to leave them alone, although their silence made me even more curious. I wanted to find at least one collector who would tell me more about his or her 2am hunting sprees through the darkened streets.

One night I left home, as usual, soon after midnight. To reach the street I had to first step over Eva, who was playing with a boy's hair as they lounged on the stairs, and then passed a young man in Ray-Bans waiting at Big Steve's front door on the first floor.

Soon after crossing into the Upper East Side I saw three women collecting. Small and dark-skinned, possibly from Nicaragua or Guatemala, they had a very organised routine. After each of them had scoured a part of the street on her own, she would wait at the corner for the others, where they compared discoveries and bagged them, and then moved to the next street. Their quest was also quite singular: toys, stuffed animals, dolls, anything for children. All in all, it was as rare a sighting as three cheetahs on the veld.

Fascinated, I wanted to ask them about it, and I was sure they would talk. Unlike the homeless men collecting cans, the women and I had more in common. We were not only fellow collectors but fellow immigrants. In this huge city the four of us, far from our homes, shared an interest; we couldn't believe that good merchandise was being tossed on the pavement, and were prepared to venture out late at night to claim it for ourselves. Yes, we had much in common.

As soon as the three women saw me approaching them, though, they grabbed their bags and fled. Like me, they had probably made a few assumptions of their own. I was a white man in a very white neighbourhood. I probably lived in one of these rich-people buildings. I could well be on my way over to accuse them of doing something illegal, or, even worse, of being illegal. I could be the law.

What the four of us had in common, I realised, wasn't as great as what separated us, and within a few seconds the trio was gone from sight.

By the time I got home that night, a slightly chipped gilt-edged mirror tucked under my arm, the hallways in our old building had fallen quiet. There was no shouting, no music from behind doors, no bellicose laugh from the woman on Four, no-one splayed across the stairs smoking.

Before I turned the corner to the stairs, I heard shuffling ahead of me. By the second floor I caught up with a young man, small, wiry, unkempt, his eyes bloodshot. He had also been out collecting and was carrying a black garbage bag that, from the sound of it, was full of empty cans. He gave me a heartbreaking smile as I passed, and then, on the third floor, went into the flat in back, the one I'd always thought was unlived in.

A few days later I saw someone else leaving the flat. He was the first man's twin but thirty years older. He opened the door very gently and closed it the same way, as if there was a child inside he feared waking. Dressed in serge pants, a frayed jacket and a cap that made him look like someone Cézanne would have painted, he carried a broom in his hands. He walked down one floor and fanned the broom ineffectively across the hallway in front of Noah's front door and then returned home, again shutting the door without making a sound.

His name, I soon learnt, was Rafael.

A donkey's bray

As life inside the tenement settled down for the night, the street outside came noisily to life. Even the trains, with fewer city noises to compete against, were louder. They rocketed out of the tunnel south of us – or were sucked up into it – and the carriages leaving the city made a kertuck-a-katuck sound as they sped up to Westchester, the Bronx and places called Rye, Old Greenwich and Pelham.

People complained about the trains as much as they did about the projects across the street, but I liked them. There was something comforting about the ebb and flow of the locomotives during the night, the single most familiar thing in a world that was still alien, especially at night.

In between the train sounds, car alarms punctuated the darkness, and almost all of them played the same trio of harsh sounds in sequence – a horn, a whistle and the bray of a donkey.

Parp-parp-parp, weeeeeeeeee, awe-eee-awe-eee-awe.

Mister Winston's was one of them, although he took an hour or more to get to it. Triggered without provocation and usually at 2am, the alarm was not in his green van but in a faded blue Chevrolet that he never used. He seemed to own it for nothing more than rousing the neighbours out of their sleep.

Parp-parp-parp, weeeeeeeeee, awe-eee-awe-eee-awe.

As I lay in bed waiting for Mister Winston's Chevy to sound its siren again after a delay of twenty or thirty seconds, I listened to the night. Another train burst from the tunnel, and the engine driver, for no obvious reason, blew his whistle.

Kertuck-a-katuck, kertuck-a-katuck, kertuck-a-katuck...

Another car alarm went off on the far side of the projects, although this time the trio of sounds was different.

Waaaaaaahhhhh, bleep-bleep-bleep, trrrrrr.

Parp-parp-parp, weeeeeeeeee, awe-eee-awe-eee-awe.

An ambulance squealed up a faraway avenue. Somewhere else, an air horn was blown.

Parp-parp-parp, weeeeeeeeee, awe-eee-awe-eee-awe.

Waaaaaaahhhhh, bleep-bleep-bleep, trrrrrr.

A light arced across the sky. A shooting star, I thought, but then another followed. They were planes landing at LaGuardia Airport.

Words detached from sentences floated through the window like unstoppable emissions from a spluttering car engine.

"It was like you said." "Hey nigger." "Yo." "I din' say that." "I liked it."

The voices moved to another location.

"Yeah, yeah. Fights... now... lunch... told him... me." "When... never... stop... tomorrow. What?"

Silence.

"When?"

Silence.

"Where you going?" "Even then... but you. Hey. It's better." "... did it. When?" "Fuck you. They never. Where?" "Okay." "Night." "Pizza." "You gotta lie down." "No, *you* lie down."

Then, as suddenly as they had started, the voices were gone.

Unable to sleep, I went to sit in my window. A large dark car playing rap music pulled up at a lone fire hydrant in front of the projects, the only open space amidst the tightly parked cars, which included Mohammed's Toyota and Mister Winston's van.

...I just wanna fuck bad bitches,
All them nights I never had bitches,
Now I'm all up in that ass bitches,
Mad atcha boyfriend, aint'cha?...

A big man got out of the car, his white shirt luminous in the night. He talked into his cellphone and, leaving his car door open with the music still playing, sauntered over to the playground in the midst of the projects, some thirty yards away, where he hovered at a bench, all the while talking into the phone, which he held in front of his mouth. The acoustics on the fifth floor were so good that if it weren't for the music I could hear most of what he was saying.

...wanna fuck bad bitches...

Two more cars stopped near the fire hydrant and the first car, but the drivers didn't get out. One of them kept his engine running, his vehicle pulsating with hip-hop, while the other opened his door and played his fingers along the roof of the car. The man in the white shirt came back, killed his music and then talked to the other two. The hip-hop in the second car was also turned off and the three men went back to the bench. Before long one of them returned to turn his music on again.

60

A short stocky woman in jeans that were too small for her, badly affecting her gait, approached from the direction of the viaduct.

"Janice!" someone shouted.

"Yeah?!"

Her voice had broken in two a long time ago, possibly from constantly shouting to be heard, and she had a laugh that was on the wrong side of infectious. It was more like a cackle. She told someone halfway down the block, someone standing in the shadows, that she was on her way to the McDonald's a few streets away.

"Hey," she yelled, remembering some news, "I'm gonna be a grandma!"

Cackle, cackle.

Parp-parp-parp, weeeeeeeeee, awe-eee-awe-eee-awe.

By the time Janice was out of earshot, another car playing music had pulled up at the fire hydrant and a guy in a baseball cap and sunglasses was dancing next to it, occasionally talking to whomever was in the driver's seat. The men on the bench shouted to the newcomers, and the dancer joined them. A light flickered between the group and within a minute or two the smell of marijuana reached my window. By 3am the cars had taken off and our street, which had little through traffic because it was virtually cut off by the viaduct at one end, was like a cemetery once more.

Finally asleep, I found myself dreaming so intensely that I could smell cheeseburgers and French fries. I woke to realise it was actually Janice on the street returning from McDonald's laden with food.

Cackle, cackle.

Rats by night

Janice spent most daylight hours on her front stairs, which faced the blackened viaduct. Sitting with her were her three daughters, one pregnant and the others a lot younger, although they were all replicas of one another – right down to the broken voice.

It was impossible to tell how old each of them was, especially Janice, who hadn't aged well if she was thirty-five but didn't look bad for fifty-five. The others could have been anywhere from four to twenty-five but seemed way beyond their years, not only because of their size and weight but because of the frequent use of words like "Christ", "shit", "bitch" and "nigger". Their voices met you long before you turned the corner.

Cackle, cackle.

Janice's tenement, clad in burnished orange bricks, was easily the filthiest building in a radius of several blocks, possibly in the entire neighbourhood, which took some doing. No-one ever cleaned up outside – in our building at least Noah made an effort, no matter how feeble, once or twice a week – so the garbage accumulated on the pavement until it ran from the bottom of Janice's stairs to the street. To get past it your choice was to walk over it or in the traffic. Even though it meant risking being hit by a car, most people took the detour.

At night the garbage came to life, the bags rustling and crinkling as rats searched inside, coming up every now and then like scuba divers to check their location before submerging themselves again. More than once there was also blood on the pavement, as if people purposely chose Janice's building to get wounded – or, worse, to die – in front of. Usually the blood had dried by the time I saw it, although one Sunday morning a particularly thick and viscous red pool about twenty centimetres in diameter lay at the foot of the empty stairs.

On a second set of stairs, barely twenty metres away but not visible to Janice, sat someone else. It was Carmen's friend, the skinny woman with lupus, who took up a perch on the lowest step of the corner tenement on our street.

Her eyes incuriously watching anyone who walked by, she could have been waiting for a lift, except no car ever arrived for her. She held a cigarette that she rarely smoked, and only moved off the steps in order to come over to our building.

"Kar-ma! Hey, Kar-ma!"

As she called for Carmen her voice lost none of its volume, despite her poor physical condition.

"Kar-ma, you there?"

Carmen's front window was right below where I sat at my desk, so everything that happened on the street, like the lupus lady's shouting, the enormous mechanic working on his cars, the conversations of passersby, came up to me. It was a window on our little world.

"Kar-ma!"

Carmen eventually came to the window.

"Hey, honey. How long you been there?"

"You coming down?"

"Nah. You come up."

"Nah. Not feeling so good today." There was a pause before she shouted the inevitable explanation. "It's the lupus."

Medusa

Unlike Janice and the lupus lady, who were almost always seated and short of energy, Lucrezia Salazar was forever on the move, a small cyclone swirling and whirling up the avenue and down the side streets like something gusting out of the tunnel along with the trains.

Passing in front of my building numerous times a day, she diverted into the projects across the street or continued north, someone with a mission most urgent. She resembled an unfortunate victim in a Vittorio De Sica movie, her face squinched, her skin never missing its shiny film of grease or sweat, and her eyes always boasting periorbital shadows (although I preferred the American expression: raccoon eyes). If any attempt had ever been made to restrain her wiry hair, she had long given up on it.

In between rushing hither and thither, Lucrezia took time off to do her favourite thing, which was to stop people and talk. Her manner, however, was less to converse than to badger, and she would soon have ascended an invisible soapbox, hands flying, fingers pointing, hair springing up unappetisingly and Medusa-like. Words she favoured included "white people", "welfare", "the mayor", "this fucking city" and "you!"

Given the paucity of pedestrian traffic on our street, Lucrezia's victim was invariably some unsuspecting visitor or someone who'd lost his way. Poor Raymond the postman couldn't avoid her while doing his rounds, and you could see him steeling himself for a confrontation whenever he saw her. Other men, however, quickly took to tending their cars or hiding inside them when they saw her. Noah was never around when Lucrezia was, while Mohammed burrowed away inside his Toyota.

So women became Lucrezia's easiest targets, probably because they were too scared to say they had more pressing business to attend to. The only woman who she never talked to, curiously enough, was one who was always available and had all the time in the world as she sat at the bottom of the stairs of the corner tenement: the lupus lady. But Lucrezia walked straight past her without even saying hello.

For a long time I thought there might be some history between them, some bad blood. It turned out that I was right, but it wasn't the kind of history I had imagined.

A death in jail

A favourite spot for Lucrezia to set up her invisible soapbox was directly in front of my building. Sometimes she came inside and visited the back flat on the first floor. The quiet old lady who lived there and went shopping with her small cart in tow was Lucrezia's mother.

Like everyone else, I actively tried to avoid initiating conversation with Lucrezia because I knew that once she'd got got going, it would take a crowbar to pry her loose. But one morning, my guard down, I found her blocking the front stairs. I muttered a quick hello, but before I could make my getaway she gave me some bad news.

"My husband died last night," she said. "The father of my boys – he died."

Lucrezia had two sons – aged about four and six, I would guess, although big for their years – who kicked a ball around our street after dark and sometimes visited the old lady, their grandmother, on the first floor. I found it odd that Lucrezia was outside the tenement, smoking and announcing her tragedy to anyone who passed by, instead of mourning at home with her two boys. Maybe sensing my question, Lucrezia explained that she was actually divorced from the deceased man. The cause of death had been a heart attack, she carried on, and he'd been in jail at the time it occurred.

The facts of the story got repeated in various dramatic ways – "Dead father", "Boys' father", "Father of my boys", "Heart attack", "Fell over dead", "So sudden", "All alone" – until I told her that, sorry as I was for her loss, I needed to get to work.

No less theatrically, she made a second announcement.

"My daughter!"

Lucrezia's daughter, who looked at least twenty years older than the two boys, also came by the building, following pretty much the same route as her mother, and just as often, but not nearly as fast. Big-boned, she had greasy, long black hair and wore glasses that she tried to look over the top of. She had for a while also used a cane, dragging her right foot behind her, but lately had started walking unaided, holding one hand as if she was using it to force herself in the right direction, the long hair falling into her face like a stringy curtain.

"A stroke!" Lucrezia cried out, explaining her daughter's limp while lighting another cigarette without inhaling. She poked her hands into the air as if she was challenging it. "Twenty-six and a stroke!"

As Lucrezia continued – "Poor girl", "Six months", "Stroke", "Fucking Medicaid", "So young" – I noticed a woman, obviously lost, wandering up the street. It was my cue.

The moment Lucrezia noticed the approaching stranger, I quickly said goodbye. As I hurried away, I couldn't help noticing in a nearby car the familiar sight of Mohammed, his jacket collar pulled up far enough to almost conceal him.

Sour Patch Kids

In the first week of May – with the northern-hemisphere spring in full bloom – Lucrezia opened a nursery school in her mother's flat on our first floor.

A less likely vocation for Lucrezia was hard to imagine. Her own young boys were regularly left unattended, playing in the street at night, dodging any cars that sped through. They also used their spare time, Mohammed told me, to scratch the paintwork on cars and, on the rare occasion that the pavement was being repaired, to inscribe their initials in the wet cement next to words like "Cunt" and "Fuck you". It was hard to believe anyone would entrust their child to the mother of these boys.

But they did, and late every morning Lucrezia would lead a dozen very small children through the building's broken front doors and down the dirty long narrow hallway. They all held hands obediently as they trooped into the dimly lit hole at the far end, and I always got an uneasy feeling, as the door of the Old Lady's flat closed behind them, that it might be the last they were heard of. But reappear they did, walking out in a neat file and leaving the first-floor hallway littered with a fresh layer of wrappers and half-chewed sweets/candy that looked like Wine Gums, which here they called something else. The closest was probably gumdrops or – quite appropriately, given the kindergarten's Medusa-haired leader – Sour Patch Kids.

A resignation

A month later Lucrezia's nursery school had, quite unsurprisingly, closed its doors for business. It ended as suddenly as it began.

The very same week, with the flies gathering in bigger numbers every day on the garbage at her front door, my downstairs neighbour Carmen made an uncharacteristic trip down to the front door, to which she stuck a piece of white paper.

Handwritten by Carmen and bearing her signature, the notice announced that she had too many things going on in her life and would no longer be serving as a member of the board. The notice itself meant nothing to me, but the word "board" did. My South African friend's building, where I had first stayed in New York, also had a board, which meant the building was a co-op or a co-operative and the residents were owners.

Until that point I had been under the distinct impression that our ugly, sullied tenement was, like most residential buildings in New York, a rental property and owned by some mystery landlord, a man who was forever absent. But Carmen's notice put a new spin on things. There was no landlord of this ugly old building. Carmen and the others – the little man on Three, the 140-kilogram mechanic – all owned their flats.

The idea of the tenement being a co-op was mind-boggling. You might as well call a dilapidated cottage a villa or a wooden shack a country home. Co-ops were, by definition, like my South African friend's building. They had doormen and awnings. They were stately, Beaux-Arts, Italianate, well looked after, rich, clean, controlled, prewar and postwar. They were the epitome of order. But the adjectives that immediately came to mind where I lived were dark, grubby, careless, smoke-filled, noisy, forlorn, undesirable and chaotic.

In an entire year, moreover, I had heard no-one in the old building mention the words "co-op" or "co-operative", and co-operation seemed to be the furthest thing from anyone's mind. There was never any talk of matters you'd imagine communal property owners would be concerned about: broken locks, stuck windows, graffiti, garbage, loitering, marijuana in the hallways, fire hazards, Noah being paid for standing on the pavement and not much else... No-one said a thing.

In truth, it was only a matter of time before neglect and decay got the better of us.

CHAPTER 3
PRESIDENT

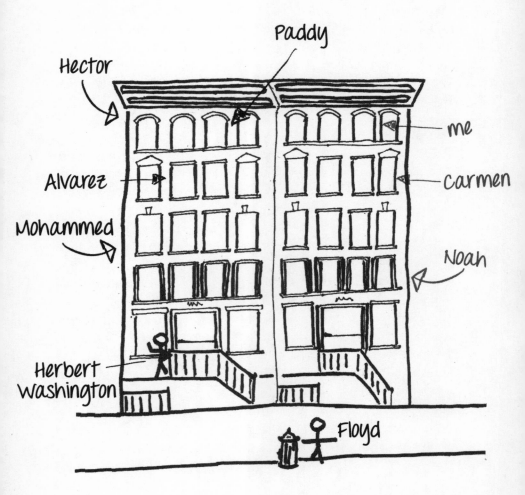

At the St Regis Hotel

In the following weeks I fleetingly mused about who might be the leader of the co-op or who might serve on its board of directors. The woman on One, Maria, who woke her son Wally with foul language? What about the Polish girl next door to me? The ruddy-cheeked man who sat on the stairs with his team of adoring friends?

The president, in fact, turned out to be none of the above but someone I had never met before. I had seen him, however, on Saturday mornings when I sat in my front window drinking coffee. Without fail, Paddy Murphy would be standing across the street with Noah, two men who, when they stood side by side, looked like physical opposites. Noah had unkempt black hair, a deeply tanned face that rarely saw a razor, and always looked like he had just rolled out of bed. Paddy's hair, meanwhile, was prematurely white and neatly trimmed, his face shaven, his skin pale, and he always wore clothes that were freshly pressed.

For an hour or so, the two men – the dark knight and the fair prince – held their positions, never saying a word to each other, both terribly upset about something. Even five floors up their anger was palpable, and you couldn't help wonder why they bothered meeting, saying nothing, apparently achieving nothing and then, a week later, carrying out the same routine all over again.

Paddy lived in the tenement next door to mine, the second one with mud-coloured front steps. He worked as a doorman at the St Regis, one of the city's most prestigious hotels, just off Fifth Avenue. When he came home, which was usually in the morning after a night shift, he walked up our street with his uniform jacket tossed casually over his shoulder, his tie removed, his shirt collar undone, his gold-brocaded hat sticking out of his briefcase.

One of those mornings during my first summer in the building, I was on my way to *Vanity Fair* when I saw Paddy returning home. As always I smiled and greeted him, even though he usually didn't respond and walked straight by, looking at the ground with singular purpose. His body language screamed three words: "Leave me alone!" But this particular morning Paddy Murphy stopped and greeted me back. His voice was gentle and he had a nice smile that you seldom got to see, especially on Saturday mornings.

"Do you like living in the building?" he asked me.

I didn't yet know what Paddy's role in my building was, but it was clear from his meetings with Noah, who also worked as the superintendent of Paddy's tenement, that he had one. Like Noah, Paddy sometimes also went into the basement of his tenement or mine, the only two people who ever did.

For the briefest moment I was tempted to get things off my chest. I wanted to tell Paddy – although he would've been blind if he hadn't already noticed – about the garbage, the dirty hallways, the graffiti, Lucrezia's boys and the mess they made on the first floor, the cars parked outside at 3am that brought an inexplicable amount of traffic between the ruddy-cheeked man's flat and our front doors, which, if he hadn't noticed, were both broken...

But I didn't say any of that. I had been in my flat for less than a year, and the rent was unbeatable. For that price, I would put up with a lot worse.

"It's great," I said. "I really like living here."

Paddy paused for a moment, and I was sure he didn't believe me. Then, as if he was casually talking about the weather or a baseball game he'd watched on TV the previous night, he asked me if I wanted to buy my flat.

"Buy what?" I asked, even though I'd heard exactly what he said.

"Your apartment," he repeated. "Do you want to buy it?"

He reached into his jacket for a fresh pack of Marlboros, unwrapped it and eased out a cigarette that he tapped against the box but left unlit. He told me that my flat belonged to the co-op and a decision had been taken to sell it to me. Was I interested?

Paddy, who was probably on the board that Carmen had resigned from, its president even, must have known how little I earned as a copy editor. So he would also have known I couldn't afford to buy a flat. How much they were asking for it I didn't know, but even in a run-down building like mine I couldn't imagine getting away for less than – what? – a hundred thousand dollars? Two hundred, even? (At the time that equalled/equaled a million rand.) This was, after all, New York City, the most desirable real estate in the world, and even the old building had a price.

"It will cost you $10,000," Paddy said.

Putting his jacket in the crook of his arm, he turned to leave. His head inclined once again to the ground, he started walking the last stretch to his tenement, before he called out a last few words.

"You think about it."

Musgrave v Baltic

There was nothing to think about. Ten thousand dollars was not only a fraction of what a flat in Manhattan would cost but a fraction of what a flat in the middle of Johannesburg would cost. In other words, it was practically free.

I had been warned of the challenges of buying a place in New York City and that it could take months, often much longer. You needed brokers, inspections, mortgages, loans, fees of all kinds, taxes, board interviews and then board approval and, of course, lawyers, who seemed to take their merry old time clocking up countless hours to peruse your documents and fine-tune them.

But that's not what happened. I was asked to meet no-one on any board and was interviewed and approved by no-one. The deal was cash, so there were no banks. Inspections: none. Fees: none. The only thing I had to do was pay a lawyer a few hundred dollars to look over the lease. After paging through it she had just one comment, besides the fact that she couldn't believe it was true.

"Buy it," she said. "You would be mad not to, even if it's a scam. And if you don't buy it, I will."

Both of us knew that she couldn't, though, because she earned too much. In the same way you had to be low-income to rent in the old building, you had to be low-income to buy. And the old building already had my papers proving I qualified.

Everything went so smoothly, in fact, and the transaction was so lacking in the headaches and stark realities of buying property, it often felt like we were playing Monopoly. The two tenements with the mud-coloured front steps would have been the equivalent of the starter properties on the game board, the brown ones on the South African version like Musgrave Road and Gillespie Street. In the American version, that would be Baltic Avenue and Mediterranean Avenue.

I begged, borrowed and scraped together the $10,000. I raided my small retirement fund for which *Time Out New York* and *Vanity Fair* took measly amounts out of my pay every week, and I got a loan from my father in Cape Town.

The night before the transfer/closing, I went through the lease one last time to see if I'd overlooked anything: a loophole, a crack, something I'd missed that would prove this was all a big mistake.

The lease said, in essence, what you could and couldn't do with your flat, what your responsibilities were and how you could, in certain situations, forfeit ownership. Most importantly, I was getting not possession of my flat but a share in the co-op – or, rather, in the two tenements. That's how co-operative all us owners were meant to be: We were shareholders and we were in this together.

I was also buying my flat *voetstoots*, which here they didn't have a special word for, so the document just said "as is". From the moment I signed the contract, all changes and improvements would be my responsibility.

Other paragraphs in the lease dealt with liens, restrictions on use, requirements for alterations, and building finances, although I couldn't imagine we had any. There were regulations detailing what was good behaviour (one of which, I couldn't help but notice, was that the hallways had to be kept vacant at all times, day and night, and not be used as a storage place for Carmen's garbage or a salon for Eva's smoking and hair-braiding). There were sections too about unsold shares, rights of possession, fiscal management, foreclosures, inspection of books of account, and meetings of shareholders, which, as far as I could tell, never happened or, if they did, no-one ever talked about.

The one thing that wasn't mentioned, and very noticeably too, was the price. Who had decided what it should be? Why was it so shockingly low? Could it ever be raised? And if someone ever decided to sell, would it be for the same price?

So many questions filled my head that night I could barely sleep, petrified that by morning someone would have changed their mind about selling the flat to me or increased the price by a hundred thousand dollars.

Even more Monopoly

Late the next morning, exactly a month after Paddy had approached me on the street with the deal of a lifetime, I headed to the basement of his tenement next door. You reached it by going down some stairs underneath the mud-coloured entrance – stairs used almost exclusively by Noah the superintendent by day and the rats by night.

A narrow main room resembled the inside of an old, badly patched-up submarine. A low ceiling was crisscrossed by countless pipes, the floor had been freshly painted a military grey and the walls were peeling so badly they might have been suffering from a disease. Three backless red wooden benches had been put out. Paddy and I sat on one, Morgenstern, the co-op's lawyer, on another.

Morgenstern was in his late sixties or early seventies and a bit rumpled-looking. His jacket was creased, his tie badly put together, and he kept digging in his briefcase for something he couldn't find.

"You gave me your paperwork, right?" he asked me for the third time.

I nodded. He burrowed away in his papers some more.

"Do I have the co-op's blank shareholder certificates?" he asked Paddy. "Or do you?"

Paddy said Morgenstern must have them because he only kept the seal. He held up a metal contraption as big as a nutcracker that was used to imprint the co-op's name on documents.

"I seem to have forgotten your shareholder certificate," Morgenstern told me, then laughed for no reason. "Never mind. I'll give it to you some other time."

Paddy sighed irritably and shook his head, but Morgenstern didn't notice.

Every few minutes, a stranger wandered down the stairs from the street and, possibly drawn by the sound of our voices, stuck a head in the door to see what was going on. I had never seen any of them before on our street – a place where you got to know the regular traffic, seeing there was so little of it – but they appeared to be quite at home walking into other people's basements.

Paddy paid no attention to them.

"What are we waiting for?" Morgenstern asked no-one in particular.

"Hector," Paddy said, visibly annoyed.

"Is Miss Carol coming?"

"No," Paddy replied curtly. "She never comes to meetings."

A scraping on the stairs signalled that someone was on his way down. The man who appeared at the door was in his fifties, had thick wavy grey hair liberally dosed with oil, a generous moustache and bushy eyebrows, and the lenses on his glasses were tinted so you got only the vaguest impression of his eyes. He pressed the large spectacles to his face and then looked at us as if he was focusing or getting used to the light. This, I gathered, was Hector.

"Morning!" he called out, but no-one responded to him.

He reached for a comb in an inside pocket of his jacket and, in a well-exercised move, slipped it through his hair a few times. He took a seat next to Morgenstern, who was still smiling at some joke he had heard and wasn't going to share.

Hector was the vice-president of the board and lived in Paddy's tenement. In a year I had seen him maybe once or twice, both times carrying a small brown paper bag in the crook of his arm.

"Welcome to the building!" he said to me as if he really meant it.

Paddy bristled. He addressed Hector without facing him.

"Did you bring those papers I asked for?"

Hector didn't reply, so Paddy tried again.

"Well?"

"I will get to them," Hector said.

"That's what you always say. It's been a month already."

Hector went rigid.

"Fuck you!" he shouted, the words almost launching his body off the red bench.

"No," Paddy shot back, unfazed. "Fuck *you*!"

"What's your problem, man? It's always the same old shit with you. 'Do this and do that'."

"Fuck off!"

They kept on like this for a few moments, during which time a surprising sense of calm fell over me, as if I was detached from their battle, a foreign mariner passing through a stormy sea. Theirs was a world I was in, but not exactly part of. None of it, in any case, seemed real: my neighbours, the conditions we lived in, the price I was paying for my flat, the simplicity of the sale. It could have been a dream.

Given all of that, the present display of two grown men behaving badly while trying to carry out an important piece of business didn't surprise me at all. I just watched them bemusedly from my passing skiff, unaware that a tidal wave was heading my way.

Paddy stopped swearing and groaned, looking down at the floor so that all you could see was the white crown of his head, a crown, it was now quite obvious, our fair prince didn't wear easily. Everything made him angry: Noah, Morgenstern, Miss Carol, Hector. He had clearly been president of the old building for far too long.

"I don't even know why you are on the board," he said to Hector. "You do nothing."

Unable to think of a clever rejoinder, Hector tried the usual.

"Fuck you!"

The comb appeared and went through his hair three times.

"Well, it's true," Paddy said. "I can never get hold of you or Miss Carol."

"Fuck off!"

Paddy gave up and turned back to Morgenstern.

"Let's get on with this," he said. "We're here to sign the lease of a new shareholder."

Morgenstern, who hadn't stopped smiling the entire time, momentarily lost his train of thought.

"Oh, yes," he said, suddenly remembering.

He asked me for my cheque/check of $10,000, which I quickly handed over before the two feuding men had second thoughts about why they were here and decided to postpone the transaction indefinitely. I signed the lease, after which Paddy and Hector signed, making sure not to get too close to one another. With the metal contraption he had been holding, Paddy impressed the co-op's official seal on the final page.

"Now you are a shareholder," Morgenstern said, then added yet again, "I forgot your certificate. Did I tell you that? I don't know where I could have put it."

Paddy sighed, while Hector stared into the recesses of the basement, where everything was in darkness. For a few moments we sat in silence and then Paddy tapped a cigarette on his box of Marlboros like a small gavel.

"I have something to say," he announced.

I hoped it wasn't going to be something about Hector, which would set off another swearing match.

"I have decided to sell my apartment," Paddy said.

"What?!" Morgenstern said. For the very first time his smile disappeared. This was not good news. "You're leaving?"

"Yes. My wife and I are selling up and moving to Riverdale."

Riverdale was far to the north of the city, across the Harlem River.

"But who's going to run the building?" Morgenstern asked.

I looked at Hector, who, as vice-president, would have seemed the obvious choice. But he seemed interested in little else except his facial hair.

Paddy had already turned to me.

"What about you?" he asked. "Do you want to be president of the board?"

Me? Run a building?

I did some quick mental maths (which, unlike antique store, here did not get an *s*, so it became *math*). I knew people in the old building by name and sometimes even by history. I had found out that Noah wasn't Noah's real name, as I'd first suspected; it was Santiago, although I had heard it used only once or twice. Maria, who screamed for Wally to wake at 6am, had been born on our street, in a building that had since burnt/burned down. Her elder son lived with an ex-husband in Connecticut because he'd been arrested for running with a gang in the neighbourhood, and she didn't want him influencing his younger brother, Wally. Carmen, as she'd confessed to me on the landing one night, had once been an airline stewardess. Esperanza, who had raised three children in her small flat on the third floor, now worked as a cleaning lady at an expensive gym Downtown. I even had nicknames for some of them, like the woman with the sputtering car-engine laugh on Four who prefaced many an attention-seeking comment with the words "Choose me!" – which turned out to be "Excuse me!" The Polish girl, the jazz musician, the Indian man Mister Singh who was married to the moustachioed Guadelupe – I knew them all.

The only person I hadn't talked to was the quiet old man who lived on the third floor, Rafael, although I wasn't quite sure he knew how to talk at all.

Yes, I could tick off every resident in the building, and then some. In Paddy's tenement, I knew Herbert Washington, the old man who stood on the stoep/stoop/porch every morning swaying his head to inaudible music. I knew about the woman who lived on the fifth floor and did laundry she threw to someone waiting in the street. Even Mohammed, who lived two floors below Paddy, I had got to know well enough for him to finally confess his true origin – which I was never quite sure why he'd hidden from me – which was not Yemen but Ghana.

Be president? Of course I could. And why not? How hard could it be to run these two small tenements? I knew exactly what and whom I was dealing with. I knew the people and I knew the place. Besides, what did I have to lose?

"Are you sure I can do that?" I asked Morgenstern. "Don't you need to have an election or something?"

Paddy was full of authority, like he'd already plotted out everything.

"Of course you can," he said. "You can be co-opted by the other board members." Then he added, possibly to reassure me, "No-one else wants the job anyway."

He had a point. Carmen had resigned. And it seemed that the treasurer, Miss Carol, whom I'd never seen, had no interest in board affairs. Hector the vice president, meanwhile, didn't even seem to be following the course of our conversation. Paddy was right – there was no alternative.

I once again asked Morgenstern if becoming president with no election was legal.

"Of course," he said. The smile on his face had come back and should have reassured me, but it didn't really. "So long as the others agree, it's fine."

We all turned to Hector, who still hadn't said anything.

"He doesn't want the job," Paddy said.

Hector sprung back to life suddenly. "Fuck you!"

He took out his comb and pointed it threateningly at Paddy.

"Well, do you?" Paddy asked him.

"No," he said, then added as an afterthought: "Asshole!"

The insult made no impact on Paddy.

"So you are okay with him being president?" he asked.

Hector patted the hair on top of his head lightly, careful not to muss it up.

"Go ahead," he said. "I don't care."

Paddy looked at me expectantly.

"So, do you want to be president?"

It took me all of five seconds to answer.

"Sure," I said. "If no-one else wants the job, I'll take it."

The secret door

And so it was, a few days later, that I found myself on the pavement outside my building waiting for Paddy to take me on a tour through the two basements. Down there was the engine of the building, the machinery, our heartbeat. As soon as we met at the top of my basement stairs, Paddy handed me a heavy set of keys more numerous than there were doors in the two tenements.

"Go on," he instructed me, and, in my first act as president-elect, I unlocked the door to the first basement.

The room was almost an exact replica of the basement next door, where I had signed my lease. Dozens of water and gas pipes of all sizes spread trellis-like below the ceiling, although the floor hadn't been painted military grey and the space was filthy. Other words that came to mind were "eerie" and "a good place to hide a body".

Cramping the room on the right was a raised area the size of a large Jacuzzi that had been filled with sand. Below it, Paddy explained to me, lay an old decommissioned oil tank. On top of the sand were strewn used car tyres and broken furniture, a hodgepodge that spread throughout the basement, where they were joined by shattered lamps, road barricades, wires, bricks and filthy cushions. The filthy public hallways in the tenement were, by comparison, immaculate.

Opposite the sand-covered oil tank was a fair-sized room, empty except for a rusty filing cabinet that stood in its very centre. Paddy, trying to force open one of the battered drawers, told me that most of the older documents for the building were kept there. Flakes of disintegrating paper powdered the surrounding floor.

The next room was smaller, the one after that minuscule, their walls and floors inexpertly torn out and the lights broken. Walking past them, to the back of the basement and the boiler room, I could hear a broken pipe dripping ceaselessly in one of the darkened spaces.

In the boiler room, the floor was slippery with leaked oil and suffocating humid fumes clung to the air. The boiler itself resembled something out of a 1950s sci-fi movie, with two big interconnected box-shaped metal containers, the larger one about three metres long, tubes and pipes running arm-like in various directions, and a gauge in front to measure the pressure. Out its back ran an exhaust covered in foil that linked it to the exterior wall.

The two buildings got their hot water and heat from the boiler, Paddy told me. This old machine created steam that coursed through numerous pipes running into the building and each flat. Bizarrely, however, the oil tank that fuelled the boiler was in the second basement. The two tenements might have had separate entrances and different lives, but they were inextricably linked by the heating system. Cut the oil in the one or the old spaceship boiler in the other, and our 30-flat enterprise ceased to function.

Paddy opened a nearby door that was meant to be an emergency exit, although it led only into a small enclosed yard that faced a side wall of Floyd's tenement. The only egress was up a rickety metal staircase to a door on our first floor that was locked from the inside, so this was no emergency exit at all. Paddy also had to push very hard to let us out because the exit was partly blocked by a congealed mass that, on closer inspection, turned out to be wads of toilet paper, tissue and tampons, studded with dozens of cigarette butts. Looking up I saw that poorly aimed projectiles streaked the wall below Carmen's bathroom window on the fourth floor. Right next to that window was the public hallway window through which Eva, lounging on the stairs, threw her cigarettes.

Before we left the basement Paddy stopped at a little hatch in the wall that I hadn't noticed earlier. It looked like a secret door – small and metal – and was situated at the height of a window. Paddy pulled a latch to expose the very bottom of the air shaft, a dark area I could barely see looking down from my flat

Pigeons nesting on the sills above us ricocheted off the walls, aiming for safety higher up, while Paddy and I crawled into the claustrophobic space. The walls on either side of us, my tenement and Floyd's, were blackened with a century of age, making the small hexagon of sky at the top almost blindingly bright. The windows on the first floor were too high to reach, but someone could jump down from them if they really wanted to. For anyone who didn't want to be found, or someone trying to escape the law, this would be the perfect place to hide.

The baseball bat

The keeper of the filthy basements, Noah, didn't exactly like me – I'm not sure that Noah liked anyone – but he tolerated me, which was the best you could hope for. When he and Floyd were hanging out on the pavement, I sometimes joined them for a few minutes, just listening to them, Floyd pointlessly tossing countless verbal grenades at Noah's impenetrable wall of silence.

Sometimes the quiet old man from the third floor, Rafael, stood near them, saying nothing, his head bent, as defenceless as a puppy. If Noah said anything, it was to bark an instruction at Rafael to go to the corner store, which was barely a few minutes away by foot, and get him some cigarettes.

"Hing crazy," Floyd said, as old man Rafael shuffled off.

Noah twirled a finger at his ear in case I hadn't understood, but "crazy" was one of the few words Floyd pronounced that I did actually understand.

The squat, talkative Floyd was the person you saw Noah with most, but I don't think he was so much a friend as a sidekick, a foil, Sancho Panza to Noah's Don Quixote.

The only person I ever met who might have qualified as an intimate friend of Noah's, in fact, I met only once. But this man knew Noah so well that he was privy to his deepest secret – the reason why Noah had fled his own country and come to America.

It was a weekday afternoon and the three of us were seated in Noah's bakkie/pick-up, a lavender Ford that had shiny wire hubcaps with spinners in the middle, gleaming silver. The vehicle, which never went a day unpolished, was always parked close enough to the tenement so Noah could see it. We were driving to a huge hardware store outside the city to pick up supplies for a small job I had asked Noah to do in my flat. The stranger, who was small and neatly dressed, sat between Noah and me.

On the way, without any warning from Noah, we took a detour to City Island. A little-known enclave not far from Manhattan, the small island was somewhere you could find cheap seafood and, for anyone in the city who owned a boat, somewhere not too expensive to keep it docked. No-one I had come across in New York had a boat, but Noah did: a small fishing vessel he kept not in a marina, but on land in a sort of boat parking lot.

As we wandered through the sea of stationary vessels, and Noah peeled off from us to find out where his boat had been parked, the stranger made small talk. I'm not sure how it came about, but he suddenly announced that Noah had come to America after an incident with a man and a baseball bat in a bar in Puerto Rico. It didn't sound like things had gone well for the other man, and Noah's parents had thought it best for him to leave the island. (Maybe it was then, too, that the man who had once been known as Santiago changed his identity to the ill-fitting name he had now, Noah.)

At some stage after arriving in America Noah had landed up at the old building, where he, too, had become an owner.

The little kingdom
A week later, out of the blue, Noah invited me to come see his inner sanctum – a place that I'm sure no-one else in the building had ever seen – his flat.

He lived in the back of the tenement, above the Old Lady on the first floor – Lucrezia's mother – and below old man Rafael on the third. Like the railroad flats in front, his had four rooms, although they were laid out in a square cut in quarters, not a straight line. The back two rooms faced the yard, which, like all the adjoining yards behind us, went unused and was strewn with garbage and debris from old could-have-been-forgotten construction projects.

As I headed down to Noah's floor, I had to step over Eva's hairdressing paraphernalia on the stairs, an ashtray and a bottle of nail polish that had leaked a deep fuchsia across one of the steps. Stale smoke commingled with the smell of something foetid, Carmen's garbage. Eva had recently taken a black bag down to the pavement, her route clearly demarcated by a trail of coffee grinds and egg shells. Someone had also spilt a carton of milk that was going sour.

I knocked on Noah's door and when he opened it I pointed at Eva's aftermath.

"It's disgusting," I said.

I was not president yet – a few weeks remained until I officially took over – and I was at an uncomfortable juncture in my relationship with Noah. How did I go from being his friend – or rather, a person whom he felt comfortable having in his pick-up, showing his boat, inviting to his flat – into being the person who told him to pull up his socks and do his job? After all, I'd said nothing about the same hallways for almost a year. Why start now?

"Peeg!" Noah declared, meaning Carmen.

Noah hardly ever said anything, so his remark took me by surprise. Then, in perhaps the longest speech I ever heard him make, he told me – I'm not sure how exactly, given his poor English and my limited Spanish – that Carmen's behaviour used to be far worse. She once used to throw her garbage directly out of her front window to the street far below. It was a measure of how far the building had progressed that Eva now took it down by hand.

"Ease good," he concluded.

"But look at the mess she makes when she does it," I carried on, pointing out the obvious coffee grinds and spilt milk in case he hadn't noticed. "It goes all the way from her front door, down the stairs and outside."

Noah wasn't interested and changed the subject.

"Venga," he said, motioning me inside his front door.

Behind it I didn't expect to find much. This, after all, was a man who appeared to sleep in his clothes and who let litter gather outside his front door rather than bend over and pick it up. He didn't live alone – in another strange twist in his relationship with Paddy, Noah was dating Paddy's sister-in-law – so I knew there would at least be a woman's touch in the flat. But what I found left me astounded or, more appropriately, as they said here, gobsmacked.

The floors in Noah's place were marble and the kitchen cabinets and the wardrobes in the bedroom were handcrafted from mahogany and oak. The bed, a huge ornate affair, had also been carved by hand. Not a single thing was out of place, not a dish in the sink, not a jacket tossed over a chair, not an open box of biscuits/crackers on the counter, not a surplus ornament on a shelf. The flat was neat, spotless, well thought out and, if your taste ran to marble floors and oversized wood furniture, most desirable.

In the living room, set up in a prime position that you couldn't avoid noticing as soon as you opened the front door, was a small glass display case. Instead of containing an old model sailing ship, which one might have expected, this one had a house made of balsa wood and was nicely painted. Raised off the ground on stilts with a wide porch decorated with doll-house-sized furniture, a neat sandy stretch below it all, the structure was someone's dream property on a beach somewhere.

"Mi casa Puerto Rico," Noah announced proudly. His house in Puerto Rico.

Noah, whether or not he was trying to, had impressed me. Within a few weeks I had learnt that he not only knew how to handle himself in a bar with a baseball bat but that he had, since coming to America, been able to buy a lavender pick-up that he kept spotless, a speedboat, a beach house and a flat he had renovated beautifully.

And that wasn't all.

Noah opened the front door with uncharacteristic enthusiasm.

"Venga!" he instructed me again.

We both stepped out of the immaculate flat into the stinking hallway, careful not to slip in the pool of old milk. With his cigarette protruding from between his knuckles, his keys jangling like a small sabre, Noah led the way to the basement of Paddy's tenement. After unlocking the door, he walked across the military-grey floor, past the room housing the oil tank, and stopped at a door that was the only one in either basement that anyone bothered to lock – and not only once, but three times.

Behind it lay a workshop, which, like Noah's flat, was carefully looked after. Two electric drills had their cords wrapped around them, a huge lathe stood squarely in a corner, boxes of floor tiles were piled high in another corner, an open metal trunk displayed neatly arranged tools, wood off-cuts were packed tightly together against the wall, and a 250-horsepower boat engine was propped up in a huge drum. On the workbench was a rocking chair Noah was busy fixing. It was here, he told me, that he did jobs for people in the building and outside.

Even more pieces of wood, metal, drywall/sheetrock and ladders that couldn't fit into the workshop were stored in other parts of the basement. Every room, in fact, had been co-opted by Noah for his equipment and supplies.

"Mira!" he said. "Look!"

Standing in the middle of the grey-floored main room, dishevelled and happy, he waved his hand around what was clearly his little kingdom.

September 11

I was sitting at my desk early one Tuesday morning, my attention diverted by the lupus lady shouting for Carmen, when the phone rang. It was my brother in Johannesburg.

"Are you alright?" he asked.

The date was September 11, 2001, and two planes had flown into the World Trade Center. It was barely ten kilometres away from me, Downtown at the southern tip of Manhattan, but people far across the Atlantic Ocean had heard the news before me.

First I panicked. A very close friend of mine sometimes worked in the basement of one of the Twin Towers. I tried to call him, but there was no answer. Did he work there on Tuesdays or Thursdays? I turned on the television and I watched the same images – one plane flying into a tower, then another into the second, the shaky amateur footage picking up the panicked movements of people and the cries of disbelief – over and over again. Then my friend called. No, he only worked at the World Trade Center on Thursdays. He was fine.

I felt relieved and then, oddly enough, I felt nothing. My little skiff, once again, was sailing by this turmoil without being part of it. All around me other people were outraged by what had happened, fearful of going outside, nervous about taking public transport, crying at the slightest provocation, even though they hadn't known anybody who had died. Me, I felt like someone at a funeral who knows he should be in mourning but for some reason can't do it.

A few days later, I happened to talk to another South African journalist, who worked at a major news magazine and had lived in America longer than I had. He was equally mystified by the reactions of people around him.

"I have colleagues who don't even want to come to work," he said. "And they are journalists, mind you. They're scared another bomb will go off."

What was wrong with us, we two immigrants? Why couldn't we be angry and scared and mourn like everyone else? Were we cold and inhuman? Or were we just immune to this kind of event?

My mind also kept going back to Pretoria, 1983. It was a Friday afternoon in May, when people were leaving work for the start of the weekend. In front of the Poyntons Building, the tallest building downtown where the military had an office, a car bomb went off. Nineteen people were killed and more than two hundred injured. Television was heavily censored back then and there was no CNN, but I remember photographs in the paper of bodies lying in the street. It looked like a scene from a movie about the end of the world.

A terrible sense of depression and dread came over me at the time. My country was doomed. The Nationalist Party would never accept that apartheid was wrong, and the African National Congress would keep fighting and setting off bombs. A year earlier the South African military had raided an ANC base in Lesotho, where forty-two people were killed. In Mozambique, the anti-apartheid activist Ruth First had been killed by a parcel bomb sent on the orders of the South African police. The spiral of violence was getting worse and the end would not be good for anyone.

From that day in 1983 onwards I mentally prepared myself for a new reality – at any minute a bomb might go off. When it finally did, it was on another continent eighteen years later. And my reactions, or lack of them, were so different from everyone else's around me that I felt more than ever like an immigrant and a fraud.

Morocco and insurance

With the city still on edge – you could see it mostly on the faces of people packed tightly on the train underground – I headed to Midtown on one of my days off from copy-editing. At the Il Forno pizza parlour, I waited in a grimy alcove where I had stood once before and was buzzed up to the second floor.

The last time I had been outside Il Forno, just over a year ago, I had been nervously holding a year's supply of *Vanity Fair* and desperately hoping that Shoshanna the real-estate agent would let me become one of her tenants. Now I was, in effect, her boss.

"Let's go see Abbie," she said as soon as we met.

Abbie, Shoshanna's sister, was the head of the agency, which, it now became clear, consisted of just the two of them. She was smaller than Shoshanna, clipped her hair short, wore shorter skirts and talked with a lisp.

"Where are you from?" she asked when she heard my accent.

I told her.

The mention of South Africa for some reason triggered Abbie's desire to be from somewhere else too. Maybe it was a way to stand out in a city of millions. To me the sisters sounded American – maybe from Queens or Staten Island, going by their accents – but Abbie claimed another nationality I never would have guessed.

"We're from Morocco," she said.

Her phone rang, and as she picked it up Shoshanna suggested we go back to her office.

Once we were seated in her little cubicle she opened a file with numerous papers she wanted me to sign, most of them blank cheques. In preparation for this moment, I had visited our bank the previous week to arrange becoming an official signatory for the building, a procedure that turned out to be not only lengthy – four return visits and about twenty phone calls – but very confusing. It was the kind of inefficiency and bureaucracy people always said you got in Africa, not America.

Our old building, I discovered, had no debt, no mortgage and about $30,000 in reserve. It was the one healthy limb we had left, although it's a wonder no-one had lopped it off yet. At least six people were authorised to sign cheques for whatever amount they wanted on our behalf, although only one of them – Hector – still lived in the building. The five other names, none of which I recognised, did not include Paddy, even though he had been signing cheques for several years. No-one at the bank had picked up on any of these mistakes.

"Just sign at the bottom," Shoshanna said, pushing one paper at a time across her desk.

There was a cheque for Morgenstern but several too for another law firm whose name – Maguire & Cohen – I saw for the first time. There was a payment we owed for the maintenance of the boiler. There were cheques for Noah, both for his job as superintendent that he didn't do and for other "miscellaneous" jobs.

We had also received numerous fines from the city for garbage messed on the pavement.

"Noah needs to keep the garbage sorted out," I told Shoshanna.

Looking after Noah was one of the agency's primary duties.

"I will tell him," she promised.

"The hallways are a disgrace too," I added. "How come they aren't being cleaned?"

"They aren't?" She was credibly astonished by this piece of news. "I'll talk to Noah."

"That would be good. And mention the basement too."

She nodded, pushing another paper across at me. It was a renewal of our insurance policy, which was for a big amount, and there was lots of tiny print on its pages that I felt I should go through before committing the building to it.

"Never mind," Shoshanna said. "It's the same one every year." She indicated a big blank space under the word OWNER. "Just sign there."

"But I'm not the owner," I replied, uncomfortable about authorising something I hadn't read and understood.

"It's okay," she said reassuringly. "You're the president. That's what you do."

Death threats

Paddy's tenement was identical to mine, right down to the two-tone, shit/vomit-brown walls in the hallways and the tiles on the floors more suited for an old prison. The litter and cigarette butts on the floor only seemed less severe because they lacked Eva's weekly spillage as she trekked to the garbage cans.

Most distinctive, though, was a very strong odour. Hitting you like a sledgehammer as soon as you walked through the front door was a combination of wet dog, toxic old paint and cigarettes extinguished in flat beer, creating a potion so acrid it made you turn the colour of the brown walls. By the fourth floor, the smell had eased up somewhat and been replaced, probably on purpose, by a very strong and expensive perfume.

Paddy lived in the exact same flat as me, fifth floor, front, west side. His wife – pretty, petite and slightly nervous-looking –

answered the door, and Paddy stood protectively behind her. He was the happiest I had ever seen him, as if he'd let go of all his troubles along with the post of president.

Their flat felt more cramped than mine because they had turned one of the small middle rooms into an office, with heavy floor-to-ceiling built-in cupboards. On the desk were two boxes containing papers and files, as well as a plastic bag with the metal seal of the building. To these Paddy had added the blank shareholder certificates, which he had obtained from the lawyer Morgenstern.

"You don't keep these in the basement like the other documents?" I asked, referring to the rusty filing cabinet he had shown me.

"No," he said. "And if I were you, I would keep them in my apartment too. They're not safe down there."

"How do you mean, 'not safe'?"

"Someone might get to them," he said. "Just keep them with you."

The basements were always locked, so I wasn't sure who Paddy could mean by "someone". Noah? Hector? Carmen? Was there a thief I should know about? Why would anyone want to get into these particular files anyway? What could be so important?

"Okay," I said, promising to keep the two boxes in my flat.

I tried to sound nonchalant but it was quite obvious that things had changed. For the very first time Paddy had actually said something about the building that made me think this maybe wasn't Monopoly we were playing, after all.

I knew there were problems – filth and decay mostly – but I was sure I could deal with them. Unlike Paddy, I was the hail-fellow-well-met guy, on good terms with everyone, and I was eager to make the co-op work. Maybe Paddy just had the wrong disposition for the job.

Paddy's wife, who had been on the phone, exchanged a few words with her husband as I flipped mindlessly through the pages in one of the boxes. When she left, Paddy came over to me smiling so much he looked ready to burst into song.

"That was my wife's sister on the phone," he said, meaning the sister who was involved with Noah. "You know they've split up?"

I shook my head, although I hadn't seen her recently.

"She's been telling my wife a lot of things about Noah," Paddy continued, "things that Noah says about you."

"About me?" I asked in surprise.

I couldn't imagine Noah talking to anyone about anything, let alone me.

"Yes," Paddy replied. "He says he has nothing to worry about now that you are president. He has you in the palm of his hand and he can do anything he wants with you. He says you won't give him any trouble."

What I had expected to be a simple trip to Paddy's to pick up some files was turning into something darker. First, I had learnt there was someone who might want to tamper with, destroy or steal our building's documents. Second, Noah was not going to take me seriously and it was unlikely I would ever get him to do his job. The building would stay filthy. But there was a third piece of news from Paddy, and it had to do with why he was moving.

Paddy's sale had never entirely made sense to me. I could understand him giving up his role as president, but that didn't mean he had to move. His newly purchased flat was in Riverdale, far to the north and west of us, which meant that he had almost tripled his commute, in time and distance, to the St Regis Hotel.

Besides that, he was selling his flat for a fraction of what it was worth. What you could sell your flat for – a point the lease referred to in vague terms no-one had ever been able to decipher – was still a mystery to me and, clearly, also to Paddy. And that was also maybe why no owner in the building had ever sold a flat before.

So Paddy was going to be a trailblazer. He was asking for only $30,000, which, though it was three times as much as he had charged me for my flat (another figure the origin of which still mystified me), was a lot less than he could have asked. He was turning his brown property on the Monopoly board into a pale blue one when he could have at least gone for pink.

None of it made any sense at all to me, until I found out why Paddy was really leaving. He was trying to get away from our building and our street as fast as possible.

"Somebody has been threatening us," he said, his old seriousness back again.

For an entire year, a man had been coming upstairs at all hours of the day, pounding on the door, shouting abuse and promising to kill them. The man knew that Paddy worked at the hotel at night, leaving his wife all on her own, so he made sure to come by more often during those hours.

"My wife is scared out of her wits," Paddy said, holding her hand. "He makes our lives a living hell."

The man making the threats was, in fact, a neighbour, a fellow owner who lived one floor down named Alvarez. I had never seen Alvarez or anyone who looked like he'd kill you – besides Noah maybe – so I didn't know who Paddy meant.

The incident that had started the battle was, it appeared, a small one. There had been a leak in Alvarez's flat, apparently caused by the washing machine in the flat above his owned by the woman who did laundry. She wasn't actually allowed to own a washing machine, according to the lease, but that was another issue altogether.

Alvarez demanded that the leak be fixed by the building, but whenever someone came by to fix it he wasn't home. The damage to his ceiling got worse, and he retaliated by not paying his levy. Paddy, angry at Alvarez for withholding his monthly payments, told the sisters, Shoshanna and Abbie, to send Alvarez a letter from the lawyer. The fight quickly got ugly after that.

Paddy had gone to the police about the threats but they said they had to actually catch Alvarez in the act of threatening someone. Paddy's wife was no longer able to sleep at night when Paddy wasn't there, and he was always worried when he was away from home.

"That's why we can't live here anymore," Paddy said. "We have to leave."

CHAPTER 4
A NEW ORDER

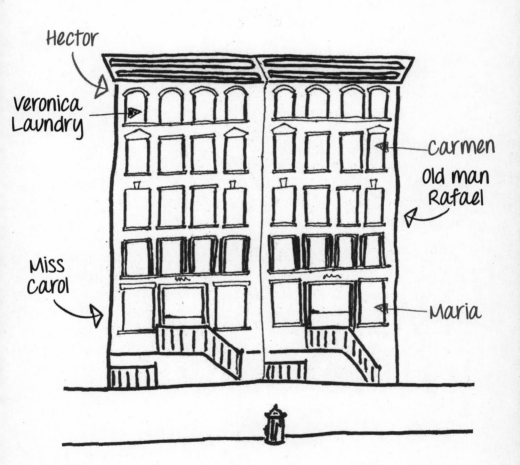

Hector

Veronica Laundry

Carmen

Old man Rafael

Miss Carol

Maria

Black marble

Hector was my vice-president and Miss Carol the treasurer. The one I knew from my lease-signing as a man who played with his moustache, and the other I hadn't met. Both of them, I had been warned by Paddy, did little on the board and he had not managed to get Miss Carol's phone number out of her in four years. But she gave it to me the first time I asked her for it, which I took to be a good sign.

It wasn't.

I tried to arrange a meeting with the two of them several times, but in vain. In the course of doing this, though, an inadvertent routine started developing, a sort of mobile conference, with me being mobile, them not. I would pay a visit to Miss Carol and then to Hector in their respective flats, where I'd make a short presentation on my ideas for the building, and then I would shuttle between the two to iron out any differences, convey their responses and come up with a plan of action.

I say "ideas", but I really had only one, which was to clean up the hallways: paint the walls, put down new floor tiles and change the harsh fluorescent lighting. Do that, I firmly believed, and we could wipe out the mess and the garbage in one fell swoop. A better-looking public space, I was convinced, would improve everyone's spirit, make them happy to live in the two tenements.

We had $30,000, which wasn't a lot in real-estate terms in New York, but a fortune for a little building that looked like it didn't have enough to afford a coat of paint. I figured that if we kept our expenses to $15,000, half of what we had, we would be fine. This, of course, was random guesswork at best – I had never run a building or been in charge of thirty flats or $30,000 – but guesswork is all I had to go on in the new job.

First of all, however, I had to convince the other two board members to agree with me.

Miss Carol and Hector lived in the second tenement, in the back of the first and fifth floors, respectively. Miss Carol, in fact, had been born in that very first-floor flat during World War II, and there she had lived her entire life. She remembered when the neighbourhood was, like her parents, Irish. Now she worked in a city agency Downtown, came home by 4pm every day, walked her two old dogs, and led a quiet life.

When I arrived at her flat, she was sitting in her kitchen, an ashtray on the table piled high with old butts. Her dogs' long nails made sharp clicks against her floor as they moved aimlessly from room to room. The combination of the two – old cigarettes, ancient dogs – was the cause of the acrid smell that hit you on first entering the second tenement. Inside Miss Carol's place the smell was so overwhelming it made you count the seconds until you could run out the door.

Miss Carol's streaky grey hair was always pulled back into a bun, and though her teeth were brown from smoking and quite a few of them were missing, that didn't stop her from showing them off, which she did quite often, when she let loose a laugh you couldn't help liking.

Even though she didn't offer to help with anything, and she let it be known from my first visit that if you asked her to she would refuse, she always sounded very enthusiastic. She also knew the lease backwards, and those parts she didn't know she made up, always adding words that ended any further discussion.

"That's just the way it is, honey."

Unfortunately, Miss Carol also disliked making a decision in haste. Renovating the hallways was a big undertaking, the biggest that anyone seemed to remember in two decades, and she needed time to think it over. Without her vote, however, the work was unlikely to happen. I needed her backing.

"Fixing the place up will make people happier to come home every day," I said, brimming with enthusiasm, "and to live here."

One of Miss Carol's dogs was stuck under the kitchen table, its nails marking time in the same place.

"But we've lived like this for a long time, honey," she replied.

"It's been okay until now."

"You like the graffiti and words scratched into the walls?" I asked her. "The garbage?"

Miss Carol shook her head, but she was concerned.

"All that money. Can we afford it?"

Miss Carol, even though she was the treasurer, had no idea how much we had in the bank.

"We have thirty thousand," I said.

She took a short drag of her cigarette and leaned back in her chair. Our liquidity impressed her.

"We just need to do the renovations very modestly," I carried on. "If we can keep it down to half of that – no more than $15,000 – we should be fine."

Reflecting on the two numbers, she smiled. The dog under the table had given up trying to find a way out and stood motionless.

"It's an investment," I said. "It will make the buildings more valuable. And the lease says the board should do things that are for the shareholders' benefit. This is for our benefit."

Using the lease as a backup helped my case because Miss Carol suddenly gave in ever so slightly.

"What does Hector say?" she asked.

That was my cue. I headed up to the fifth floor to Hector's place.

Hector had a job working for a local community organisation that assisted low-income people, and before that he had been a barber, which probably accounted for his fascination with his hair and moustache. His flat was done with some style: the living room, which the front door opened into – as it did in all the rear flats – was painted in a nice eggshell blue with Frida Kahlo-ish works of art hanging on the walls. To the right was the kitchen, and at the back, in a room facing onto the yard, an old movie with Jimmy Stewart was playing on a very large TV positioned in the centre of a wall. On either side of it were shelves loaded with DVDs and videos, all of them neatly arranged.

"Name a movie, I've got it," he said, casually pointing at one of the shelves. "Classics here, Westerns here, comedy over here."

When I told Hector about the renovation, he was very pleased.

"About time," he said. "When do we start?"

"As soon as possible," I said. "Maybe I can get some tiles and paint samples and bring them by for you and Miss Carol to choose from."

"Good," he said, already used to the convenience of not having to attend a meeting but having the meeting come to him. "Tuesdays during the day suit me best."

The following Tuesday I visited Hector armed with an array of paint colours I'd collected from a few hardware stores – various shades of orange, blue, cream, mauve, grey and green – and samples of Novilon, a word that I gave up using right after the first blank stare it drew, switching to the local version, vinyl flooring.

Miss Carol, when I showed the colours to her, liked cream or blue.

I then lugged everything up to Hector, who had a drink in his hand when he opened his front door.

"Come on in," he said. "Thirsty?"

"No, thanks."

I put the paint samples and different types of flooring on the bar counter that lay between his living room and kitchen. He quickly went for the pale green. I took the paint colours back downstairs to Miss Carol, and then, after consulting her, returned to Hector. I told him she was not displeased with the pale green.

Hector was seated on the kitchen side of the bar counter looking intently at the floor samples, as if he had suddenly noticed something unusual. All the tiles were standard, square and inexpensive, except one – a heavy black marble with very fine streaks of white in it that cost about ten times the price of the others. I had brought it along merely to illustrate how much we would be saving by keeping the renovation simple.

Afraid that Hector might be having second thoughts about the entire renovation while I was downstairs, I exaggerated Miss Carol's response to the pale green.

"Actually she likes the green a lot," I said. "Very much."

Hector wasn't listening.

"These tiles," he said, fanning his stubby fingers over the samples. "They look cheap."

"Yes. That's because they *are* cheap. They're Novilon," I said, then quickly corrected myself. "Vinyl."

He picked up the black marble.

"What about this one?" he asked. "I like this one."

"That's way out of our price range," I replied, sure he was joking. "We have to keep costs down. Ten floors of marble would bankrupt us."

He ran a finger along the tile, possibly checking for dust. His nails looked like they had been manicured.

"What about using it on my floor?" he asked.

For a moment I thought he was suggesting that he wanted to use it in his own flat, but then realised he meant for it to be put down in the hallway of the fifth floor.

"Your floor *only*?" I asked.

He nodded.

"Don't you think it would look a bit odd having black marble on only one floor, while all the other nine floors get pale green vinyl?"

Hector patted his hair with extreme caution but said nothing. Thinking he maybe didn't understand I tried again.

"I'm not sure people would be happy if this floor had better tiles than the rest of the building."

He considered this possibility for a moment.

"They won't notice," he said finally. "No-one comes up to the top floor anyway. They would never find out."

The rusty filing cabinet

The third Thursday in November was Thanksgiving. Everyone at the magazines where I worked started planning long before the event to head across country and do whatever they needed to do – climb mountains, ford raging rivers, deal with snowstorms and clogged airports – in order to spend a few days with their family and loved ones.

If you were a new immigrant, Thanksgiving was a time to feel more spare than usual, your family and loved ones suddenly feeling more distant than ever. So, without anything to do that Thursday night, my steam pipes hissing now that the cold weather had set in, I sat on my kitchen floor surrounded by piles of papers for the old building. Some of the papers came from Paddy's two boxes and others I had dug out of the rusty filing cabinet in the basement.

There were tax certificates, insurance documents and fines from various city departments. One especially thick wad of forms did little to explain why the city was supposed to – but didn't – subsidise the monthly levy for two flats. The most obvious pile of papers, however, was the one that was not there, which would have been for all the people who were in legal trouble of some kind. There were three very distinct groups: the debtors, the devious and the dead.

Out of thirty flats – fifteen in my tenement and fifteen in the other – only two flats were in court, and they had been there for quite some time. Those were also the two flats just mentioned, which the city was meant to subsidise but didn't. They belonged to two residents who had been in the building the longest, the screaming Maria on the first floor and the woman on the fifth floor next door who threw just-washed laundry to someone waiting on the street several times a week. Her name was Veronica.

As I tried to make sense of the documents, I found out some of our old building's history. It had been transformed into a resident-owned co-op in 1988, at a time when the city was taking over hundreds of run-down tenements and trying to improve them. For a nominal sum of one dollar each for two hundred and fifty shares – that would have been about R2.20 per share at the time, or R550 in total – each resident had been given the option to buy their flat. The city's plan was to give people who could never afford property the chance of a lifetime.

Some of the residents, amazingly, said no, while many of those who said yes didn't survive. Going by the names in the rusty filing cabinet, new owners failed to pay their levy each month, whereupon they were evicted and their flats repossessed by the old building. My own flat on the fifth floor had gone through numerous owners until the last one was evicted and the pigeons moved in. All that was left of those people were names and files in the basement, forgotten and disintegrating.

Maria and Veronica Laundry had not only managed to survive but had at some stage got an extra perk. The city began subsidising their monthly levy, but then, because of some bureaucratic glitch, took it away. Indignant, both women refused to pay any levy at all until the city started subsidising them again.

Maguire & Cohen, the law firm the sisters used instead of Morgenstern, had been trying to sort out this muddle for years, but nothing had come of it. Maria and Veronica Laundry kept insisting they'd been screwed, the city wanted more paperwork it never got, the sisters said they'd tried everything to sort it out, and Maguire & Cohen kept pulling a regular pay cheque from us.

The only one losing out – probably tens of thousands of dollars so far, by my calculation – was the old building.

As for the twenty-eight remaining flats, three of them were still owned by the building, the same way mine had been. Of these, one was empty and two were being rented out, although the building was, inexplicably, charging one tenant half the rent being paid by the other.

Three flats were in the names of people who had died without a will.

At least four flats were claimed to be owned by people who had no proof of ownership.

Nine flats were being sublet, or rented out, by their absentee owners, who were legally required to have had their tenants approved. No-one – not Shoshanna or Abbie, not Miss Carol or Hector – could tell you who lived in any of the nine flats. As for the absentee owners, not one of them ever visited the old building. We were out of sight and out of mind.

Finally, ten flats hadn't paid the building any levy for months, if not years, and together they owed a total of $30,000, which was enough to buy three of my flats or one of Paddy's.

But that wasn't the worst of it. Half of that amount, $15,000, was owed by just one person, who hadn't paid anything in more than four years. And that person was none other than the little old man who lived on the third floor and sometimes swept the hallway outside Noah's front door – Rafael.

The sad fate of old man Rafael

By this stage already, an uneasy pattern had started developing with Shoshanna. I phoned her, she was never there, I left a message, and she didn't call back. I kept trying to reach her without any luck, and when I finally did she assured me – like she had the very first time I called her – that she hadn't received a single one of my messages.

"Patty!" she would shout accusingly at the receptionist, the latest of many receptionists who didn't last for very long.

In this roundabout way, it took me some time to find out what had been going on with old man Rafael's flat.

At first, Shoshanna expressed total shock – "Four years? That's a lot of money" But slowly, like she was trying not to disclose too much information all at once and had to do some detective work to find out the truth, the story came out.

Old man Rafael's brother was, in fact, the owner of the flat, but at some stage – dates were always vague with Shoshanna – he had died and, predictably, hadn't left a will. Old man Rafael, who had been living with him at the time, stayed on in the flat. Someone in the family could have gone to court to get the property transferred to his name, but no-one did.

"This is, in fact, a very simple procedure," Shoshanna told me, although she clearly hadn't bothered to tell the dead man's relatives.

Old man Rafael had probably been taken care of by his brother, but since his death the job had been assumed by their sister, who lived somewhere else. She received Rafael's social security payments, out of which she was meant to pay the levy every month – which she had not been doing.

"You mean she stole his money?" I asked Shoshanna.

"We can't prove that," she replied, adding quickly, "and you can't tell anyone what I just told you."

Shoshanna, it seemed, wanted to stay in everyone's good books. She divulged secrets and then pleaded ignorance of the fact. Should the secret ever come out, she wouldn't be the one taking the blame.

"Does the sister understand that Rafael has to pay something?" I asked.

Shoshanna didn't have an answer.

"Let's call Abbie," she said.

When things got a bit beyond Shoshanna she roped in her sister.

"We need to take him to court," Abbie said, suddenly eager to make up for the four years of inaction.

"What will happen?" I asked.

"He might lose the place," Shoshanna said.

This wasn't the outcome I had hoped for.

"But where will he go?" I asked.

Shoshanna was unforgiving.

"He can go live with his sister. She's taking his money."

"I thought you said we couldn't say that she was taking his money."

Abbie added something that was probably meant to make the decision easier.

"It's okay," she said. "This happens in New York courts every day."

The sisters were suddenly fired up, obviously grateful that the spotlight had been diverted away from the fact that for four years they hadn't been doing their job. Old man Rafael, not their ineptitude, was now the problem.

"Let the court decide."

"And then?" I asked, fearing the answer. "What will happen then?"

"We take the apartment away from him."

My heart sank. Old man Rafael was the last person in the building who deserved to be evicted, a meek soul who did nothing to offend anyone, was mocked by Noah and Floyd, and who was the only one to make even the slightest effort to clean the place. Yet he would quite possibly become the latest name to join those in the rusty filing cabinet in the basement.

"Can't we reach some agreement?" I asked, sounding a bit desperate. "Maybe he can pay off the debt monthly."

Shoshanna raised her voice.

"Fifteen! Thousand! Dollars!" It came out in little bursts. "Monthly?!"

She was right. Old man Rafael had no income. And where would his sister come up with that kind of money? They would be paying off the debt for the next decade.

"You want us to take the apartment?" Abbie asked again, full of fighting spirit. Her voice had a nasty edge to it. "We'll take it. Just say the word."

I told them I would have to think about it, and then hung up. Nothing short of a miracle, I knew, could save old man Rafael.

The Jewish lawyer

Not sure who to turn to for advice, I thought of calling our lawyer Morgenstern, but Shoshanna quickly advised me not to. I thought it was because Morgenstern was forgetful and not particularly good at his job, but that wasn't the reason.

Morgenstern, it appeared, was what in New York City they called a tenant lawyer. His speciality/specialty was to help renters who were threatened by their landlords with eviction. (In this scenario, to my horror, I had suddenly become the mean landlord while old man Rafael was the helpless tenant.)

Furthermore, and quite unbelievably, Morgenstern was

apparently very good at his job of being a tenant lawyer. Indeed, he had perfected that art on his very own flat.

I had been to Morgenstern's flat several times, because that was where he ran his business from. The building was a large co-op on the Upper West Side, halfway up West End Avenue. I had never been to West End Avenue before visiting Morgenstern, but someone had told me it was created back in the day as an alternative for Jews who had been shunned by anti-Semitic buildings on Park Avenue. Whether or not this was true I don't know, but the random statement stuck in my head, partly because Morgenstern, the only reason I had to visit West End Avenue, was Jewish, partly because he was being ostracised by his building (even though it wasn't for anti-Semitic reasons), and partly because of my South African tic. If anyone mentioned an ethnic barrier, my radar pinged.

For many years already, Shoshanna told me, Morgenstern had been locked in a vicious lawsuit with his building for running his legal practice out of his residence. He wasn't an owner, and as a tenant in a co-op, working from home was immediate grounds for eviction. But Morgenstern had fended off one legal challenge after another, and you only had to visit his flat to see why he was fighting so hard. He had one of those fantastic deals that were legendary in New York – four bedrooms, huge view, minuscule rent. When I first saw his place, it struck me that might be the reason he was always smiling.

The sisters were right, though. Morgenstern, as a tenant lawyer, would probably help save old man Rafael but would at the same time leave the old building more screwed than it already was.

"How did this happen?" I asked Shoshanna. "How did we come to have a tenant lawyer in a co-op, representing a building full of owners?"

"Paddy liked him," she said dismissively.

Shoshanna blamed anything she could on Paddy Murphy, now that he was gone and couldn't defend himself. The battle lines were becoming more obvious by the day. The sisters hadn't liked Paddy and didn't like Morgenstern, neither of whom liked the sisters.

Instead of calling Morgenstern, I climbed the five flights of stairs to see Hector, who I was sure would have a solution. Working for a community organisation that assisted low-income people in distress, he had the means to help old man Rafael. But Hector, who had trouble remembering anyone's name, including mine, didn't have a clue who old man Rafael was.

"You must know him," I said. "He's the guy who sometimes sweeps the hallways."

Hector walked to his front door and opened it.

"Look at our hallways!" he said. The old prison-style floor tiles looked filthier than usual. "Do they look like someone sweeps them?"

A miracle

In the first weeks of being president, I always seemed to be on the phone. I called anyone in the city or anywhere else I could think of – agencies, institutes, welfare groups – that might know something about how a low-income building of resident-owned flats like ours came into existence and how we were meant to function. Instead of answers I usually got more questions.

What had started out in the 1980s as a philanthropic scheme by the city to create a new breed of property owners had, for reasons I was quickly finding out, not worked out as well as had been intended. If ever there had been a grand plan, the person in charge was hiding the blueprint somewhere.

One call, however, led me to a small NGO / non-profit agency that had been set up to help buildings like ours with advice. That was where Siobhan worked.

The first time I called Siobhan, I started describing our two tenements to her: their location, the infuriating muddle created by the sisters' incompetence, and how the president of the board had fled because he and his wife were receiving death threats from a downstairs neighbour. At that point, she interrupted me.

"Oh," she said, "you must be talking about Paddy's building."

Siobhan, it turned out, had helped Paddy with advice a few times, although he had left so fast he hadn't mentioned her name to me. Something about our building amused her, and throughout the conversation she sounded on the verge of laughing, like our tenements were some kind of Fawlty Towers.

I explained our latest dilemma – old man Rafael.

"Can he be saved?" I asked finally.

Her answer wasn't encouraging.

"New York courts are very pro tenant and like to keep someone like Rafael off the street if they can," she said. "But it's unlikely a judge will rule in his favour. He owes too much. He hasn't paid for too long."

"And then?" I asked. "What happens then?"

"He will be evicted."

"There's nothing else we can do?" I asked.

"This is your building and you're in charge of it," she said. "This is what you have to do."

Clearly, there would be no miracle to save old man Rafael. The next day I called Shoshanna and, hating myself, gave her my decision.

"We need to go to court."

Thieves

In the two boxes Paddy had left with me for safekeeping were countless notes he had written to himself about the sisters. Some of them began with words like "Find out why... hasn't been done." (You could fill in the blank with any of the things I was now seeing for myself that the sisters repeatedly neglected to do.) Another note also became a refrain: "Why has... still not been done?" That gave rise to "Ask *again* about...". Finally, like a cry for help, "What's happening?!"

Along with the neatly handwritten notes were receipts, although figuring them out was like fitting together a puzzle that had numerous pieces missing. Falling basically into two categories, the receipts were for work done 1) by Noah and 2) by anyone else.

Noah got paid for his job as superintendent but also for extra work. Even though many of the jobs were ones he should have been doing anyway, such as fixing leaks and carrying out small repairs, any suggestion of the kind was met with him puffing on his cigarette and mumbling something as he walked away from you.

No-one knew what Noah's duties were exactly, and even if they did, it didn't matter. In the same way that he looked after his own flat, he neglected the old building around it. Most work he did needed to be done all over again by an outside contractor, which meant we were paying for the same job not once but twice, and often, if an outsider had to be called in, three times.

I noticed one particular payment of $6,000, for a job that hadn't been done at all – not by Noah or by an outsider. Studying the receipt, for work to replace numerous windows and some stairs, I saw that the contractor had a very unusual surname, one I'd seen only once before. It was the same as Abbie's. I wasn't surprised that the sisters, besides being useless, might be stealing money from us. But now I had proof.

My mission suddenly became a lot clearer. Whereas I had taken over from Paddy with only one idea – the renovation of the hallways – now I had three more: to get rid of the sisters, Noah and the lawyer Morgenstern.

The only problem was I had no idea how to do it.

The renovation

As soon as the sisters heard that I wanted to renovate the old building, they wasted no time suggesting their favourite contractor. They insisted I come to their office to meet him, a small German man named Hans whose previous job had been to redecorate a hair salon. Noah, meanwhile, assumed that the renovation job would be his – and there would be no discussion about it.

Without saying anything to either of them, I started phoning numerous contractors around the city for quotes. Most of them were too busy or not interested when I told them how small our building was. The quotes that I did get were far too high for us — so high, in fact, I couldn't imagine what kind of renovation they were planning. Maybe I had totally miscalculated how much a job like this would cost.

I asked friends and people at work, even though painting and tiling public hallways wasn't the normal conversation you heard around the offices of *Vanity Fair* and *Entertainment Weekly*, another magazine I'd started working at. Most people rented and, going by the small rental buildings I'd seen around the city, the state of the public hallways was usually an afterthought, a landlord's last concern.

The few people who didn't rent but owned their flats, meanwhile, had paid enough for them to leave all future thinking about their building's upkeep to a management company that was big and had an official-sounding name like Orion Properties or Boustead Services, Inc. It wasn't left to the devices of two sisters scheming above a pizza parlour.

One colleague said he thought his superintendent did odd jobs on the side, but he wasn't sure. The superintendent, when I contacted him, put me in touch with a friend of his in Brooklyn. His friend sounded interested, but his quote was also too high.

With nowhere else to look, I finally took to the streets, the same way I once had for a flat to rent, and the way I still did looking for furniture to collect. Going from door to door was time-consuming and often embarrassing, but it was the one thing I knew how to do.

I spoke to random superintendents and doormen who were standing on the pavement outside upscale buildings, whistle-in-mouth, ready to hail a cab for a resident, or hosing down the pavement. My questions invariably took them by surprise.

"What kind of building is it?" they asked in reply.

"A really small one," I answered.

There was a pause usually, which, if it had been anywhere else, I would've assumed had something to do with my accent. But these men were often immigrants too and had accents of their own to worry about other people understanding.

"Are you the manager of the building?" they asked, still unsure whether I wasn't one of those people who walked the pavements talking to themselves and waving their hands about erratically.

"No," I answered, "but I'm on the board."

At the mention of the word "board", things always took a turn for the worse, and any price they quoted was seldom lower than the ones I'd received from official contractors. The word "board" meant co-op, rich, Park Avenue, deep pockets.

"But it's not *that* kind of co-op," I said, hoping they would sympathise, especially as fellow immigrants who had probably arrived in New York City with little except a dream. "We don't have much money."

That confused them even more.

"But it's a co-op, right?

"Yes, it is. But it's a low-income one."

Saying we were "low-income" did the reverse of what I expected, and actually turned many of them off. Associating themselves with our building was a step backwards for anyone hoping to succeed in their new country. Maybe it brought to mind parts of Tirana or Caracas that they wanted to forget. So I immediately cut the word from my advertising spiel.

After two weeks, I chanced upon Julio, a Mexican doorman working on the other side of Central Park who found nothing odd about what I was doing and quoted me exactly what we could afford: $15,000. He promised to bring two helpers and to start the job within two days. And he was as good as his word.

Community Chest

Even before Julio arrived with his ladders and canvas sheets to cover the hallway floors, Noah had been informed – by the sisters, no doubt – that he hadn't got the job. His kingdom was diminishing and he wasn't happy about it.

Things between the two of us had, in any case, been getting progressively worse in direct proportion to the number of times I asked him to do a job and he refused. Whereas he had previously been happy to simply ignore me, now it was open rebellion.

"You no president," he snapped at me.

I wasn't sure how Noah, who until then had accepted me as president without question, had deduced this. The answer was obvious: the sisters. Annoyed that I was cutting them off, rejecting their contractor Hans and any of their other suggestions, they had probably told Noah that being co-opted as president wasn't legal.

And they were probably right. Despite the fact that Morgenstern had vetted the change of power, there had been nothing democratic about it. But I saw my presidency as part of the ongoing game of Monopoly. I had casually accepted taking over the building, and now I thoughtlessly started undermining Noah's role as easily as I might have picked up a card from the Community Chest stack on the game board. I didn't even think there might be consequences.

For a while I tried to reason with Noah, explain that he needed to do his job more effectively, but he turned away from me each time, his body rigid. I was convinced he hated me.

"It's useless talking to Noah," Hector said to me one day. I had gone up to tell him about finding Julio to renovate the hallways. "Paddy tried to fire Noah many times."

Why Paddy had never managed to get rid of Noah was only one of the questions that kept coming back to me. Why hadn't he noticed the $6,000 missing from our account? Why hadn't he got rid of the sisters? Why hadn't he done something about old man Rafael owing $15,000? Maybe he had tried and failed, which would have explained all his notes and forever being angry with the world.

"Mother, Daughter Kill Each Other – Knives Used"

Late one Friday in December, the hallways half-painted by now, a scream from Carmen's flat pierced the frigid night air. Then another scream. Then more. No cars thudding an irregular beat had arrived at the fire hydrant yet, so the screams travelled clear and unhindered. They cut through my floor like a dagger, at the same time penetrating Carmen's windows and shooting up the air shaft.

You got to know the sounds and smells in the tenement and the time of day or night they could best be expected. About tonight's screams there was definitely something out of the ordinary. Maybe it was the pitch of the voices, the duration of the screams or the silences in between. Occasionally a heavy object got thrown. The little boy interrupted his mother, which only made things worse.

After about fifteen minutes a hush fell over everything. The shrieks were there one moment, gone the next. There was no gradual easing off, no screaming fading into shouting into crying. One minute it was there, the next it was gone.

I listened for a few minutes, waiting for something to happen – murmurs, footfalls, objects hitting walls – but there was only the faint thud of rap music coming from a car that had just pulled up at the fire hydrant.

...Cause I got mo' hoes, mo' dank
Mo' cheese in da bank, mo' rank,
My dawgs on dubs, yours ain't,
My dawgs do whatever, yours cain't...

I opened my front door and looked down the narrow stairwell to see if anyone else had heard what was going on. All thirteen other flats must have heard Carmen – there was no way you could have missed it – but no-one else appeared. Back inside I waited a bit longer, imagining the following day's headline in the *New York Post*, a tabloid that often had the kind of stories I was more used to seeing in Johannesburg papers – murder, rape, child killed by parent, drive-by shootings. MOTHER, DAUGHTER KILL EACH OTHER,

KNIVES USED, it would say, or POLICE ACCESS TO CRIME SCENE BLOCKED BY GARBAGE.

I went to my kitchen window, one of those facing the air shaft. From there, and from the opposite window in the third boxy room, I could get an oblique view of the same two windows in Carmen's flat. I tried to see if there was any sign of life, but Carmen's windows were dark and covered in too much dirt to see even if a light was burning behind them.

Opening my kitchen window I stuck my head out, trying to hear something, anything. A dozen pigeons gathered on nearby windowsills fluttered around anxiously, then settled back on their perches clucking softly. A faint light shone in one of the lower flats in Floyd's tenement, but the air shaft was otherwise so dark you couldn't see anything below the third floor. I leaned out as far as I could, fearing more than once that I'd lose my balance and end up dead and squashed at the bottom of the air shaft.

I strained my ears for any sound at all but heard nothing except the words thumping into the black night from the fire hydrant outside.

...mo' hoes, mo' dank, Mo' cheese in da bank...

CHAPTER 5
THINGS GO BADLY

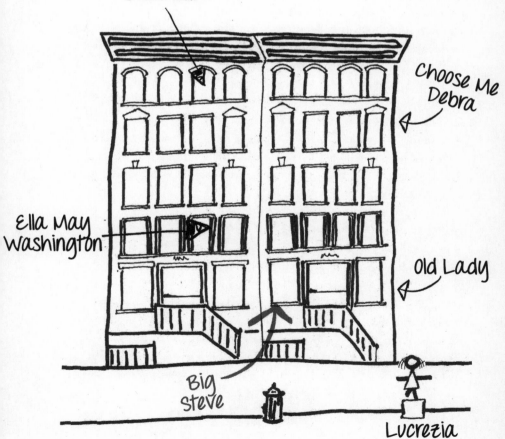

A winter wonderland

Right after Thanksgiving, in November, dozens of windows in the projects across the street from us were suddenly draped with Christmas lights, each flat trying to outdo the next. The two normally nondescript buildings exploded with colour, even in the daytime, putting me in a better mood every time I saw them.

As Christmas got closer, it was publicised that there would be an evening of carol singing not far from the tenement, and I decided to attend. Christmas carols in the southern hemisphere, even though we did sing them, had always sounded a bit off-key – sleigh bells and mistletoe and white Christmas and winter wonderland – especially when the temperature outside was 30°C and everyone was standing around the braai dressed in shorts and slip-slops. Turkey, which no-one seemed to eat, we swapped for cold ham and tomato aspic and potato salad.

Some festivities just didn't transfer very well, especially when they weren't adapted to a new climate or geography, and none more so than Christmas.

But on the night of the carols in New York City, with the weather crisply cold and the forecast predicting snow flurries, it seemed everything would be perfect. This would be the Christmas that the cards and the music piped into South African stores on balmy December days had prepared us for.

The carols were taking place within walking distance of the tenement, but in the pretty part of town, the affluent Upper East Side. I set off by foot in the direction of the Split, the infamous dividing line between our forlorn section of Harlem and the wealthy apartment buildings to the south.

What I saw in front of me was indeed a winter wonderland. The entire Park Avenue below the Split and all the way to Grand Central Station, a distance of about four kilometres, was festooned with several hundred very large fir trees, each one dripping with lights.

The avenue was closed off by the police for several blocks either side of a cute red-brick church where a choir standing on its steps led the carol singing. Hundreds of people wrapped up in fur and expensive overcoats greeted each other like it was a country club. Fathers held their young children on their shoulders to get a better view of the choir.

As we sang *Silent Night* and *Away In A Manger*, a gentle sprinkling of snow fell on us. The avenue of fir trees glowed brighter than ever, as did the lights strung along penthouse terraces and visible through countless apartment windows. You could almost feel the goodwill to all men. At that moment, more than any other, New York was the most beautiful and perfect city in the world.

After we sang the final song, *Joy To The World*, the people applauded and then broke ranks in an orderly fashion to go home and probably drink eggnog and unwrap presents. Unlike everyone else, I headed north and back across the Split. Immediately overwhelmed by the dark shadows of my neighbourhood, I made my way past Janice's building, the rats furiously gnawing at the snow-dusted mound of black garbage bags. A lone train exited the tunnel, making a quick escape up the viaduct.

Turning at the corner tenement into my street, the carols still ringing in my ears, another kind of music reached me. Very earthy and un-carol-like, it crackled from broken speakers in a car parked at the fire hydrant.

...*Fuck you hoes, I'm the baddest lady,*
All my shit niggas hear, I know it drive them crazy...

Lucrezia on a soapbox

The news of old man Rafael being taken to court, and possibly being evicted, spread quickly. It went not only through the building but spilled onto the street.

One morning in January I noticed a group standing outside the corner tenement. There was often a small gathering there – two people joined by a third and then a fourth – talking about nothing in particular, standing for fifteen minutes, an hour, watching the cars go by. But today it was different.

In the midst of about seven or eight people stood Lucrezia, waving a cigarette-pierced hand, seeming to tower above them all on her invisible soapbox, her most important words audible as I approached them.

"Old man", "lies", "kicked out", "old people", "fucking asshole".

It was a random assembly quickly turning into a lynch mob.

As I passed them I could feel their eyes following me, led by Lucrezia's. Once I'd turned the corner, I stopped outside Janice's building, so deep in thought I didn't notice the garbage I was standing in the very middle of.

They were talking about me!

My immediate impulse was to go back and tell them the truth: I had no choice. I wasn't after old man Rafael. I'd tried to save him. It broke my heart to do what I did.

But I didn't go back. Instead, later that day, I put up a notice at the front doors of the two tenements.

MEETING IN BASEMENT, SATURDAY. SUBJECT: CO-OP MATTERS. ALL WELCOME. PLEASE COME.

Five residents turned up in the basement on Saturday morning: Esperanza from my third floor; our useless treasurer, Miss Carol; Maria, the swearing mother from the first floor, who kept looking at the ground as if she might be turned to stone if she looked directly at me; an old African-American woman of about eighty, petite and neatly dressed; and Brunhilda, a fussy pear-shaped woman who had bought Paddy's place.

They sat in silence until the end, after which everyone left except the African-American woman, who came up to me and introduced herself. Her name was Ella May Washington and she said she was the wife of Herbert, the old man who stood on the front stairs of the second tenement swaying his head to music only he could hear. She wore glasses almost as thick as her husband's. She and Herbert owned a flat in the second tenement, but lived in a huge constellation of projects a few blocks away. Herbert visited the building daily, standing on the stairs or sitting in their flat, and

Ella May seemed to like what I was doing.

"You keep up the good work," she said, touching my arm.

A week later, I again put up a notice in each tenement.

INFORMATION MEETING IN BASEMENT THIS SATURDAY AT 11AM. PLEASE COME! ALL WELCOME!

Someone wrote "Fuck this" on one of the pages, while the other one got torn down.

Choose Me Debra rebels

It wasn't even two days later when someone demanded that another meeting – a different kind of meeting – be called immediately. It was Choose Me Debra, the woman with the sputtering car-engine laugh who lived on the floor below me with her teenage son.

"Choose me!" she called out, needlessly trying to get my attention as she blocked the narrow first-floor hallway. "Choose me!"

Standing with her arms folded and legs almost touching the walls on either side of her, she gave me no choice but to stop and hear her out.

"Choose me!" she said, her tone one that was familiar with being listened to.

Why, she wanted to know, were the hallways being painted, and why, of all colours, pale green?

I stood silent for a moment, surprised not only because it was a stupid question but also because of who was asking it. The painting was virtually completed and the floors had already been tiled, so even if we'd wanted to, there was no stopping the renovation at this point.

Besides that, though, Choose Me Debra had no right to be questioning anything in the building. Neither owner nor renter, she was living in one of the three flats owned by the building and was paying us something every month, but she didn't have a contract, never had one, and was, it seemed, living among us on borrowed time.

But Choose Me Debra did have something that I had never even contemplated when I took over from Paddy, and that was a history in the building. In fact, Choose Me Debra had history in spades. She had served time in the tenement and her connections ran deep. The enormous mechanic on the second floor was her brother, who was friends with the ruddy-cheeked guy on the first floor. She regularly chatted not only to Carmen but also to Maria, who was friends with Veronica Laundry in the second tenement. She was on excellent terms with the sisters, Shoshanna and Abbie, whom she called weekly.

Most importantly of all, though, Choose Me Debra's mother was Bella.

Bella's name I knew from the rusty filing cabinet and from Paddy, who didn't like her. She lived in Florida now, but she still owned the mechanic's flat on the second floor and she had once been president, ruling the building with an iron fist.

It was during Bella's reign that Shoshanna and Abbie had been hired as managing agents and that many of the present owners had bought – Hector, Carmen, Noah and Alvarez, the man who had threatened to kill Paddy and his wife. For some reason, though, her own daughter, Choose Me Debra, hadn't even got a rental contract.

Bella had also been responsible for painting the hallways shit- and vomit-brown and putting down prison-ready tiles, work I was now undoing. And Choose Me Debra, I suspected, didn't like that.

"Choose me! All contracting work must stop immediately," she insisted. "The shareholders must be called together to discuss the matter."

Choose Me Debra, a non-shareholder with no rights, wasn't making a request but a demand. Mumbling something incoherent, I managed to squeeze past her and headed up the stairs.

"Choose me!" she shouted after me. "We want a meeting! Choose me!"

Not knowing how else to deal with the problem, I did what I'm sure Paddy had done on many an occasion. I closed my front door.

Advice with Dewar's

Things were going badly, and my plan was quite clearly failing.

The newly painted, nicely lit hallways were supposed to make people happier, as I'd told Miss Carol months ago, and not the opposite. But Noah was angry, the sisters were angry, Choose Me Debra was angry, my notices were being torn down with anger, and people were massing in front of the corner tenement whispering angrily about me. Even Carmen and Eva's unusual behaviour after their murderous argument – they hadn't shown their faces in public for two weeks, hadn't appeared once on the fourth-floor landing for a cigarette or to paint their nails – somehow boded ill.

What was going wrong? Maybe it should have been obvious to me, but it wasn't. Couldn't people see I was trying to make things better? Who would want the old building dirty? Who would want us to be mired in debt? Who would want chaos?

Desperate for an explanation, I instinctively sought out Hector and Miss Carol, both of whom had been in the building long enough to know what might be going on. Miss Carol wasn't home and all I could hear were her dogs' wet sniffles a few inches away, behind her front door.

Upstairs, Hector was watching a musical in his TV room. He poured himself a Dewar's, sat down at the kitchen table, and took a sip.

"You're going too fast," he said, as if the reason had been quite obvious to him all along.

"What do you mean?" I asked.

"People aren't used to things happening quickly."

"But it's been three months since I took over from Paddy. That's not fast."

"The painting, the hallways," he said, then paused. "You know, Noah's not happy about what's going on. You didn't give him the renovation job."

Hector didn't care for Noah, didn't trust him, and wanted as much as I did to see him fired.

"But you don't like Noah," I reminded him. "You told me Paddy had been trying to get rid of him for years."

Ignoring me, he continued.

"And what's this I hear about taking someone to court?"

He meant old man Rafael, who, no matter how many times I mentioned him, Hector never remembered.

"I told you about him before," I said, although I don't know why I bothered.

Retrieving his trusty comb from a jacket pocket, he ran it through his hair several times.

"You know," he said, "people think that you're a racist."

The words came out detached, like he had nothing to do with them or them with him.

"You are white," he said. "Most of the people you are taking to court are Hispanic. It's like you are picking on them."

The third part of his accusation came as anticipated, like clockwork.

"And you are from South Africa."

Spanish in Africa

Until that moment I had confessed my origin to three people – Mohammed and the sisters, Shoshanna and Abbie – not because I wanted to hide it but because no-one really seemed to care. For all the questions I asked my neighbours about themselves, they seemed genuinely incurious about me. I could have been a wanted criminal, and no-one would have cared less. And gone were the days that people made the connection between the name Botha and South Africa.

I suspected that the sisters, eager to fan the flames of discord, had quite probably mentioned my background, and Hector had taken the bait. Perhaps they had even planted a thought in his head, a thought that so many of us who'd grown up with apartheid and racial division had become used to outsiders assuming: he's white and South African, so he must be a racist.

Instead of arguing with Hector, I immediately felt guilty as charged. Maybe he was right. Maybe I *was* a racist. While I thought I'd been doing things in the old building in order to better the place (categorising people in terms of Good Resident v Bad Resident, Paying Resident v Non-Paying Resident), was it possible that I had been driven by some terrible, deep-down bias, singling out people purely because of their background?

The only trouble with this theory was that I hardly knew anyone's background. Random facts I had about Maria and Carmen, but that was all. I wasn't even entirely sure what the word "Hispanic" meant. Ask me about the Dutch, the Xhosa, the Zulus, the Portuguese, the Setswana or the Khoi Khoi. There I had some idea of what to look and listen for, intonations and expressions that told me where someone might be from. There I was on terra firma. But Hispanic? Thanks to the early colonists, Spanish words and things Hispanic didn't crop up much in Africa.

I had always assumed that Hispanic referred to any part of the world that had Spanish links, or to the people who came from there. I had recently come to think that maybe it was more a Latin American and South American connection. But what about Brazil, even though its language wasn't Spanish? And what about the Philippines? And was Spain Hispanic, or was saying that tautologous? Did you even need to be able to speak Spanish to be Hispanic? Could you tell someone was Hispanic by looking at them? Were there any telltale signs?

Noah seemed to be the most obvious candidate, with his preference for Spanish rather that English and his features that came straight out of a painting by Goya. I also knew that his real name was Santiago. His friend on the pavement Floyd, meanwhile, had an unidentifiable name and spoke English except when addressing Noah/Santiago. Esperanza's name suggested she was of Spanish origin, although she said barely a word, and when she did it was while holding her hand over her mouth, so any accent was muffled. And what of Carmen or Choose Me Debra, both of whom never spoke Spanish but had olive-coloured skin? Hector, too, might have been Hispanic, especially given what he'd just said to me, but I couldn't tell for sure. He never spoke Spanish and I had a deeper tan than he did.

It didn't strike me until long afterwards, but the whole situation was full of sad irony. The very thing that I and many others from South Africa were busy trying to unlearn and to not do again – namely, to not judge people differently because of their race – Hector was now telling me I should have actually been doing all along. If I had, things might not be going so badly.

So busy had I been focusing on my own possible biases that I didn't think that the old building might have one or two of its own.

"I told you before," I repeated my words to Hector. "I did everything I could think of to save old man Rafael. Nothing could be done."

Even as I said it, though, my head filled with more doubt and self-recrimination. Maybe I could have done more.

"And Noah – you know yourself that Noah does nothing," I added.

Or does he, I wondered. Have I been sympathetic enough to Noah? Have I perhaps been too hard on him and the others? Does Noah have redeeming qualities I have been blind to?

Hector, curiously, didn't seem to care either way, and he went to get a refill of Dewar's. Maybe he wasn't Hispanic after all, I thought. But then I looked up again at the fake Frida Kahlo paintings on his blue walls and drew a connection. Kahlo being Mexican, it occurred to me, might suggest that Hector was Hispanic too.

As ice tinkled around in his glass, a new round of merry singing broke out on the TV in his back room. My eyes strayed back to the paintings, and one of them, a portrait of a woman, seemed to be looking straight back at me.

"I'm just telling you what I've heard," Hector said, taking a sip of his drink as he came back into the living room. "Don't say I didn't warn you."

The fugitive

A few days later, I was downstairs very early, not long after Maria had sounded the alarm up the air shaft for Wally to wake up. Six or seven cars had pulled up in front of the building the way police cars might at a crime scene. All of them were black and nondescript, some without hubcaps and in serious need of a wash, and they pointed in different directions, like they had come racing into our one-way street from both ends and screeched to a halt outside.

Half a dozen men dressed in civilian clothes were coming out of the basement of my tenement. Noah was standing to one side, and it was obvious that he hadn't been in the basement with them.

Never before had I seen Noah let anyone downstairs without him being there too, his keys jangling to clear the way. It was his kingdom, after all. But these men he had left alone, and the look on his face was one I had never seen there before: fear.

When I asked the men what was wrong, already positive that they must be policemen, one of them asked sternly who I was.

"I am responsible for the building," I said, still uncomfortable about using the word "president" for myself.

A gaggle of people was watching us from the corner tenement. One of them was a sour-faced woman who was friendly with Lucrezia. Mister Winston leaned against his van, his cowboy hat pushed back uncharacteristically far so you could see the surprise in his eyes. Maria, now that she'd woken Wally, watched curiously out of her first-floor window, her elbows on the windowsill and her eyes wide as saucers.

I motioned to two of the policemen that we should go back into the basement, and they followed me.

"I think it's better if we talk here," I told them, not wanting anyone to overhear us.

"Name's Sergeant Steinberg," said the man in charge. "This is Detective Motta."

He handed me his card and explained that they had been chasing someone. He pulled out a picture of a man with an ugly

123

face that was so bloated he could have been beaten up before the picture – his mug shot, I assumed – was taken. The look in his eyes was emotionless and dead.

"You know him?" Steinberg asked.

I shook my head. That puffy, dead-eyed face wasn't one you'd easily forget.

"We're looking for him on charges of dealing drugs and burglary. We chased him into your building. We think he went into one of the front apartments."

Sergeant Steinberg lowered his voice.

"That guy upstairs – the one with the cap," he said, meaning Noah. "You trust him?"

"Noah?" I asked. There were lots of things I didn't trust about Noah, but they all had to do with his code of ethics as superintendent. I was sure, though, that he would never help a criminal. "Oh, yes, totally."

Steinberg wasn't convinced.

"We think he helped the fugitive," the policeman said.

The way Steinberg figured it, Dead Eyes had got into one of the flats and from there had jumped into the air shaft between my building and Floyd's. Steinberg walked over to the small secret door in the middle of the wall, the one that led to the air shaft.

"See?" he said, standing at the secret hatch and opening it. "The superintendent could have opened this door and let in the suspect, who fled out the back into the yard."

The only flat that Dead Eyes could have jumped from was on the first floor facing the air shaft. That would have been Maria's, and she was now sitting quite innocently at her front window watching the police go about their business. I couldn't imagine a single mother who made sure to walk her son to school every day so no-one would snatch him away opening her door to a dead-eyed fugitive.

When I took a second look at the photograph of Dead Eyes, I noticed that his surname was Salazar, the same as Big Steve, the ruddy-cheeked guy who lived opposite Maria. It wasn't an uncommon name, but it was worth mentioning.

"Oh yes," said Steinberg, "they are brothers."

In fact, the police suspected Big Steve of also being a drug dealer, but they had very little information to go on.

"He's clever and very careful," the policeman said. "All we know is that he has two Rottweilers."

"Rottweilers?" I repeated in disbelief. "On the first floor?"

He nodded.

"That's not Big Steve," I said. "We don't have Rottweilers in our building."

It was common knowledge that there was only one dog on all five floors, and that was Esperanza's brave Chihuahua, Tiny, who lived on the third floor. It was impossible that someone could have kept a Rottweiler, let alone two, without someone noticing, especially if they lived right next to the front door.

"Oh, we know he's got them," Steinberg insisted. "And he's trained them so well they don't bark. That's also a sign he's a dealer."

My mind had already started doing some building maths again, connecting the dots between several flats, whose residents' lives fitted into each other like Russian nesting dolls. If Dead Eyes was Big Steve's brother, then Lucrezia was his mother, which meant the quiet Old Lady who lived in the back of the first floor was his grandmother.

I mentioned this to Steinberg, who threw a look at his colleague.

"No, we didn't know that," he said, annoyed.

"They don't have the same last name," I said.

"Oh, that would explain it."

Maybe, I suggested, Dead Eyes went into the Old Lady's flat, climbed out of her back window and onto the fire escape, dropped down into the backyard, and then fled from there. No-one would have seen him escape.

Steinberg nodded.

"We've lost him for now."

With that the two detectives started moving towards the basement door to leave. Steinberg told me to contact them if I happened to see

Dead Eyes around the building. The men outside had already piled back into their dirty black cars, and within a few minutes they pulled off in different directions. As the last vehicle turned into the avenue, Lucrezia's sour-faced friend in the corner tenement shouted something in defiance and raised her middle finger at the parting cops.

Moron

In America the words were dumbass, dipshit, moron, asshole. In South Africa, it could be anything from chump to mampara to moegoe to arsehole. And at that moment, I felt that any or all of them could have applied specifically to me.

Things had been staring me in the face for more than a year, but I hadn't seen any of them. Suddenly I did: front doors always broken only days after the repairman came by, nails jammed into locks to keep them that way, sometimes the entire locking mechanism ripped out. Cars parked outside ever so briefly, long after midnight, young men driving, the passenger (always in sunglasses) visiting the same flat, one next to the front door, and staying there for only a minute or two before leaving in a hurry.

What I had previously thought was simply more building chaos was, in fact, a very neatly worked-out entryway, an easily accessible trail to Big Steve's place on the first floor, and an equally easy way back out.

Big Steve was a drug dealer, and the old building had one more problem.

The model tenant

As soon as the agency opened that morning, I called Shoshanna. Unusually, as if she'd been tipped off that I would be calling about something like this, she answered on the first ring. When I told her about the police raid, she immediately called Abbie to get on the phone too.

"Well, I can't believe it," Abbie said. "Big Steve!"

As much as I didn't trust the sisters, and was convinced that they were stealing money from us, I was sure they had their limits. They would never side with a drug dealer.

"The police also said he has two Rottweilers."

The sisters didn't like dogs being allowed in the building.

"He does?" Abbie asked.

Incredulity came to her easily, but a solution didn't. The speed with which Abbie and Shoshanna had moved to get rid of old man Rafael was nowhere in evidence.

"He has to go," I said suddenly, surprised by my own words. "If someone is selling drugs, we need to get rid of them."

There was silence on the other side.

"Big Steve has never done anything wrong before," Shoshanna said. "He pays his rent on time. He even brings it down here personally. He is a model tenant."

"The police are convinced he is dealing drugs," I said.

The sisters were out of arguments.

"What should we tell him?" Abbie asked.

Suddenly I realised that Sergeant Steinberg had given me no actual proof I could use against Big Steve. All I had were allegations of a fugitive brother and two dogs that I'd never seen or heard bark. So I qualified my statement to the sisters.

"If we take action against him," I said, "we cannot use the word 'drugs'."

"Well, we can't do anything then," Shoshanna replied quickly. "We can't just kick him out."

In fact, it struck me, we *could* just kick him out. Big Steve's was yet another one of the many flats waiting to be taken to court. Like Choose Me Debra on the fourth floor, Big Steve had no legal right to be in the building.

"Big Steve doesn't have a lease, does he?" I put it to the sisters. "He's not even a legal renter."

Shoshanna and Abbie spoke excitedly at the same time, but then stopped. Abbie continued.

"No," she said, "but he does claim to own his place."

This was news to me. Nothing in Paddy's two boxes or in the filing cabinet said anything of the kind.

"How could he own it when the name on the monthly roll is Gomez," I asked. "There's no paper trail showing he bought it."

Shoshanna replied quickly.

"Big Steve says Lady Gomez sold it to him before she left."

The disappearance of Lady Gomez

Lady Gomez had apparently lived in the first-floor flat with her children, all five of them in that tiny space. Then one night the family had disappeared without anyone seeing them leave. By the next day Big Steve had moved in.

"She was there one day, gone the next," Miss Carol told me when I asked what she could remember about Lady Gomez. "Just vanished."

Miss Carol made it sound like there was something more devious and clandestine about the incident, as though Lady had been given no option but to pack her bags, hand over her keys and leave.

Later that day I went down to the agency, where the sisters pulled out a document that Big Steve had given them at some point. (Dates, as always, were vague.) Perhaps because every crisis seemed to have originated on their watch, the sisters produced information unwillingly, and only when it was way too late to fix.

The document was only four lines long, was full of spelling mistakes, and the wording was vague. It didn't specify what rights were being transferred to Big Steve, and nowhere was the word "sale", "sell" or "purchase" used, although a figure of $2,000 was mentioned. The signatures of Big Steve and Lady Gomez bore a striking resemblance, while that of the notary public as well as the date were smudged. Even to my legally untrained eyes, the words "phony" and "fake" were written all over it.

A second page, also only four lines long, was meant to serve as a reference letter. It was signed by someone named G Happy Smith, Chairman of The Awareness Group. G Happy Smith claimed to have known Big Steve for a long time, and vouched for him as a good upstanding member of the community who often helped out at The Awareness Group, which described itself as an organisation that helped rehabilitate substance abusers. There was an address in the Bronx and a phone number that I later tried calling. The phone had been disconnected.

All the other formalities that the sisters were meant to have carried out before anyone bought a flat – a credit check, a background check, a review of their income to prove their low-income status – were missing.

"I'm not a lawyer," I said, holding up the two pages, "but this won't stand up in court."

The sisters had clearly been hoping the two documents would settle things.

"Doesn't it seem fishy," I asked them, "that a man accused of selling drugs has a reference letter from someone at a centre that treats substance abusers?"

There was, of course, no answer.

The barometer

During these two wintry months, someone in our old building had been conspicuously absent, as if she had gone into hibernation: Carmen.

Ever since the night of her blood-curdling screams, when I thought mother and daughter would turn up in the headlines the next morning, the movements in the flat below mine had become less gay. Carmen's shoes didn't make their clippety-happy sound as she headed downstairs on shopping day, and she lost her temper more often than usual. The lupus lady hadn't visited in a while, and no-one on the street called for Carmen to come to her window. Her night-time visits onto the landing to talk to Choose Me Debra had all but ceased.

Maybe it was my imagination, but there seemed to be a direct correlation between the painting of the hallways, old man Rafael being taken to court, Choose Me Debra demanding a meeting, the police raid and Carmen's absence and radical mood swings. She was a barometer right below my floorboards – the more things changed, the more volatile she became – and I kept wondering what it would take for her to finally explode.

Quite appropriately, it was the heating in the building that finally blew the top off everything.

By late January, the weather had become bitterly cold again and the wind found all the cracks and bad insulation in our cheap windows. To fill them I used rolled-up newspapers and towels, and I daily offered up a silent prayer that the old boiler in our basement wouldn't break down.

Heat, or rather the lack of it, was the one thing in the building that could single-handedly cause a riot. Someone downstairs regularly hit one of the metal steam pipes if it was unusually cold, as if they were trying to send a semaphore message to the boiler: S-T-A-R-T-N-O-W. Each clank sent a shudder through the five floors.

Unlike South Africa, where you had your own geyser and heater, everyone in the old building got their heat and hot water from the oil-leaking boiler in the basement.

The 1950s sci-fi-looking boiler was a fragile cantankerous contraption with some very odd quirks. The hot water regularly changed its mind mid-stream, so that anyone taking a shower had to be ready at all times to jump to safety or get scalded. That someone hadn't been seriously burnt yet was quite a marvel.

As for the heating, some of the steam pipes that ran through the building didn't work. Each flat had not only a radiator but three vertical pipes running outside of the walls from the basement to the fifth floor. When the heat kicked in – which it was supposed to do below a certain temperature, but you could never be sure it would – a valve at the apex of each pipe hissed, sometimes to the point that it sounded like an explosion was imminent, or it dribbled pathetically like a runny nose.

One of my three pipes, the one in the bathroom, hadn't worked since I'd moved in. Fixing it would have been no harder than replacing the valve at the apex and would have cost almost nothing, perhaps a few dollars at most. But to do that the boiler had to be turned off. And to turn off the boiler required the involvement of Noah.

I lost count of the number of times I asked Noah and the sisters to see to the broken pipe – and I was sure there were others – but like most requests it went unheeded. And as more and more things started going badly in the old building, the steam pipe lost relevance. Eventually I forgot about it.

Centre Street, not Center Street

Early one Tuesday morning, I got a call from Shoshanna. Because her phone calls were such rare occurrences, I knew that it had to be important.

"You have to go to Centre Street," she said.

Centre Street, which was spelt the British way for some reason, was not far from Wall Street – which meant it was way Downtown, way beyond *Time Out New York*. I had walked along Centre Street before, but with the eyes of a tourist, admiring several gorgeous Beaux-Arts buildings that covered numerous blocks and whose function I wasn't paying attention to. I had since learnt that they all had a common purpose. They were courts.

While I was used to South Africa's simple three-tiered judicial system – magistrate's court, Supreme Court, Appeals Court, and no juries – Centre Street was a salmagundi of courts. There was criminal, civil, district, county, supreme, city, financial, surrogate – some with juries, some without. And somewhere in the midst of them all was one that dealt specifically with housing.

The case against old man Rafael was scheduled for 10am that Tuesday, and someone from our building needed to be there. Hector and Miss Carol weren't about to cross the city on the building's behalf when I couldn't even get them to set foot outside their flats.

"If someone from the board isn't there," Shoshanna warned me, "the case might be postponed for several months."

She was lying, of course. One of the sisters could have gone as

131

our representative — that's what they were paid to do — but they were refusing to. Vague battle lines had already formed between us. I was taking their advice less and less, while I kept digging up more problems that they'd been responsible for creating. They had probably figured out that I was looking around for an agency to replace them, so in the meantime they were going to make life as difficult as possible for me.

I had no freelance copy-editing job that day, but Shoshanna had given me exactly one hour to get Downtown, find the right exit at a subway station that had numerous, locate the right building out of dozens on Centre Street, and then figure out what floor and courtroom to go to for old man Rafael's case.

I hung up, grabbed my things and ran for my front door. I had barely started down the stairs when I saw Carmen blocking my way. Being Tuesday it was her shopping day, and her entourage was in the middle of its expedition between the fourth floor and the Cadillac waiting downstairs.

Carmen was looking at the new NO SMOKING sign Julio had recently put up above where Eva usually smoked on the stairs. Carmen's boyfriend in the fur-necked cream jacket held the pram, looking at me as if I'd insulted him.

"Hey! You!" Carmen shouted at me.

Shit, I thought, now I was not only late but had Carmen to deal with.

My response — and I knew it the moment it left my mouth — couldn't have been worse.

"What is it?" I said abruptly.

Carmen's high heels made her a lot taller than usual, and her perfume was overpowering.

"The heat in my bathroom don't work," she said. "I got a baby. He gets sick, I got hospital bills. Who's gonna pay? You?"

The heat in Carmen's bathroom, which was below mine, hadn't worked for as long as I'd been in the building, probably a lot longer. So why was she complaining now, several months into the winter?

I also knew that she was in regular contact with the sisters – a fact they often bragged about – so why hadn't she complained to them?

Obviously this had nothing to do with the heat at all but with what was going on around her. Something had suddenly pushed her over the edge. Was it one of the changes? Was I going too fast? Was it because I was new and had no history in the old building? Was it because, as Hector had said, I was white?

With her fedora-wearing boyfriend, the lupus lady and Eva watching us, I should have felt intimidated, but instead, and quite stupidly, I lost it. I was suddenly sick and tired of all this building silliness: board members who did nothing, police raids, drug dealers with their fake contracts, the sisters lying and stealing, Noah not working, residents not paying, Choose Me Debra's demands to stop renovating the filthy hallway, and now Carmen's ridiculous bathroom pipe. They did nothing but complain, while I was wasting more and more of each day trying to make the old building better.

I'd had enough.

"Call the sisters!" I snapped back at Carmen. "I have to get Downtown!"

I squeezed past the entourage and took the stairs two at a time, my neighbour's piercing voice trailing me.

"Hey, asshole! Who the fuck you think you are? Where you going? Get the fuck back here!"

As I pulled open the broken front doors, I bumped into Rafael coming up from the pavement. The old man whom I was this moment going to court to get evicted smiled shyly and then looked down at his feet. I ran for the subway, unhappy about what I was on my way to do and anxious about what I'd just done.

Carmen was the queen of the building – everyone knew that – with a lot of history there. And now I had not only changed the old building but I had disrespected her. The battle that had been looming for some time now was upon us.

Thirteen

A tense quiet fell over the two tenements, but it wasn't to last long.

Shoshanna called me several days later, and I at first suspected it would be to again send me running down to court on Centre Street. Instead she began by asking me how things were going at *Vanity Fair*. Pleasant conversation not being part of our usual exchanges, I knew something must be up.

"There's a petition going around," she finally said. She sounded cheerful. "It's about you. They want you out."

I asked her where the petition was.

"I don't know," she said, "and I haven't seen it myself. I don't know who is behind it."

Shoshanna was probably holding a copy of the petition in her hands and knew exactly who was behind it. A day later she admitted that she had managed to acquire a copy and would fax it to me. Once again, though, she demanded total anonymity.

"You can't say where you got it from," she said, the noncommittal bearer of bad tidings.

The petition, I could tell even from Shoshanna's fax, was smudged and had been folded and unfolded countless times, as if it had been repeatedly retrieved from someone's pocket. I pictured the ringleader going from door to door – Carmen probably, although I somehow couldn't imagine her having enough energy to repeatedly climb five flights of stairs and knock on numerous doors.

The copy editor in me couldn't help proofing the page as I read it. The board was referred to as an Executive Board, the letter was written because of "concern for the wellbeing and protection" of not only the shareholders but also the tenants. And a request was being made for the "immediate resignation of the Entire Executive Board".

A line about the sisters had been crossed out, and someone had scribbled a signature next to it, as if they were authorising a correction on a cheque.

"Therefore," it continued, "we the below signers have concluded that a proper election of a new board will take place in the basement on February 15."

There were thirteen signatures, although at least half of the names and their flat numbers were illegible. Carmen's name was there, and so was that of her neighbour, the illegal tenant Choose Me Debra. The Old Lady on the first floor, Lucrezia's mother, had signed, as had Maria, the loud mother on One. There too was the imprint of Lady Gomez, whose whereabouts had long been unknown, her handwriting bearing an uncanny resemblance to the signature below hers, which belonged to Big Steve.

Of the seven people whose names could be made out, most of them were not living in the building legally. Seven flats out of thirty shouldn't have concerned me, but it did, because the names included a drug dealer, his grandmother who had probably helped a fugitive escape the police, a woman who had gone missing under questionable circumstances, another woman whose mother had almost solely been responsible for the composition of the old building and had hired the sisters, and, last but not least, Carmen.

A few days later, a notice went up at the two front doors. It was brief and talked uncompromisingly about lives and flats being in danger. The demand was for action to be taken before everyone's homes were snatched away from them and for an election and an emergency meeting, in that order, as soon as possible. The signature at the bottom was Carmen's.

The faint rumble of war was in the air.

Gertrude pays a visit

The rats that brought Janice's pavement to life at night migrated in stages. Using a trench that ran from under her front steps and then along two sides of the corner tenement, the rodents travelled back and forth unseen.

From the corner tenement they branched out to Floyd's trash, which was kept under his entrance steps, and then, following Eva's trail of leftover food on the pavement, they infested ours. After dark, even on the coldest nights, our black garbage bags rustled and shook and our basement stairs became a little highway of agile bodies.

"We need to get those rats killed," Miss Carol said, closing her front door behind me. I hadn't seen her for a week or two, and I wanted to find out what she thought about the petition.

Miss Carol's best friend, Gertrude, was visiting her. They had known each other since they were children. Gertrude was missing several front teeth, smelt of liquor and reminded me of a woman I sometimes saw when I went out collecting furniture late at night. The odour of cigarettes, from the ashtray and the two of them smoking, was more noxious than usual.

"I've spoken to the sisters about an exterminator," I said.

"Good," Miss Carol replied. "Have you seen how big those things are?"

"Fat rats," Gertrude said, adding a phlegmy laugh.

I turned to Miss Carol.

"You've seen the petition?" I asked, trying not to sound overly concerned.

Miss Carol nodded.

"People are talking," she said, as if it meant something.

"People are talking," Gertrude echoed her.

I was hoping for support from Miss Carol and Hector, but I had never seen her more troubled.

"You see how many people signed?," she asked. "Thirteen."

"Mohammed didn't sign," I said. "Esperanza didn't. I could find only four legal signatures."

"Yes, but thirteen," she said, unable to get that figure out of her head.

Miss Carol knew many things about the building, such as the lease and who the old-timers were. She remembered when there had been six more tenements like ours on our street, which had become so dilapidated they'd been knocked down. How much we had in the bank, though, she didn't know. Nor could she tell you who was in the building legally and who wasn't. I explained to her that most of the signatories owed money, should be in court, didn't have leases, and so on – the debtors, the deceitful and the dead.

Once again she shook her head pessimistically.

"People are talking," she repeated, like a mantra or a curse.

She had lived in the building long enough to know when things were going badly.

"So you think we should give in?" I asked her. "They want an election. You think we should have an election?"

Miss Carol didn't answer, but Gertrude for some reason let out a manic, phlegm-filled laugh.

"Fat rats."

Casablanca

My visits to Hector's floor that week outnumbered those of any previous week, even at the height of the renovation. Each time I got to his front door, however, he wasn't in or he chose not to answer. My phone messages got no reply either.

Shuttling between Hector and Miss Carol had become a frustrating and hopeless exercise: trying to find them, get them to answer phone calls, get them to consider proposals, get them to make up their minds. It took three times as long to get anything done. More and more I started doing things on my own, and then telling them afterwards.

The only thing I didn't mention was the police raid in search of Dead Eyes. Other than telling the sisters, I didn't speak a word about it. Nor, for that matter, did anyone else. For a building as small as ours, and despite personal networks that were as intricate as the steam pipes coursing through its bowels, the raid by Sergeant Steinberg never got a single mention.

Noah must have spoken to someone about it; Maria must have gossiped to Veronica Laundry; Mister Winston and Mohammed must have said something to people parking their cars; and more than a few neighbours must have been looking out their windows that morning – but you wouldn't have known it. The raid could easily have been an illusion, a bad dream.

I thought of telling Miss Carol about it, but something stopped me. She had lived in the building her whole life and could well be friends with Lucrezia or Lucrezia's mother, the Old Lady on the first floor, or Choose Me Debra. I had no idea who was in whose network. By saying something bad about Big Steve, I might alienate Miss Carol and then Hector. And right now I needed all the friends I could get.

After I had made numerous trips in vain to Hector's place, he opened his front door. His thick glasses did little to hide his bad mood.

"I told you you were going too fast," he said. For once his hair was uncombed and stood up in the middle like a small tepee. "I don't like it when people come up to me on the street and ask me what's going on in our building."

"Which people?" I asked.

He walked through to his TV room, where *Casablanca* was playing.

"What's this about us taking some poor guy to court?"

"Rafael," I reminded him. He still couldn't remember who old man Rafael was. "I told you about the case. The guy who sweeps the hallways sometimes."

"Yeah?" he said. "Well, you're too pushy. You're like Paddy. I don't like what's going on around here. All these court cases and Noah and the sisters. What the fuck's going on?"

"We talked about it," I said. "I told you about every court case. I brought you documents to sign. You could have said no."

"Fuck off!" he said, then again, "Fuck off!"

Not even five months had passed since the Saturday morning Hector, Paddy, Morgenstern and I had gathered in the basement for the signing of my lease, Hector and Paddy exchanging curses, my skiff passing them, me uninvolved in their crazy antics. But now I was not only in the midst of the problems but I seemed to be the main one.

CHAPTER 6
CHANGE

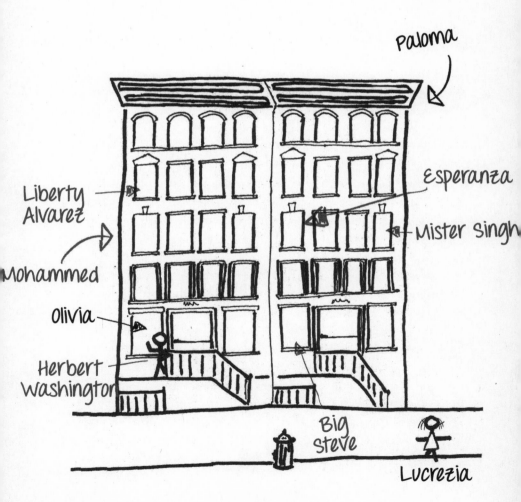

He loves me, she loves me not

Walking out of the tenement a few days later, I saw Mohammed sitting in his Toyota. Mohammed, my fellow African, had his fleece collar pulled up around his neck and the flaps of a hunting cap hiding his ears like a bloodhound. He cracked open his window and the smell of coffee greeted me.

"There was a drug raid," I told him, "and Carmen's upset she's not getting heat in her bathroom… and Noah's gone on strike… and suddenly everything's going badly."

I ran on and on but I could see Mohammed wasn't interested. He smiled at me sympathetically.

"This happened to Paddy," he said. "You can't fix this place. Give up trying."

"If there is an election," I began, "can I count on your support?"

He shook his head, not meaning no but meaning he wasn't interested.

"Paddy tried to get me to come too."

"Please," I begged, "you have to."

"I don't go to meetings. It gets too crazy. You'll see."

"Please. It's your building. You have the right to vote."

I felt like a disgraced politician begging for votes.

Mohammed started rolling up his window, signalling the end of the conversation. He mouthed two words from behind the glass.

"Good luck."

Esperanza was coming up the pavement with Tiny, her Chihuahua. She had worked the night shift at the gym Downtown and looked exhausted.

"There's going to be a meeting and an election," I told her. "I hope I can count on your support."

"Carmen, she very angry," Esperanza said into her raised hand, which she lowered only a fraction when she talked. "Debra, she no like the green paint."

"And you? Do you like it? Do you like what I'm doing?"

She looked around furtively, checking whether anyone was

watching us. There was nobody on the pavement, and only Herbert Washington was standing on the stoep of our second tenement, staring mystically into the distance. Her hand still poised in front of her mouth, Esperanza nodded.

"Yes, I like."

"I'm glad."

Leaving her, I made a beeline for Herbert Washington. If his wife, the petite eighty-year-old Ella May who had come to one of the basement meetings, liked what I was doing in the building, they would surely support me. When I greeted him he didn't look at me but swayed his head back and forth, as if he had already decided that his answer was going to be no, whatever the question. I gave him a very brief version of the latest events.

"Oh, I don't come to meetings," he answered. After a long pause, he added, still moving to an inaudible beat, "Ella May might come. Can't say for sure."

Walking away from Herbert, my mind fell to calculating, a terrible habit I'd developed over the last few weeks. I counted up, subtracted, considered variables, starting at thirty flats and then ticking each one off. Who was with me and who was against me? Whose support could I count on, now that I really needed it? For me the two sides were quite obvious: those who wanted change and order versus those who, for some reason, didn't.

But the sums never came out well. My opponents seemed too numerous, or maybe that's because they were the ones who were so visible, vocal, angry, shouting, massing on pavements, drawing up petitions. Against them were Esperanza, Mohammed, Mister Singh, the Washingtons, Miss Carol – quiet, law-abiding, passive and, I suspected, just a bit scared.

I needed more support. I had to make more allies – and fast.

Turned tables

Several months earlier I'd had more friends than I could count on two hands. From the moment people heard that I'd managed to buy a flat in New York for $10,000, I received countless emails, phone calls and supplications – yes, people actually begged me – sometimes even from total strangers. They had somehow heard the news and they wanted a cheap flat too. How could they get in on this fantastic deal?

"There's nothing for sale," I would say.

"Can I come see your place anyway?" they pleaded, trying to get a foot in the door, "just in case an apartment becomes available? Please."

"Sure," I replied. "But it won't help."

Anyone who actually came to my flat and saw the neighbourhood, the street and the tenement immediately had a change of heart.

"Oh, you have projects across the street," one of them said.

Then another said the same.

Then a third.

The two twelve-story buildings facing us, even when decorated with their Christmas lights, might as well have been a toxic waste dump.

"But there are projects all over the city," I said, the enthusiastic buyer now thoroughly disinterested. With the tables suddenly turned, I wanted to make them see the value of our two tenements.

"Look," I said, "the hallways have been painted and we have new lights. It's only $10,000. Where could you get a deal like this in New York?"

"Thanks," the response came each time. "But this isn't for me. I'm not a pioneer."

The pioneer

In the end, only one person showed any interest in being a pioneer – crossing a frontier into possibly hostile territory for a cheap piece of land – and did she ever show an interest! A friend brought Olivia by to see my flat and she had barely walked through the front door when she got very excited.

"Oh, your place is adorable!" she said. "It's the cutest place I've ever seen. I love what you've done with it. I love these kinds of apartments. You ever have one of these to sell, you let me know."

When Paddy was selling his flat, I told my friend to let Olivia know there was a place she could look at. She immediately came to view it, but she said five flights of stairs were too many for her old dog to climb. She wanted something on a lower floor.

Afterwards, Olivia was relentless. She phoned me regularly and asked how things were going in the building. With each conversation, I confessed a bit more about what was going on – first the small problems and then the nastier ones – until she knew more about the two tenements than anyone who lived in them.

"If I had an apartment in your building I would help you," she said, unwavering.

No news, no matter how catastrophic, could faze her – not even the police raid and the description of Dead Eyes.

"Together we could sort things out," she said. "Keep doing what you're doing. It's the right thing. You're doing the right thing."

Given the general hostility and the lack of support around me, it was hard not to be smitten by Olivia. So, somewhere in between fending off Carmen and Noah and Big Steve, I sneaked her into the second tenement one day to show her a flat owned by us but which no-one had lived in for many years. And it was obvious why.

On the ground floor, it was the smallest flat out of all thirty. There were only two rooms, the one barely larger than a walk-in cupboard, and the entire place was covered to about knee height in old newspapers, even older magazines, bursting garbage bags and broken bits of furniture. Electrical wires hung from the walls, and the ceiling was caving in.

"It's adorable!" Olivia exclaimed the moment she saw it.

Nothing about the flat was adorable, and it was hard to imagine anyone living there, least of all Olivia. As she stood in the midst of the garbage and the pendulous wires, the contrast couldn't have been starker. Her hair and makeup, as always, were impeccable, her heels ferociously high, and she was dressed as if she might be on her way to a very important meeting, which she often was. She belonged to one of the city's most high-profile women's charities, known for its tea parties and money-raising events. She was, in fact, a vice-president.

Olivia looked so high-income, in fact, I didn't see how I could possibly get her into a low-income building. But on paper she was poor, having been unemployed for at least a year. She claimed – although I would never see any evidence of this – to be a magazine editor.

As things in the building got worse, the idea of selling the tiny flat to Olivia turned from being a crazy notion into, quite possibly, a fairly brilliant solution. Olivia understood what it meant to live in a co-operative, that work was required, that people had to obey the rules, that there needed to be order. If anyone would support me, Olivia would.

So, in the midst of shuttling between Hector and Miss Carol to talk about rat exterminators, the boiler breaking down, the renovation, the legal cases, I threw in a casual remark about it maybe being a good idea to sell the tiny flat on the first floor. It could bring us an additional $10,000 instead of lying there empty and earning us nothing.

They both agreed – or rather, they didn't disagree – and after letting another week pass, I mentioned to them that I might have found a potential buyer. Both Hector and Miss Carol met Olivia briefly, and neither had any argument with the sale, although Hector passed a casual remark that made my South African radar go ping again.

"She's white."

Olivia and pigs

The sale of the tiny flat went through in record time, even faster than mine had. In only a few weeks we were sitting in the sisters' office above the pizza parlour preparing to sign the deed of sale.

The atmosphere was as thick as pizza dough. The lawyer Morgenstern glared at the sisters, whom he didn't like because he was being used less and less. They glared back at him when they weren't glaring at Olivia, who was wearing a designer suit and very high heels and who'd had her hair done for the occasion. I'd told her all about the thieving, scheming, duplicitous Shoshanna and Abbie, and she was determined to upstage them, which she did.

The sisters, meanwhile, knew exactly what I was up to. They were the only ones who'd cottoned on to it. I was sidelining them more and more, and they were very unhappy about it. For a reason I would never figure out – either they were hiding something very bad they'd done or we were just an easy pay cheque – the sisters desperately wanted to cling on to our old building. But if more people like Olivia were brought in, their days would be numbered.

Once the documents had been signed, Olivia and I left the meeting and walked up a noisy New York avenue. Within a block we were both laughing out loud at what had just happened in the sisters' office. I felt as if a load had been lifted off my shoulders. Now I had someone who would back me, support me, tell everyone I was doing the right thing. Two was better than one.

"We will turn things around," Olivia said, her toothy smile more expansive than ever. "We will get them out." Then it came, finally: "They're *pigs!*"

I felt myself jolt.

Olivia might as well have scratched her beautifully buffed nails down a long blackboard or blurted out the words "motherfucking cunt". Who she meant exactly I wasn't sure, but I suspected the sisters, Noah, Choose Me Debra, Carmen, Lucrezia, Big Steve, even Hector; basically anyone who had broken the laws of the old building and made things go badly.

As we walked further up the avenue and conversation fell to other things, non-building things, I thought that maybe Olivia's two-word outburst had been a sign of frustration. She was, after all, the local vice-president of a highly influential women's group whose ranks included former judges and even former president's wives. Yes, it was a once-in-a-blue-moon comment that I should just forget.

But the word "pigs" stuck in my head, along with the other doubts I'd had about her from the moment she set foot into my flat – simple and furnished from the street – and called it "adorable".

Why, for instance, would anyone in their right mind want to move into such an obviously troubled old building? Why was she so enthusiastic about a place so unworthy of being enthusiastic about? Did the $10,000 price tag really make it that attractive? Her excitement seemed out of proportion with what she was getting in return.

But whatever concerns I had, I kept reminding myself that Olivia would be living in the old building and would help me. Having her was better than having no-one. Come what may, it was a less-than-ideal pact that I was prepared to make because the outcome, I was convinced, would be good.

Several weeks after Olivia bought her place, the petition went around the building and then Carmen put up a notice at the front door demanding an election. When I called Olivia to tell her what was happening, her response was immediate and unequivocal.

"Pigs!"

Kisses for the ladies

One morning in late February, an especially icy wind blew down the viaduct towards the heart of the city. I went to the basement in the second tenement and placed the peeling red benches in a neat U-shape. Behind them I arranged a couple of folding chairs.

I had prepared as well as I knew how to, since I'd never held an election before. I had written a speech. I had reread the lease and the bylaws, which also dealt with the procedure to follow at a building election. There were lots of fancy terms that I knew I would have no use for: Reading of Minutes of the Preceding Meeting, Reports of Officers, and Reports of Committees, of which there were none.

I had also, a few days earlier, contacted Siobhan at the non-profit agency to ask if she had any last-minute advice. I quickly updated her about the case against old man Rafael, the petition, Carmen's fury, Hector's reaction and the countless warnings I'd got that any meeting in our building would quickly turn into chaos. Once again, Siobhan sounded amused; our version of Fawlty Towers offered no end of entertainment for her, it seemed.

"I can be there if you want me to," she offered. "To make sure things go properly."

"Yes, please," I said quickly. "Please come."

When the meeting started, Siobhan sat to one side of me, Olivia the other, dressed not for our tenement but for the Upper East Side, her hair done, a full face of make-up, and a fur collar around her neck. It suddenly struck me that we were three white people in a row, and I wanted to get away from them, sure that everyone else would interpret it the wrong way.

Morgenstern took a place on his own at the end of one of the red benches, smiling mindlessly again. There were eight or nine other people – the usual suspects: Ella May Washington, her sister-in-law Mrs McGreevy (who, like Ella May, lived somewhere else and kept her flat opposite Ella May's unlived in), Miss Carol, Brunhilda, Esperanza – but far fewer than we needed to proceed.

I waited fifteen minutes longer, but still no Carmen, no Noah, no Hector, no Big Steve. Not even the tall Mister Singh.

"Maybe this is all that's coming," I whispered to Siobhan.

I stood up.

"Good evening, ladies and gentleman," I began.

With no previous Minutes to read and no Committees or Reports of Directors to talk about, I went straight into my speech. In it I told everyone who I was and how I had come to be president of the board. I tried to be upbeat. I pointed out all the things that had been done over the last few months – the painted hallways, the new floor tiles, the pleasant new lighting, the exterminators – plus we still had money in the bank. I used the words "we" and "the board" all the time, like we were a properly functioning team in a normal building.

No-one looked at me except Ella May Washington and Mrs McGreevy, a buxom, grave woman. Every now and then Olivia shouted, "Here, here!" which drew unnecessary attention to her and the fur collar at her neck. With the ink barely dry on her lease, her flat still a wreck she didn't live in, no-one knew who she was. Siobhan looked at Olivia like she was an unwanted visitor.

Random clapping followed my speech, and I stupidly believed that I would get away with it. But as soon as I asked if anyone had questions, people started to come down the stairs into the basement. Lots of people. More people than there were seats for. More people than the basement seemed capable of holding.

Carmen stormed in, a puffy ski jacket pulled over her T-shirt.

"Fucking asshole," she said in my face as she passed.

She pushed a bench out of her way and sat in one of the folding chairs with her back to the wall. She kept muttering words in Spanish that sounded something like, "Fucking creep. Asshole. Who's he motherfucking think he is? Fucking fucker."

Almost invisible behind her were the sisters, Shoshanna and Abbie, who had never visited the old building as far as I recalled. Shoshanna took a seat right next to Carmen, an odd couple if ever there was one, the two extremes of the opposition. The one: screaming, foul-mouthed, tight T-shirt bursting from her pillowy jacket, bright lipstick. The other: heavy overcoat, no make-up, dowdy, clutching her polio arm. They said not a word to each other the whole evening, but they were obviously together. It was an alliance made long ago, inexplicable but somehow crucial.

A few of the late arrivals I knew from the tenements. Lots I didn't know. They reminded me of the people who had walked in off the street the day I signed my lease, random passers-by drawn by the commotion. Some of them knew Carmen, Veronica Laundry and Maria, greeted them like old friends, although that didn't seem to be a prerequisite to come in and join us.

One face that I did know but hadn't seen for a long time belonged to a beautiful young woman in her thirties who stood in the back on her own, wearing a baseball cap pulled low over her eyes like she didn't want anyone to recognise her. She was the mother who had lived behind me with her husband and small son but had moved out.

Her name was Paloma.

Still missing: Hector, Noah, Big Steve.

"The meeting is only for shareholders," I pointed out to Siobhan. "I don't know who most of these people are."

Siobhan, who was clearly concerned, had not been smiling for a while.

"It's probably not a good idea to say anything right now," she replied. "Just carry on."

"Should I read my speech again?"

Before she could answer, Hector stumbled in. He regained his balance and planted a big kiss on the cheek of the first woman he reached. Then, like a politician doing a last round of campaigning, he made a fuss of kissing every woman in the room – even Olivia – after which, having misjudged the location of one of the red benches, he fell to the floor. Several people helped him get up, whereupon he took out his comb and ran it through his hair. He was drunk.

In front of us all, in the very middle of the quadrant, like he was on trial, sat old man Rafael, scared and confused, a caged animal. He had somehow become the focus of the meeting, the rallying cry. No exact grievance had been spelt out yet, so this poor silent man had unknowingly come to represent the collective anger.

Perched on the end of a red bench nearby was his sister, a grey-haired woman with the face of an angel who clasped her hands in her lap. It was hard to believe, if Shoshanna was correct, that she was the person who had stolen all old man Rafael's money. She was probably also the mother of the bloodshot-eyed can collector who sometimes lived with her brother.

When she spoke, it was in Spanish, and after a few sentences Hector leaned in as if he was going to kiss her.

"I will translate," he announced.

The woman carried on, with Hector struggling to follow her

words. It was the first time I had heard Hector try to speak Spanish.

"'I don't know how this happened,'" he translated. "'The city was meant to...'"

He couldn't think of the right word, so a woman with a big hairdo sitting on the other side of Siobhan interrupted.

'... was meant to give me assistance.'

"Yes," Hector nodded at the big-haired woman, whom he had kissed but didn't seem to know. "That's right. *Gracias.*"

Old man Rafael's sister bent her head miserably. She sobbed more, spoke a bit more, Hector translating pointlessly, half the people engaged in their own conversations. The impact of her words suddenly hit him, and he stopped, flabbergasted. Old man Rafael was being evicted? Was this true? Scandalised, he turned to me.

"How did this happen? We must do something," he said loudly, making sure everyone heard him. "We need to help this poor old man."

Hector, for the first time, surprised me. He might not know anyone's name, but he knew how to play a room, even when he was drunk.

On my other side I could hear Olivia sighing in frustration – all this back-and-forth about an old man she didn't know, Hector lying, some woman with a big hairdo we'd never seen before interrupting as if she belonged there – and I was sure I heard her mutter the word "pigs".

Gloria

The woman with the big hairdo was in her late thirties, dressed very well compared to the rest of us, and held herself very erect, which made her appear taller than she actually was. She was the only stranger in the basement who was given a name. People called her Gloria.

"We are your friends," Gloria said in English to old man Rafael's sister, before turning to the room. "We can't let this man's home be taken away from him."

"You tell him!" shouted Carmen, looking at me. "Let's vote! Fucking *cabrón!*"

Old man Rafael's sister mumbled softly and cried some more. Olivia shifted in her seat and finally, unable to control her irritation, she leaned in towards me.

"She's a liar," she muttered, meaning Rafael's angelic-faced sister. It was a pointless remark, since I was the one who had told her about old man Rafael's missing money in the first place. But I suspected her words were intended not for me but for Gloria, who, unfortunately, heard them.

"Excuse me?!" she shouted at Olivia, leaning across Siobhan. "What the fuck do *you* know?!"

Siobhan and I were sandwiched between Olivia and Gloria, neither of whom seemed at all intimidated by the other. They were the two best-dressed, best-coiffed women in the room facing off against each other. If a fight broke out, though, I didn't think Olivia would stand a chance.

"A liar?!" Gloria went on in disbelief. "How can you call this woman a liar? Can't you see how upset she is? Her brother is being kicked out onto the street." She motioned at poor old man Rafael, who clearly didn't understand what was happening. "You are a fucking racist!"

The word "racist" triggered Carmen, who, like most of the people in the room, had no idea who Olivia was. But they didn't say a word about it. No-one really knew who belonged here and who didn't – it was basically a free-for-all.

Carmen focused on me again.

"Motherfucker!" she shouted. "Let's vote!"

Siobhan grew more bewildered by the minute. If she was acquainted with low-income buildings, they hadn't been like ours. Our Fawlty Towers that had amused her when we talked on the phone was a joke no more.

It was of continuing amusement, however, to Morgenstern,

who kept chuckling to himself; the more lawless things became, the more he seemed to enjoy it. His choice of scenarios to watch kept multiplying: Gloria screaming at Olivia; Carmen cursing me; Hector walking about the room greeting strangers; various arrivals shouting support for someone or other; Veronica Laundry airing a grievance – the only grievance so far – about about her toilet not working properly and demanding it be fixed immediately.

The situation was so out of control, in fact, that it struck me that the only solution was to let everyone carry on screaming until they were too tired to do it any longer. Let them scream themselves into exhaustion.

At that point, in the midst of the madness, Lucrezia walked in. Smoking a cigarette, her Medusa hair pointing out like a thorny crown, she sauntered between the benches, said something to Veronica Laundry and waved at the big-haired Gloria. Finally she returned to the back of the room and leaned against the wall, her arms folded threateningly over her chest. I could imagine what she was silently shouting from her invisible soapbox as she looked at me: "You! White man! Racist!"

Standing nearby was someone I hadn't notice come in after her. He slipped into the shadows, stood there for a while, then momentarily came into the glare of a low, bare ceiling light. I had never seen him in person before, but I had seen his picture – on a flyer held by Sergeant Steinberg. It was the fugitive, Lucrezia's son, Dead Eyes.

At that moment, I was ready to give up. What the hell was I doing in that basement, trying to lead this broken old building? It was the stupidest idea I'd ever had. What was I thinking when I had accepted Paddy's offer? A white South African taking charge of a wild building in Harlem, New York? Mohammed had been right – the meeting was crazy, and so was the building. Maybe the hallways had best been left alone, brown and graffiti-coated, Noah undisturbed, the sisters pilfering money, the drug dealers in business, until the two tenements finally collapsed from abuse, bankruptcy or neglect. I didn't want this job and I didn't need it. I wanted to be like other people in New York, like the people I worked with at *Entertainment Weekly* and *Vanity Fair* who didn't get involved, didn't know who their neighbours were, used their flats only as a place to sleep. Now I knew why they did it.

Life was simpler as an itinerant, a passer-by, a renter, someone who didn't put down roots – and I wanted to go back to that place.

Liberty's other meaning

During an unusual lull, I stood up and made a last-ditch effort to reestablish some sense of calm.

"Thank you, ladies and gentlemen," I said.

There was a moment of silence, a mixture of disbelief and incomprehension. Not only was I daring to say something, but I was doing it with an accent that most people in the basement hadn't yet heard. It was English but not the kind they were used to, and that threw them off for a moment.

"I would be happy to make copies of my speech for anyone who is interested."

Everyone, Ella May and her sister-in-law Mrs McGreevy in particular, looked at me as if I was out of my mind. Carmen broke the silence.

"Asshole! We don't care about your fucking speech."

I carried on, probably looking as awkward as I felt.

"Does anyone have any questions?" I asked.

A heavy-set man was standing in a corner near the door leading to the oil tank, Dead Eyes to one side of him. He had a shaved head, a narrow Koki pen / Magic Marker of a goatee and moustache etched across his face, and cheeks polished a shiny red. Quite improbably for our ragtag meeting, he wore a tie. Not once in sixteen months in the building had I seen him, but I knew as soon as he opened his mouth that he was the man who had threatened to kill my predecessor Paddy Murphy and his wife: he was Alvarez.

He stepped forward.

"Liberty!" someone shouted.

He took in the accolade for a moment or two.

"Yeah, I got a question," he said. But instead of asking it, he introduced himself. "Everyone here knows me. They call me Liberty. I been living in this building my whole life. My mother, everyone knows my mother."

He mentioned her name, whereupon there was some muttering.

"Yeah," he carried on. "She helped this building. When times were bad, she was there. You all remember, right? She fought for this neighbourhood." He looked at me accusingly, to remind me that I hadn't. "When everyone else gave up, she fought. She is the reason we have this building today."

"Hey, Liberty!" a lone voice cried out.

Of all the many names I had come across in the rusty filing cabinet and Paddy's two boxes, Alvarez's mother was not one of them. Even Alvarez – who seemed to prefer being called Liberty – had been in the building for only six years and not, as he had just told everyone, his entire life. Both histories, his and his mother's, were made up. But it didn't seem to matter. People weren't listening to what he said, just how he said it. Volume equalled conviction, and he had lots of it.

"Liberty! Liberty!"

Alvarez/Liberty didn't need any encouragement to carry on, but he took his time as the voices died down.

"Yeah, I got a question for you," he said finally, pointing a finger at me. "Who! The! Fuck! Are! You?!"

Quorum

Carmen was growing impatient and Shoshanna was shifting around uncomfortably, literally trapped in her corner.

"Let's fucking vote!" Carmen said. "Jesus!"

Siobhan, sitting next to me, finally stood up. No-one knew who Siobhan was, but some of them knew the non-profit agency, at least by name. It was somehow related to low-income buildings like ours and, like Liberty's speech about his mother, it went unquestioned. Certain things about life in the old building were just accepted, and the agency was one of them. That was enough to give Siobhan a smidgen of authority, which in this room was a lot.

"For the voting to be legal," she said, "there has to be a quorum."

The word "quorum" meant nothing to anyone, and no-one knew if there was one or who was eligible to vote. What with all the dead, departed and delinquent residents, not to mention all the spectators moseying in off the street, the answer was anyone's guess. Morgenstern our lawyer didn't have a clue. Nor did the sisters. I had a vague idea, from the files, but no-one was going to listen to me. In desperation, Siobhan grabbed a figure out of the air and, bizarrely, everyone accepted it, so long as voting could begin.

Then Siobhan announced another rule that no-one seemed to recall: if you owed more than two months' levy, you couldn't vote. Liberty found out he was one of those people.

"Jesus Christ!" he shouted, turning to those nearest him, one of whom was the fugitive Dead Eyes.

"Liberty!" one of them called out.

For the second time, he launched into his speech about having lived in the building his whole life, his mother having saved it, and so on. Ella May Washington rolled her eyes to the ceiling. She and Mrs McGreevy next to her wanted to get out of the basement fast, but they were hemmed in.

"I paid my money a couple days ago!" Liberty told the room. He turned to the sisters. "Abbie? Did I pay my money? Did I bring it to you?"

The sisters had remained unnoticed until now, Shoshanna shrinking away next to Carmen, possibly wondering how she could be associated with such a murderous, foul-mouthed person. Abbie, alarmed that she was being brought into the argument, shyly came over to consult with Siobhan. The three of us knew Liberty was delinquent but Siobhan decided to let him vote anyway. To do otherwise would only prolong a very dark night.

"Let's fucking vote!" It was Carmen again. "I have a baby upstairs."

Carmen was nominated to fill one of the five posts. So were Liberty, Hector, Miss Carol and me. It was a combination of tradition and desperation.

"Any other nominations?" Siobhan asked.

Paloma, my beautiful former neighbour from the fifth floor who now lived across the East River in Queens, looked around for someone to notice her. Oddly enough for someone who seemed to want to be incognito – hiding under a baseball cap in a dark corner, not having lived in the building for a year – the lack of recognition seemed to offend her. When her name was finally put forward, someone shouted a question.

"Who is Paloma?"

It was probably the best question of the evening. Who was she? Whose side was she on? I had no idea, but during the fuss of people deciding who they would vote for, I pointed out to Siobhan that Paloma didn't live in the building and thus, technically at least, was not allowed to be elected. Why I even bothered to mention this, I don't know, especially after so many more serious rules had been overlooked.

"She lives in Queens," I said.

Paloma overheard me and the reaction was immediate. A scowl suddenly scarred her beautiful face, she lowered her head, and her eyes were once again hidden by the brim of her baseball cap. Siobhan, who, like Ella May and Mrs McGreevy, wanted to escape the basement without any further delay, didn't care where Paloma lived and let her stand.

As all this was going on, one person was lost and forgotten, and looking more frightened than ever – old man Rafael.

Many months later, when nothing could be done about it, I found out that the election that night had been rigged. Carmen's daughter, Eva, had somehow managed to add votes for her mother and Liberty, helping them tie for last place out of the five board positions. The other three people elected were – in this order – Hector, Paloma and me.

Hector received only one vote more than Paloma and two more than me, but he assumed that this majority automatically made him president. He immediately made his first two pronouncements, which were that we should gather 1) not right away, which would have seemed the obvious thing to do, but a week from tonight; and 2) not in the basement, the obvious place, but somewhere more convivial.

"It's so ugly down here," he said. "Why don't you all come up to my place."

It sounded like we were being invited for cocktails.

Breaking the ice

When I reached Hector's flat the following Monday, Liberty was already there, sitting below one of the Frida Kahlo-ish paintings, his shaved head catching the light of a nearby lamp. He grinned at me and shook my hand, even though we still had not formally met. He had a disarming smile and pushed his shiny head forward at the same time, as if he was going to playfully butt you.

Carmen arrived fifteen minutes later, hugged Liberty, and walked straight past me without saying anything. Paloma was last, coming directly from work. Beautiful as ever and dressed in a suit, the perfect picture was flawed only by the look on her face when she saw me. She scowled.

Hector's flat, which I had been in dozens of times before, felt different, cramped, unfamiliar, tense. My role had changed, but I didn't know how. Saying nothing and just watching the others, I wanted to see what they would say, which direction they would go in.

For a while no-one said anything, and then Hector broke the ice. Literally.

"Drink, anyone?" he asked.

None of us replied, so he went into the kitchen and was busy noisily scooping ice cubes into a glass when Carmen announced that she would be secretary. Hector quickly exited the kitchen empty-handed.

"Don't you think we should vote for president first?" he asked.

"You can be president," Carmen said, queen-like. "I'm gonna be secretary."

She took out a notepad and made a big motion of turning it to the first page, although she didn't write anything down.

No-one objected to Hector being president.

"Gracias," he said.

Half a year earlier nothing on earth could have persuaded him to take the position when Paddy gave it up, but now he was obviously moved. He got his glass from the kitchen and raised it.

"Gracias, amigos."

It was the second time I had ever heard Hector speak Spanish, even if it was only two words. But two words was all it took to suddenly alert me to the gulf between the five of us, a divide Hector had pointed out to me that I'd failed to pay attention to, the divide that had caused things to go badly. All the people I had got into trouble were Hispanic. And now here we sat, one white and four Hispanics.

I knew they were Hispanic because I had made it my business to find out. Ever since Hector first mentioned the word "Hispanic", I had asked around to find out where people in the old building came from. That's when I started noticing how many New Yorkers claimed to be from somewhere else, no matter how long ago their ancestors got here. People weren't from America, they were from another place. The sisters were from Morocco, Liberty from the Dominican Republic, and the other three on the board from Puerto Rico.

The divide between me and the other board members suddenly felt immense, especially in Hector's small living room. I was fully expecting them to switch to Spanish from that moment on, the way Afrikaans people back home sometimes did to exclude an English speaker. Hector and the other three would talk about what they planned for the old building, what they wanted to do, how they would change things, how they would protect people like old man Rafael – all without me. By using another language, they would effectively shut me out.

Clink!

The ice in Hector's whisky glass, nudged on by his finger, brought me back to the small room.

"Gracias," he said again.

A new kitchen

I waited for more Spanish, but it didn't come. There was no English either. In fact, there was no conversation at all, and everyone seemed a bit lost. Once Hector had settled into his seat, and the other positions on the board had been divvied up as randomly as numbers in a lottery, silence filled the eggshell-blue room.

I had, after the uprising and the angry election, been anticipating a flood of questions. People would want answers. What had I been doing for five months as president? How much money had been spent on the hallways? Where had Olivia come from and how had she managed to buy the tiny flat on the first floor in record time? What was going on with old man Rafael now? How far along was his court case? What would happen to his flat if he was evicted? How much money did we have in the bank? Which flats were delinquent? Why wasn't Noah doing his job? Why were several steam pipes still not fixed?

But nothing; not a word.

When the silence was finally broken, it was by Carmen.

"Debra wants to buy her apartment," she said.

She meant her neighbour on the fourth floor, bellicose Choose Me Debra who had no lease. Choose Me Debra's flat was one of two that the building still owned – our last remaining sources of income besides the monthly levies that numerous people weren't paying. Once we sold that flat to Choose Me Debra for $10,000, the building would have one less cushion. We needed to either raise the price of flats we sold or think of another way to make income. But there was no discussion about any of this and, rather than participate in the meeting, Liberty was in fact craning his neck to study the artwork on the wall behind him.

"Before Debra buys," Carmen continued, "she wants the apartment painted, and a new stove. Her fridge is old too."

Again, silence. No-one seemed to care that Choose Me Debra would get not only a cheap flat but would have new appliances thrown in too – a new kitchen. And all of it would have to be paid for by the old building.

Quiet until now, I finally broke in.

"The lease says you buy an apartment *voetstoots*," I said.

Everyone looked at me that funny way they did when they didn't understand your accent. Paloma's scowl reappeared. Then I realised I had used the Afrikaans word for "as is". Before I could correct myself, Carmen carried on.

"We all know Debra. She's our friend. We know Bella, her mother."

I tried to interrupt.

"Enough!" Hector said, holding his glass up in the air like he was going to make a toast. "I am president. Debra can buy."

Carmen's pen was poised at the notepad, although she still didn't write anything down. Liberty took his chance to talk. He was still sore about Paddy Murphy, the man he had threatened to kill and who was now long gone from our building, and the court case that Paddy had initiated against him. These things he would never forget or forgive.

"I am now treasurer," he said, words that scared me a little. What would a man who made death threats and arbitrarily refused to pay his levy do with our meagre funds? "I want to investigate Murphy. I know he stole from us. I'm gonna get my accountant to look into this fucking asshole. We take Murphy to court. Where'd all the money go to?"

No-one knew what Liberty was talking about, what money had been stolen, and they didn't seem to care either. So Liberty carried on with his rant, while Hector left to get a refill in the kitchen. Carmen, now that she had finished what she'd come to do, stood up.

"I'm going," she said. "I got a baby."

Before Hector had time to fill his glass and return to the room she was gone.

Gone

At almost the same time that we were having our first board meeting, Olivia who had so recently bought the tiny apartment was involved in a very important meeting of her own. She was paying a lot of money for a country house two hours outside the city.

Unbeknownst to me, Olivia had owned a spacious two-bedroom flat across the Split, on the Upper East Side. This fact, if she had disclosed it at the time she was buying the tiny flat, would have disqualified her. But she had kept it a secret. With the money she made off the sale of the two-bedroom flat she could afford to buy not only the tiny flat in our building but a country house, and within weeks of the election she had moved there.

Over the following months I called Olivia many times. I wanted to find out when she would be coming to town to begin renovating the tiny flat and making good on all her promises to help fix up the old building. Like the sisters, Olivia rarely answered her phone, but when she did she always had an excuse.

She was sick, her cats were sick, her dog was sick, the phone line was down, there had been a flood in her house, she'd lost her cellphone, she never got my message, her phone was broken, she was away, she was renovating her country house, she was snowed in, a tree had fallen across the driveway, she had a meeting, she had run out of petrol/gas on the highway coming into the city... There was always a reason.

"I'm so sorry," she said each time, never missing a beat. "I will be there next time – definitely. I promise. I will be there soon."

Main Street, New York

Well into winter, the street and pavement outside the old building brought to mind a desolate Main Street in one of the many cowboy movies that Hector had in his DVD collection. It was blustery and empty, plastic bags and fast-food wrappers swirling around a lone small concrete picnic table in the projects and in between parked cars, from where they were carried like tumbleweeds down past the open lot, which, behind its chain-link fence, could have passed for veld/prairie.

Heading down towards the busy avenue I saw Mohammed sitting in his car. The cab of his Toyota emitted a draft of warm air as he rolled down the window.

"How was the election?" he asked, smiling mischievously.

I shrugged. He could see I was still sore about the outcome.

"At least I got elected," I said.

"I hear Carmen is on the board too. Didn't she just quit the last board under Paddy? And now she's in again." He chuckled. "I told you it would be crazy, right?"

"It was," I said. "And I could have done with some support."

"Like I said, it doesn't do any good. It's always the same. Lots of people you have never seen before turn up and take over. Then Liberty starts screaming. Am I right?"

"Yes," I said. "But it's your building. You have a share in it. It's your investment. You have a right to be at the meeting. You could help change things."

It sounded like I was giving him a lecture. Mohammed shook his head slowly, as if I just didn't get it.

Chanel No 5

The second board meeting took place in the basement room where the rusty filing cabinet was kept. To try to make it more pleasant I arranged some chairs, a table and a carpet, all of which I had gathered off the street while collecting at night. Only two people turned up, the beautiful Paloma and me, she growing increasingly annoyed that she had come in all the way from Queens for nothing.

The silence between us was unbearable – she wasn't going to forgive me anytime soon for almost sabotaging her chance to be on the board – and after half an hour she left.

After that the board met at random, and we were lucky if three people out of five attended. There was rarely a quorum, although it didn't matter because there was never anything to vote on. Hector, for all the times he didn't arrive, offered no apology. Paloma came when her schedule allowed it, and if anyone brought up her absence she reminded them that she had a son, a husband and a job. Liberty, on the one occasion he came, got angry that Paloma wasn't there and wanted her fired because she didn't live in the building.

Carmen also came only once more. For some reason her absence irritated Hector, who himself was usually missing, and on one of the nights he turned up he decided to exert his authority. When it was clear that she wouldn't be joining us, he turned to me.

"Go tell Carmen to come down," he said, like I was his flunky.

I didn't hesitate because I knew the outcome would be unforgettable. Given Carmen's temper and the fact that she was queen of the building, Hector had no idea what he was asking for.

Fifteen minutes later Carmen stormed into the basement in her slippers and a ski jacket pulled over her pyjamas. Standing in the doorway she pointed her finger at Hector.

"Don't you never the fuck tell me to come down here! I got a fuckin' baby to take care of! You never do that again! *Never!* You hear me? Leave me the fuck alone!"

"You are the secretary," Hector said. His breath smelt of mints and wine. "You are meant to be taking the minutes."

Carmen took a step forward.

"Fuck you!" she said in a way that was meant to end the conversation. "I'm going back to my baby."

"Carmen, you have to make time for the board."

I was convinced that Hector must be very brave, stupid or drunk to keep taunting Carmen. She looked quite capable of throttling him.

"I don't wanna be on no fuckin' board!" she shouted. "You get me?"

After giving Hector a last murderous look she walked out.

The three of us – Hector, Paloma and me – sat in silence. It had taken exactly three months for the newly elected board to show its cracks, and the old building was a lot more fractious than I'd imagined. Carmen didn't like Hector, Liberty didn't like Paloma, and Paloma, who still scowled at me every chance she got, didn't care for Liberty or for Carmen, whom she looked at with a mixture of pity and disdain. It was no longer me against the four of them. It was all five of us against each other.

The following month, quite out of the blue, Carmen came to the meeting without having to be summoned. But this time no-one else came. It was just the two of us, and she didn't have her notepad with her. She was dressed in black – leather jacket, very tight leather pants and thigh-high boots – and reeked of Chanel No 5.

"I'm going out after," she told me.

Carmen rarely left the building except to go out shopping on Tuesdays, and she was obviously excited about the night that lay ahead. She'd had her hair specially cut and streaked with blonde highlights.

"You like?" she asked me, tilting her head into one hand, nails newly polished.

Things between us had improved since the election. Her shopping sprees were once again festive, even though the gangster with the white Cadillac no longer came by, and she had to organise a car service to ferry them back and forth from the store. At least one night a week she came out onto the landing to join Eva for a cigarette under the new NO SMOKING sign.

Her new hairstyle, I told Carmen, was very fetching.

"I'm going blonde for a while," she said, then raised an eyebrow coquettishly. "Blondes have more fun."

She laughed, and at that moment it was hard not to like her.

"Well, I guess no-one's coming," she said finally.

Her leather jacket and boots squeaked as she got up. Giving me a mischievous smile, she headed outside, where a black car was waiting to take her into the night. A rat dashed madly out of a crevice under the stairs as I locked up the basement, the air still heady with the scent of Chanel.

Guadelupe on the bus

Coming home from work after a late shift at *Time Out New York* one night, I caught the bus up Madison Avenue. The normally bustling shopping avenue was almost dead at this hour, with no pedestrians, and yet the bus made a stop almost every two blocks.

Being a regular user of the late-night bus, I recognised a number of the passengers. They were the black and Hispanic women who cleaned offices when everyone else was gone. Some of them greeted each other, spoke about what was happening at home with the kids, greeted the driver like an old friend.

I felt a tap on my shoulder, and turned to see Guadelupe, the moustachioed woman who owned the flat under me and Carmen, on the third floor. Guadelupe, who had never lived in the flat since I'd moved in but had left her husband Mister Singh alone there, made occasional visits to the old building.

"Hi, honey!" she'd greet him in a loud voice, maintaining a facade everyone knew about.

Her visits, though, had been growing fewer and fewer, all because of a fraud she was committing against the building.

Over the last few months, I had overseen a rather odd manoeuvre she carried out that at first didn't make sense. Every few weeks she made a request to the sisters Shoshanna and Abbie to add a new name to her lease to become a co-owner with her. A few weeks later, she would ask for the name to be taken off again. Then she wanted another name added. Then the name came off again.

I think they were all her sons, but I couldn't be sure. All I knew was that there seemed to be a lot of people falling in and out of favour with her by the fortnight. Each time Guadelupe asked for a switch, Shoshanna called me up to let me know, and because there was no-one else around to sign it, I did.

When Mister Singh's name finally went on the lease, though, everything fell into place. Guadelupe was writing one extra final scene to a play we all thought was already over. It was generally accepted in the old building that Guadelupe had married Mister Singh to make him legal in America, and had received something in return for that, probably money. But now it seemed like he would be receiving something else too – her flat on the third floor.

By transferring it to him in such a subtle way – at least subtle for the old building, where no-one was paying attention to name changes on a lease – Guadelupe would also not have to pay any tax to the city. Nor would she have to give a small transfer fee to the old building, which, once again, came out the loser.

Whenever the sisters sent me Guadelupe's lease with the new name on it, or removed from it, I saw what was happening but said nothing. With so many other things going badly, I didn't want to make another enemy, and certainly not Guadelupe, who I knew had spent some years in prison. So each time the changed lease arrived in the mail, I just signed it.

In return, I got Guadelupe's friendship.

Sitting down next to me on the bus, she began talking without any provocation about the old building.

"That's a bad family," she said, meaning the Salazars, Big Steve and Lucrezia. "I know them. I dated Big Steve's cousin. I been living in the building with them for a long time. They are fucking trouble."

I had heard that Guadelupe once dated Big Steve's cousin, who had dumped her, and she had never forgiven him. So I wasn't sure whether she was telling the truth or just had a grudge.

The bus stopped for another passenger, and I looked at her get on, a stooped woman old enough to be a grandmother.

I wasn't sure what to make of Guadelupe's accusations, and I wasn't sure why she was telling me about Big Steve. She didn't live in the old building, was phasing herself out of its future by putting Mister Singh on her lease, and couldn't really help me change things there.

"Big Steve sells cocaine," she said suddenly.

Maybe it's because I was tired after a day looking at minuscule print at *Time Out New York*, but the whole scene struck me then as very peculiar. My world now consisted of taking a bus after midnight with cleaning women who were as chatty as larks, while I listened to my neighbour the ex-convict gossip about a mutual acquaintance she hated who was dealing cocaine. And the really peculiar thing was that all of this seemed normal to me.

Two Rottweilers, two trees

The building settled back into its own version of calm. Big Steve gave up his attempts to claim Lady Gomez's flat as his own, and the Rottweilers made their first appearance, but only one at a time, when Big Steve's crippled sister came by to take them out. Because of the way she walked, with her one hand in front of her, she had acquired the nickname Gimpy Hand. She took the large black dogs across the road to the picnic table in the projects one at a time and then, a few minutes later, she returned home.

Sergeant Steinberg was right. Not once did either dog bark.

Some days it felt like nothing in the building had changed – me, the sisters, Noah, Hector – but on other days it was obvious that they had. I had power, but not really.

There were things I could do on my own, without consulting anyone else, so I did them. If I didn't, they went undone. It was that simple. Carmen was disinterested, Paloma was across the East River in Queens, and Liberty was often absent. (In fact, Esperanza had this theory that Liberty had actually moved away for good. Then again, it could have been just another one of the many rumours floating around the building like bacteria.) That left just me and Hector.

The sisters, unable to get hold of Hector, gave up trying. They called me instead and sent me the building paperwork. I signed cheques for insurance, oil and cleaning equipment that, curiously, disappeared without any cleaning having been done. I opened the basement for servicemen who came to read our gauges when Noah wasn't there, which was often.

But for the important things in the old building – firing Noah, firing the sisters, evicting Big Steve – I needed Hector's approval and signature. In the past he had agreed to whatever I suggested without question, but now he wasn't as quick. He made me leave documents with him, and there they stayed, rarely looked at or signed. I suspect he was keeping an eye on me, the way I was keeping an eye on him, waiting for my chance to make some kind of move.

In the meantime, I found other things that I could do. There were free courses available for people in buildings like ours on how to repair your own boiler, how to decrease your oil bill in winter and how to minimise your building's debt. There was also a programme run by the city that offered free trees to put outside your building to make it more attractive. They would even come and plant them in the pavement for you.

It would take several months for the trees to arrive. I ordered us two.

CHAPTER 7
HECTORED

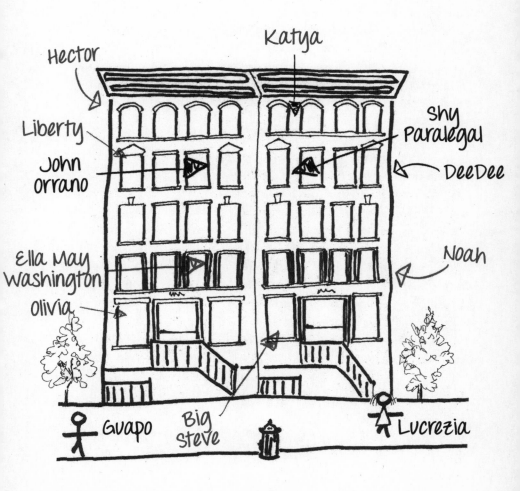

Gunshots

One morning in early March, I woke to hear someone downstairs hitting one of the steam pipes, sending more semaphore messages that would go unheeded. The heat wasn't working, and by mid-morning my flat was still cold and the water freezing.

As usual the sisters weren't answering their phone and Noah wasn't anywhere to be found, so I called the boiler company, who sent someone around. After I'd let him into the basement and he'd replaced one of the long tubes inside the machine – the third one that had broken this winter – he told me our boiler was old and would soon need to be replaced.

That night I went to Hector's place, my climbs to the fifth floor less regular now. Several gunshots went off as he opened the door, and I realised an old gangster movie was playing in the back room.

"The boiler went out today," I said.

"Oh, that's what happened," he said, oblivious and unconcerned. "My place is usually like an oven."

"Noah should have fixed that."

"Noah is useless," Hector said, moving into his back room and sitting down. A car chase in black and white was crossing his large TV screen. "Paddy tried to fire him."

"I know."

"He couldn't do it," Hector said, as if he had already given up the idea.

If Paddy Murphy had failed, Hector was sure he didn't have a hope in hell. Hate the former president though he did, Hector also knew his own limitations, and firing Noah was something he was unprepared, unwilling or unable to do.

I was ready for that. With me I had brought a letter I'd found in Paddy's two invaluable boxes that had been sent to Noah two years previously. It specified all his duties – sweep halls, mop, clean front-door windows, bag garbage, tend boiler – basically all the things he didn't do.

"Have a look," I said, handing Hector the letter.

It was hard to see through his dark lenses if he was actually reading it.

"Besides," I added, "don't you think it's a bad idea to have an owner earning money off of the building he partly owns?"

Hector liked this idea more than the letter, and I could see I was making headway. Then I mentioned how much Noah was earning. No-one had ever put a monetary value on Noah, and Hector was shocked. To keep Noah employed, the old building would need to sell one-and-a-half flats each year. If nothing else bankrupted us, Noah would.

Hector handed back the letter and reached for his drink. I could see his interest quickly flagging.

"What about giving Noah a trial period?" I suggested. "That's fair enough, right? Tell Noah to improve over a certain period, and if he doesn't…"

Another round of gunshots came from the TV behind me. Hector looked at the screen.

"Two months," Hector said. "We'll give Noah two months."

The decoy

By the end of March, old man Rafael was evicted. The court case against him, as Siobhan at the agency had predicted, was relatively quick and simple. The quietest and most inoffensive resident moved out as unobtrusively as he had lived in the tenement. The only sign of his absence was more garbage than usual outside Noah's front door, where he once used to sweep.

Even more noticeable than his departure was how little attention it attracted. Only six weeks earlier, he had been sitting between us in the basement, all eyes trained on him, the focus of all the apparent grievances. Now no-one cared.

It turned out, however, that no-one actually *ever* cared about old man Rafael. The fuss – the petition about lives and flats being "in danger", the urgently called election, the angelic-faced sister sobbing, Gloria with her big hairdo defending "this poor old man"

– hadn't been about any of the problems I had imagined. Old man Rafael had been a distraction, a decoy, taking any possible focus away from someone else I had barely considered, someone who hadn't even attended the meeting: Big Steve.

A chain of events, it seems, had begun with the police raid on the building looking for Dead Eyes. Sergeant Steinberg had told me that Big Steve was a drug dealer, which led to me talking to the sisters about him, which led to them informing him I wanted him out, which led to Big Steve telling his mother, Lucrezia, who, within a few days, had drawn up a petition and taken it around the building. (The petition wasn't Carmen's doing, after all.)

Leaving nothing to chance, several members of Big Steve's family had come to the election. Besides Lucrezia, there was Dead Eyes, who had risked appearing in public for the event, and Gloria with the big hairdo.

Gloria, I learnt soon after the election, was Lucrezia's sister. She was also G Happy Smith, the head of the nonexistent substance-abuse awareness group who had written a letter supporting Big Steve when he tried to purchase Lady Gomez's flat.

Conspicuous by his absence through all of this was Big Steve himself. But that was clearly how he worked, in a manner most unlikely to be noticed. If he sat on our front steps with his friends, he never smoked, never drank, never made a noise. He kept his dogs quiet and unseen. He paid his rent on time, a model tenant. No-one could finger him for doing anything wrong.

The plan was ingenious and had worked perfectly. Big Steve had removed the old board and got a new one elected without setting foot out of his flat. Now, with people he could trust in charge of the building, life as it had been several months earlier could resume.

"Where are you from?"
The otherworldliness of the old building probably exacerbated it, but I sometimes longed for Africa. The problems back home I at least understood. Those around me, not so much.

So I looked for random connections to Africa, although they weren't that easy to find in New York. It might be a gallery exhibit of old *Drum* magazine covers, showing home in black-and-white from forty or fifty years ago, or a trip to a curio store where the masks from Central Africa and the mud cloth from Mali were redolent of a faraway place that was fading in my memory.

I didn't know any South Africans except the friend I had stayed with on first arriving in the city. South Africans in America I'd met were mostly white and they settled in particular areas – St Petersburg, North Carolina, San Diego, Houston – that possibly reminded them of home, where the winters weren't too harsh. Maybe those were the best replicas of home in the northern hemisphere they could find, but without the violence.

In New York South Africans generally slotted into two groups. The first lived in areas like Westchester and Scarsdale that, except for the lack of high walls, brought to mind Sandton and Constantia. The second group, the ones I felt more comfortable with, were Jewish, although they often threw in their lot with New York Jews. Unlike me they were at least trying to fit in.

Australian and New Zealand expats were simpler to find, and were a good substitute. We were part of the colonies. We understood what it meant to be far-flung. We knew what Marmite and rugby were, and we were used to people not totally understanding our accents and often confusing us for one another. British expats weren't as good, because they had London, which was almost the same as New York, they spoke English that was more correct than ours, they had a longer history than us, and they weren't from an outpost thousands of miles away.

For the most part, then, I sought out other Africans, ones who came from countries other than my own. Like a radar, I picked up on arbitrary signs: accents, clothing, behaviour. The statuesque woman dressed in beautifully coloured fabric she also used to wrap her head. The man with skin the shade of ebony who wore plain clothes and thick sandals he could have bought in the marketplace of Lomé or Cotonou. The old woman with a woollen skirt and a pancake beret I'd last seen on a street in Johannesburg in winter.

Out of all the myriad noises you overheard in public, mostly indistinct and arbitrary as you passed people and walked through crowds, there were three syllables – Af-ri-ca – that somehow always jumped out at me as clearly as if they had been broadcast on a megaphone. On hearing the word "Africa", I didn't always stop but I often lingered. If I was close enough, I tried to pick up the context. The speaker had just returned from my continent, or was going there, or had lived there, or had at some point worked for three months in a far-flung village on Lake Victoria helping build toilets.

For those few moments, listening to some total stranger reminisce about Africa, I was taken back.

I also tuned in to people's voices on the subway. Even languages that I didn't know a word of I instinctively knew had to be Bambara or Wolof. I drank them in, the unknown dialects strangely familiar. If they were talking French, I jumped in because I knew that meant they were probably from Senegal or Guinea. In the rare times I caught a taxi, I looked at the name of the driver on his medallion. If it was Ouettare or Diouf or Ousmane, I jumped in again.

"Where do you come from?" I asked.

The men selling chenille scarves for $10 and cheap sunglasses and diaries on Fifth Avenue were usually Senegalese. Late at night they unwrapped a canvas sheet on the pavement to display knock-off Pierre Cardin or Yves Saint Laurent handbags that they could quickly cover up if the police came by. I always had the same opening question, which, uttered in a moment of excitement, always came out sounding quite rude.

"Where do you come from?"

On West 8th Street, I eyed out the vendors selling T-shirts saying I ♥ NEW YORK. One man looked like a good candidate. At first I took him for a local, his face wrapped in fake Oakley sunglasses,

174

aggressive and full of a don't-fuck-with-me mien, but then I heard him on his cellphone. He was talking French.

"Where do you come from?" I asked.

Still aggressive, he answered.

"Ivory Coast," he said.

"I have been to Abidjan," I replied.

It was a card that got you in the door at once, and the metamorphosis was immediate. His face lit up. Hostility gave way to a broad smile. There were two people, the American and the African. In front of me suddenly stood a trader I'd met in Abidjan or Ouagadougou, jaunty and not ready to let you go until he had made a sale. You were both here to bargain.

"I am from South Africa," I said.

Ah.

The acceptance was instant. The usual questions were absent. He didn't ask me why I was white and from Africa. He knew this was possible. Nor did he have to explain to me that there was actually a country called Ivory Coast. Our homelands might have been four thousand kilometres apart, but we shared a continent and an experience that our new country just didn't understand. We had heard all the strange tigers-in-the-street ideas about Africa. We knew that on our continent the discrepancies were huge. We knew that the world outside New York City wasn't politically correct.

Once we had chatted for a while and he had sold me a pair of knock-off sunglasses for three dollars instead of five, I knew I could not keep him from his business any longer. I said goodbye and headed further along West 8th Street. When I looked back, he wasn't there any longer. The first man, the unsmiling one who hid behind his fake Oakleys, had returned.

On one particular street in Harlem, the Senegalese liked to gather at night as the weather got warmer. Women sat out on the pavement on folding chairs in their colourful *pagne*, yakking. You could almost imagine the dry wind coming down 116th Street was the Harmattan.

175

I headed for a restaurant called Kine Afrika, which was on the second floor of a forgettable building; but people who had been there certainly remembered it. The place was packed, the menu short, the clientele African, the air rich with tomato and onion and spices.

A young man served me.

"Where are you from?" I asked.

"Burkina Faso."

"I have been to Ouagadougou."

He was surprised. No-one had been to Ouagadougou.

"Wof!" he said.

"What are you *doing* here?" I asked. "Ouaga is so beautiful. How do you deal with the winter and the summer?"

He looked surprised.

"What are *you* doing here?" he asked back.

We laughed.

"I have also been to Bobo-Dioulasso."

"Wof!"

His smile brightened the poorly lit room. I had taken him home for just an instant, and he had taken me home. It was one step closer to being in Africa, a small ray of recognition shining on each of us. I suddenly wondered whether this was why immigrants stuck together in the city, in any city. Was this why the Hispanic people in my building trusted only one another, why I sought out other Africans? It immersed you in the familiar and took you back to what you knew, when all around was alien.

"I miss the weather," he said. "I miss my family. I hate the cold."

"I do too," I said. "But at least you live in Harlem. It feels a bit more like Africa here."

It was probably politically incorrect to say that, and I wouldn't have said as much to an American, but to him I could. And he knew exactly what I meant. I had assumed that as a black man he didn't stick out as obviously in Harlem as he would on the very white Upper East Side, or as I stuck out as a white man in Harlem.

"Yes, it is true," he said. "But sometimes people here are mean to us Africans too. They say we are foreigners."

Dragon breath

By May Noah's two months of probation were drawing to a close. He didn't try to work any harder, but his defiance escalated as the deadline approached. When he stood leaning against the fence across the street looking back at the tenements, he held his position for so long the message was unambiguous: change in the old building would come over his dead body.

The newly painted hallways in the tenements had already started acquiring scratched messages between the front door and the Old Lady's flat in the back of the first floor – ADRIAN WUZ HERE, random letters of the alphabet, and inexplicable additions like 7$7 – and the floor tiles now had a darkening trail down their middle, from Eva's leaking garbage bags. The steam pipe running up to Carmen's bathroom and mine remained unfixed, and when there was snow outside Noah didn't clear it away. New Yorkers often sued buildings for slipping on a stairway that hadn't been de-iced, and I wondered what Hector would make of a million-dollar lawsuit.

Before Easter I left a message for Hector to remind him that our meeting with Noah was scheduled for the following Saturday. Given his bad memory, lack of concern and constant drinking, the chances were less than even that he would pitch up. But not only was Hector there that Saturday morning, he arrived early and seemed to be quite lucid.

When Noah came down to the basement he was smoking and giving off what could have been snorts of dragon breath. Hunched forward, he stared at me accusingly. He knew that Hector never would have got this far on his own – this was all my doing. At this stage, I didn't care what he thought of me. If being the bad guy was how you got things done, I'd be the bad guy.

Hector spoke Spanish for a sentence or two but then switched to English. For the first and only time, I heard him call Noah by his real name, Santiago. Back came Noah's response in Spanish. I tried to make out what he was saying, but mostly it was the same words. He was angry and pointed his finger at me. Then Hector got angry back. And so it carried on, a barrage of curses in two languages.

"You don't do your job, Santiago," Hector said, consolidating all the arguments I had given him over the past months. "Don't improve... How many times?... Two months you were given... Paddy told you before, many times."

Paddy Murphy's name, as it always did, triggered more fury. Now Noah started to blame Paddy.

A face I had never seen before peered in at the basement door, took a look at us, and then left without saying anything.

Hector was growing more impatient.

"I'm tired of this shit, Santiago," he said. He brought up the letter I'd given him about Noah's duties.

Noah threatened legal action. He would fight and would sue the co-op. This wasn't the end, he promised.

"You are going to sue yourself then," Hector said. "You are an owner, Santiago, and you can't be paid by the building too. See what happens?"

Hector gave a great performance and, if only for a very brief moment, I was actually proud of him.

"It's over!" Hector shouted, and then, once more, "It's over!"

Hector then stood up and without another word walked out, leaving Noah standing there, irate but still threatening to sue the building. Before he left the basement he gave me one last black stare, his eyes full of hate. He and I both knew exactly what had just happened: his kingdom had been lost.

Noah didn't ever go to a lawyer, and before too long he occupied his position on the pavement less and less frequently until you hardly saw him in public at all. With him, too, disappeared his Sancho Panza, the next-door superintendent, Floyd.

A few weeks later, in an incident that seemed entirely unrelated to his demotion, all four tyres on Noah's lavender pickup were viciously slashed during the night, and barely a stone's throw from the tenement. The culprit was never found, but I instinctively suspected Big Steve, Dead Eyes and Lucrezia.

In the strange world of the two tenements, friends and enemies were impossible to discern. As soon as you thought they belonged to the one camp, they'd moved to the other. It seemed to be a game of survival. More and more I saw that sharing a race, a language and some kind of history in the old building didn't mean a whole lot in the end.

I still didn't know where most people fitted in – the beautiful Paloma was a cipher, as was Maria, the mother of Wally – although I think in the end I figured out where Noah stood. He was in neither camp. He was a loner, the man standing across the road watching the old building. He never attended meetings, never exerted any rights as an owner. He did nothing to stop the drug dealing going on under his nose, but he clearly didn't care for Lucrezia or Big Steve either. Sometimes I even got the feeling that he despised them. I had been right to trust Noah when Sergeant Steinberg hadn't, but I would never trust him with the future of the building.

With the loss of his job as superintendent and the tyre-slashing, Noah also lost a certain standing on our street. Whatever control he had was gone, and that obvious spot by the fence he had once occupied was now glaringly vacant and waiting to be filled by someone else.

The replacement

It was, I convinced myself, a turning point.

Finally we had a chance to make the building better, and to hire someone who actually cared enough about his job to take care of the place and keep an eye on what happened there. He would be our new gatekeeper.

So, as the day of Noah's dismissal got closer, I went back to the street in search of his replacement.

If I could find a contractor by walking from door to door, I could find a superintendent. Up and down the avenues and the streets I went, asking doormen and porters standing outside buildings large and small if they were looking for part-time work, or if they knew anyone who was.

"Are you the manager?" they asked me, obviously confused by being offered a job by a stranger on the pavement.

"No, I'm on the board."

"Are you the president?"

"No. Um… but it's a great job. It doesn't take long at all. Maybe a few hours every week. You could do it part-time. Just two small buildings."

"It's *two* buildings, not one?"

"Well, it's really one building. Two small buildings put together."

Sometimes they asked our address or what kind of people lived there. When they heard it was in Harlem, some of them dropped out. If anyone quoted the salary they expected, it was always way too high for us.

"We can't afford that much," I said.

"It is a co-op, isn't it?" they asked.

There it was again, the word *co-op*, meaning rich, Park Avenue, deep pockets.

"It is," I answered, "but it's not a normal kind of co-op."

"What kind of co-op is it then?"

To me the job seemed like easy money, especially for someone new in the country looking to make some extra cash on the side. But I kept meeting fellow immigrants, the doormen and superintendents, to whom easy money needed to be *enough* easy money. It was as if they had lost sight of where they came from and had been tainted by their rich buildings.

Losing hope that I'd ever find someone for the job, I suddenly found him sitting on my doorstep one day. Julio, the man who had renovated our hallways, came by to do an odd job for me and I mentioned the position to him. I didn't think he'd be interested, but he was. And he couldn't have been better qualified. He was a good worker, and he had no connections in the building.

He was perfect.

The Lupus Lady's father
Hector had other ideas, and he didn't think Julio was perfect at all.

"I don't like him," he said.

I was surprised. The last strong opinion Hector had was about putting black marble tiles on his hallway floor when the rest of us went without.

"You liked what he did with the renovation," I pointed out.

Hector never failed to brag about the renovation to people, and always took credit for it.

"Well, you push him too much," he said. "In any case, I have already found a new super."

In the six or seven months I had worked with Hector, he had done not a single thing, had not generated one idea of his own. Even now, as president, documents lay unsigned for weeks, phone calls went unreturned, and he came to meetings on a whim. The sale of Choose Me Debra's flat, agreed to at our very first meeting, hadn't been completed because he somehow couldn't find his way to signing the necessary forms. Every few nights Choose Me Debra and her brother on the second floor – the 140-kilo mechanic had by now been replaced by another brother, a chef at a nearby jail – went up to his flat and banged on his door so loudly that we could hear it in our tenement. But Hector never replied.

How, then, had he managed to get a superintendent in a city where superintendents, especially cheap ones, were almost impossible to find? I had phoned people and walked the streets for two weeks, but Hector had found someone without even leaving his flat.

I should have been overjoyed that he had finally done something, anything, but instead it worried me terribly.

Guapo, the new superintendent, was in his sixties, wore a baseball cap, and had a deep gravelly voice that he didn't use much. He lived in the corner tenement but kept such a low profile that I had seen him maybe twice since I had moved in. He was also the father of Carmen's friend, the lupus lady, who herself no longer screamed for Carmen from the pavement and had at some stage disappeared off our street.

Early one morning two weeks after Guapo started his job – with him already in evidence less than Noah, who at least hung out on the pavement – the early morning air was filled with the sound of a jackhammer. Two men were making a pair of holes in the pavement in front of the building, and on a nearby flatbed truck lay the small trees I had applied to the city for several months earlier. It would be the first bit of greenery on our side of the street.

I was standing outside watching them when Miss Carol came and stood on the front porch of her tenement.

"I see we got a new super," she said.

Miss Carol hadn't been around much since the election. After not being elected for the first time in five boards, she had been so upset that petite Ella May Washington and her sister-in-law Mrs McGreevy had gone over to console her after the results were made known. In the following months, more tragedy struck. Her old dogs had died, one after the other.

"Yes," I replied, "his name is Guapo."

She smiled.

"Yes, honey."

"You know him?" I asked.

"Sure do. Used to sell drugs out of our basement a while back."

Instinctively, I said nothing. People had a tendency to listen through their front windows – usually Maria – and Big Steve's flat was barely ten feet away from us. My head was suddenly working overtime, though, doing the maths, drawing lines between the various dots in the building, making the connections between the intricate networks.

Guapo's daughter, the lupus lady, was friends with Carmen,

who was friends with Liberty, who was friends with Big Steve. Chances were pretty good that Guapo had come to Hector on the recommendation of any of them or their friends. Whatever the case, we now had a drug dealer not only on the first floor but in the basement.

Miss Carol and I watched as the men took the trees off the truck and planted them in the ground.

"That's nice," Miss Carol said.

"It makes the tenements look better, don't you think?"

She shrugged.

"You know, there were trees here before."

"There were?" I asked. It was hard to imagine any greenery in the vast expanse of grey concrete stretching in both directions. "When?"

"Oh, long ago, honey. But they died," she said with resignation. Throwing her cigarette to the ground, she scraped her shoe over it. "And these ones will die too."

No trespassing

Tenements like ours, a century old or more, existed across the length and breadth of New York City. Every neighbourhood had them. They all looked pretty much the same: dark brick sullied by age and neglect, five storeys, occasionally six, fronted by their blackened fire escapes. But thousands of them, especially if they were in more crime-ridden areas, had something extra that we lacked. Outside their front doors were two signs, each of which announced, in English and Spanish, the following:

NO TRESPASSING

THIS BUILDING IS FOR TENANTS AND THEIR GUESTS ONLY

MANHATTAN DISTRICT ATTORNEY'S OFFICE TRESPASS PROGRAM

"That's what you should do," Detective Sam Chlumski told me one day. "You should join Trespass."

Chlumski was the head of the police's drug squad in our area. I met him at the local precinct, where they had a community meeting once a month to talk about problems in the neighbourhood. I had started going to the meetings with the vague hope of learning how other buildings dealt with drug dealing or maybe alert the cops to the fact that Big Steve was up to no good.

Chlumski knew about Sergeant Steinberg and the raid on our old building, although Dead Eyes and Big Steve didn't seem to be high on his list of priorities. The neighbourhood had more important drug dealers than ours. Chlumski also needed more intelligence to go on, and he said it wouldn't be a bad idea if I did something to help him.

"If you join Trespass and you have signs at your front doors," he told me, "the police can make unannounced visits to the building."

Until then I hadn't known what the ubiquitous signs referred to or how they worked. Indeed, I always felt a little bit sorry for the buildings I passed that needed outside help to fix their problems, to keep criminals out, a bit like a barbed wire fence, only to now realise that the old building was part of that sad number.

As soon as I found out what the ugly signs represented, though, I saw our salvation in them. I had visions of a heavily armed drug squad led by Chlumski and Steinberg bursting into our broken front doors to find Big Steve selling cocaine and Guapo running a meth lab in our basement. Both of them would be manacled, locked up, put away forever, and our troubles would be over. Yes, that's how it would happen.

A few weeks after our new trees were planted, I happened to receive a standard form in the mail/post that came from the city. (Like all correspondence addressed to the old building, fines and summonses included, it miraculously found its way to me, as if even the mailman knew that no-one else would be interested.) It was an announcement from the district attorney's office.

"Do you want to know how to deal with drugs in your building?" it asked. "Then come hear what we have to say."

The letter mentioned a date ten days later when a member

of the district attorney's office would be explaining the Trespass programme. Out of habit and not because I thought she would actually turn up, I contacted Olivia. She still had done nothing to her tiny flat and rarely visited the city from her country house, except to come to her important women's club. Still, I never lost a chance to call her and remind her of our existence, hinting that it might be time to make good on all her promises to help me.

"Oh, I will definitely be there," she assured me. "I will come to the city specially that day."

I also phoned Ella May Washington.

Ever since the election, the petite eighty-year-old had regularly been calling me. She sometimes talked about the old building and its history, although soon it became obvious that she just wanted to talk. She was lonely, what with Herbert escaping their flat in the projects daily to come to be on his own in the tenements.

This time, though, I called her and mentioned the district attorney's meeting.

"Up for an outing?" I asked.

"You bet!"

By 6pm that night there was, quite predictably, no sign of Olivia, so the two of us, Ella May and I, set out, walking north on Madison Avenue. With the streetlights often broken, and with fewer cars than south of the Split, the thoroughfare quickly grew darker, more sinister.

Ella May talked about the 1960s, when she had first moved into the old building and the street outside was so violent that she had sometimes hidden under her bed in fear. Esperanza had also been in the building back then, but Ella May said they hadn't talked to each other for years.

"She doesn't like me," she said. "I don't know why. I don't like her either."

Indeed, Ella May didn't care for many people who lived in the tenements now. She hated Liberty, and had no idea who his mother was, despite Liberty's claims that she had saved the old building. Nor did Ella May trust Hector or the sisters. The only person she had ever liked was Paddy Murphy, the old president, and now he was gone.

"He was a saint," she said.

We reached a part of the famous avenue where low-income projects lined the block, as well as several blocks behind and ahead of us. Two police cars sped past, their sirens at full pitch and their flashing red lights bouncing off the dark buildings that towered above us like the walls of a kloof/canyon.

Just to our north, beyond the projects, was a small building made ugly by a glass-brick wall that had been added on either side of the entrance. At a security check, a large man looked sceptically at Ella May and me through a bulletproof window before letting us in. In a back room, at the end of a long corridor, about thirty people had gathered.

"Good evening! *Bienvenidos!*"

A woman with a severe face and a manner to match, her long hair pulled tightly against her head and knotted at the back, stood up front and said everything in English and Spanish.

"My name is Candida Esposito and I am from the District Attorney's office. *Mi llama es Candida Esposito.*" She paused. "Do you have drugs in your building? *Tu tienes droges en tu apartamento?* I am here to help you. *Puedo ayudarte.*"

Her voice was strong but unanimated, like she had given this speech a few hundred times too many.

"There are several ways to deal with drugs in an apartment building. *Hay varias maneras de impeder que las drogas.*"

The options Candida mentioned were to phone the police, to phone the city's emergency number or to join Trespass. She held up the familiar sign you saw all over the city – red block print on a white background – and then let it fall on the table with a thud.

The way Candida put it, the procedure sounded very simple, like we could take a sign home right now, nail it to the wall, and the cops could barge right in and do what they needed to do. It would be like an episode of a TV series, neat and one-hour-long, the good guys winning, the bad guys locked away, credits roll.

"This is perfect for us," I said to Ella May, who nodded enthusiastically. "That will give Big Steve something to think about. The sign will be right outside his front door. Everyone will see it. They won't want to come into the building anymore."

Ella May agreed.

After the meeting, I fetched some pamphlets that Candida was handing out. I told her that our building was ready to join her programme right there and then. Candida, now that she wasn't addressing the room, sounded even less enthusiastic than earlier.

"Of course," she said. "Just remember, a formal application has to be made."

"A formal application?" I asked.

"By whoever owns your building."

"But we own it," I said, pointing to Ella May and myself. "We are shareholders."

"Then your board will have to apply."

"The board?" I asked, horrified. I hadn't factored Hector or the others into the Trespass equation. "Can't I just sign it as vice-president of the board?"

"Oh, no," she said. "It has to be the president of the board. And the board has to formally vote to join."

Ella May rolled her eyes to the ceiling. Carmen and Liberty wouldn't support any programme that allowed the police onto the premises. And Hector, growing more and more wary of me, wouldn't sign any application that I brought him.

I explained to Candida that the very people who might be behind the drug dealers were sitting on the board.

"Can't you just let me sign?" I asked.

I thought she'd be happy that someone new wanted to join her programme, but instead she was taken aback that I could suggest breaking the rules in order to do so. Something about the situation suddenly left me feeling as if I and not Big Steve were the criminal.

Holding out a Trespass application form with a limp wrist, Candida ended the conversation.

"You will have to persuade them to sign."

Roller coaster

When I arrived at Hector's flat clutching the blank Trespass form a few days later, he was already in a bad mood. Choose Me Debra and her brother, the chef at the jail, had been banging on his door for half the night, still trying to get the documents signed to purchase her flat. An old movie with the voice of an actor I didn't recognise was playing in the TV room.

I had barely launched into an explanation of the benefits of the Trespass programme when Hector stopped me.

"What's this got to do with us?" he asked.

It was quite possible that Hector knew nothing about the drug problem. Liquor and isolation made him oblivious of most things. Until now I had said nothing to him about Big Steve and the police raid because I didn't trust him, and I was sure he would just interpret it as me being racist and picking on people in the old building.

But now it was time to tell Hector the truth.

"I think we have a drug problem," I said.

Hector laughed, but it wasn't a laugh you joined in on.

"I have lived here for more than ten years," he said.

Hector's file in the rusty filing cabinet told another story. He had lived there not for ten years but for perhaps seven. Like Liberty, he said things for maximum impact, not because they were true.

"There are no drugs here."

I then told him about Steinberg, Dead Eyes, the late-night traffic into Big Steve's flat.

"That's bullshit!" Hector shouted. "I have known Big Steve since he was a boy."

Maybe that was true. Maybe Hector had known Big Steve and the Salazar clan for decades, but I suspected it was a lie. At the election he hadn't even known Gloria, Big Steve's aunt. He could barely remember his own neighbours.

"The police raided the building," I repeated myself. "They wouldn't have done that without a reason."

Hector said nothing, so I added something I shouldn't have.

"As for Guapo," I said, referring to our new superintendent, "Miss Carol says he once sold drugs in the building."

The roller coaster of emotions that was Hector went into a steep dive. Appointing Guapo was the only decision Hector had made during his tenure, and I had just dared to question it.

"Guapo?!" he shouted. "What do you want with Guapo? I know Guapo. I've known him for a long time. He's doing his job."

Hector took out his comb, but instead of using it on his hair he pointed it at me threateningly.

"What are you trying to do? You want me to get rid of Guapo like you made me get rid of Noah? You trying to take over my job?"

Things between Hector and me had sunk to a new low. What slim chance I'd once had of getting him to agree to any of my suggestions was over. Random police searches of our hallways would happen over his dead body.

Before I left his flat, I held up the Trespass form and, in a last pathetic gesture, offered it to him.

"You listen to me, asshole," he said, pointing his comb at me again. "You watch yourself."

A visit by the sheriff

Even though Hector could stop the police from making unannounced visits inside the old building, there was another member of the law that he couldn't stop. A sheriff of the court, or what they called a marshal here, gained access to the old building not too long afterwards for a very singular reason.

Unbeknownst to any of us on the board – since the sisters, as was their practice with most things, had failed to mention it –

some very good fortune had come our way while everything else kept going badly. A little-noticed court case I had initiated many months ago had come to a close.

Unlike the case against old man Rafael, which had unleashed a storm of protest, the second case hadn't even raised an eyebrow. It concerned a man named John Orrano.

John Orrano's flat in the second tenement was one of those that belonged to the class of debtors, deceitful and deceased. It had been empty for a long time, although exactly how long no-one knew. Nor did anyone know whether Orrano was in fact the owner. At some stage he had simply vanished, as people were wont to do around here, and despite all the networks coursing through the old building and the speed with which bad news travelled, he was one neighbour who had somehow been unconnected, disregarded or overlooked. He could even have been dead.

When Orrano's case finally came to court, no-one turned up to claim his flat: not Orrano himself or any family. This carried on several times until in June, the sheriff of the court arrived at the old building and pasted a big yellow sticker across Orrano's front door. According to the law, the notice had to remain there for several weeks to give the tenant one last chance to come back and claim his place. When he didn't, the sheriff returned, broke the lock, put on a new one, and – hey, presto! – Orrano's flat, like old man Rafael's, now belonged to us. The board, as the guardians of the old building, could do with the two newly acquired flats as we saw fit.

The number of things that went overlooked in the building always astonished me, but in the case of Orrano's flat it was truly exceptional. No-one noticed Orrano's disappearance, how much he owed, the court case, the glaring yellow stickers that stayed on his door for a month, the sheriff coming by not once but twice, the changing of the locks – not even Liberty, who lived right across the hallway and must have seen the bright yellow stickers every day.

Here, then, were two flats that we owned and could do anything with – sell, rent, make money from – in a city where real estate was one of the most highly prized assets. Yet this fact, too, escaped everyone. The sisters must have known, of course, although they had mentioned the outcome of Orrano's case only to me, and then almost as an afterthought. If they had informed anyone else on the board, it hadn't registered.

So the pair of empty flats remained my secret, and I wondered how I could use them to change the old building.

As each of other plans failed – a new superintendant, the Trespass programme – I realised that the two flats would be my last chance to alter the course of the old building. All I needed to do was to find two responsible people to buy them. This time I knew exactly what I was looking for: not Olivia, not someone who blew in from nowhere, eager and full of empty promises. No, this time they would have to be people who I knew and who had proved themselves.

I already had my eye on several residents in the old building. They weren't owners and were renting illegally – or subletting, as they called it here – but everything else about them seemed to indicate that if they were given the chance to buy they would make all the difference. Now was the time to ask them if they wanted to.

An omen

There were four candidates, and two of them lived on my floor. Katya, the schoolteacher across the hallway, was renting from an owner, a woman I'd never seen who lived in Florida. DeeDee lived in the back, renting Paloma's place with her boyfriend. Katya was Polish and DeeDee Dominican, factors I never took into account but which, in the end, turned out to be very important.

Maybe it's because we were together on the top floor, removed from everyone else, but life up here seemed pretty normal for a lot of the time. The three of us got on well, we visited each other, and we kept spare keys for each other should one of us get locked out of our flat.

Both Katya and DeeDee had been in the building more than a year. Like all the other subletters, they had been bit players crossing our dirty stage, totally aware of the storyline but unable to change the script. They knew the old building's problems, had seen glimmers of its potential, and were totally aware of how cheap the flats were.

More than once after leaving their company, I wished that they, instead of Big Steve and Choose Me Debra and Liberty, could be owners. I broached the subject with them several times, as well as with the jazz musician who lived on Two and the shy paralegal on Four.

"If something in the building ever came up," I asked them, "would you be interested in buying?"

Only the jazz musician said no.

When the two flats – old man Rafael's and Orrano's – became ours, I went into action. I made sure to organise everything through Shoshanna and Abbie. The sisters had witnessed how I'd sold the tiny flat to Olivia from under their noses, and they weren't going to let that happen again. The three of us were still circling each other like wrestlers waiting for the other to make the first wrong move, to open up our weak flank.

The jazz musician wasn't interested in buying, so I told the other three candidates, all women, to waste no time. They should contact Shoshanna, make sure to never mention my name, and then casually ask if there were any flats for sale. Even if there weren't, could they fill in an application form?

The sudden flurry of activity was enough to make Shoshanna suspicious. She called me.

"Is the board selling an apartment?" she asked.

"Not that I know of," I told her. "But it's good to be prepared if we do."

Within no time, news had travelled from Shoshanna to Hector. Without any discussion between members of the board – meetings had in any case, ground to a halt – the following information was quickly transmitted: 1) We had two flats that we'd taken possession of, 2) there were people who had applied to buy them, and 3) we were selling them. As with the repossession of Orrano's flat, no-one asked any questions, and the sisters set a date to interview the candidates.

It was that simple; too simple. I should have seen that as an omen.

Hectored

Americans called it a last hurrah, although there didn't feel like anything to cheer about. This was my very last chance, my last gambit. Selling the flats was the only idea I had left, and if it didn't work I'd have to give up.

Firing Noah had failed, the Trespass programme had failed – both thanks to Hector. So good was Hector at screwing up anything, without even realising he had done it, that he deserved his own word. *You really Hectored things up! You've truly gone and made a big old Hector out of it!*

In the beginning his big glasses, moustache and buffoonery had made me want to laugh, but then I started noticing contradictions that were sad and dark.

He didn't like white people, Olivia especially, but he wanted nothing more than to live among them. Several times he confessed a desire to escape the tenements and their filth and move across the Split to the very Waspish, very upper-class Upper East Side.

As for Hispanic people, Hector seemed to dislike them too, although if he had to make a choice between the two it would probably have been the race he disliked less. At work, his job was to help poor people in distress, and yet he couldn't have cared less about the fate of old man Rafael.

Meanwhile, he clung to his presidency without having any idea what he was doing or where he was going, the dictator of a small nation in tatters.

Knowing how unpredictable he was, I had to take every precaution when we sold the two flats. Nothing could be left to chance. All the correct procedures had to be followed to prevent Hector from fucking things up.

No Hectoring this time. For once you can't Hector things!

I phoned Siobhan at the non-profit agency for advice. As soon as I told her of the latest events in the old building, I could hear that the lightness in her voice had returned. Once again, something about our misfortunes amused her.

"What do we need to do to sell an apartment?" I asked.

"Everything must be done according to the book," she said. "There has to be a rational policy when you sell an apartment. Ask candidates how long ago they applied and how long they have lived in your building. Do a credit check on each one of them. Find out how well they paid their rent in the past. Would they be good residents of the building?"

My candidates, as far as I knew, were all strong contenders. They had lived in the tenements for more than a year, and they had submitted their applications before anyone else got a chance. As for their finances, the sisters were busy doing a credit check.

"And if a board member is a relative or friend of the applicant," Siobhan continued, "they can't vote."

DeeDee had told me she was a cousin of Paloma's husband, Freddie. Maybe she was or maybe she was just a "cousin" in the way tenants claim to be in New York to avoid building bylaws, the way I had been my South African friend's "cousin" when I first arrived in the city. Even Polish Katya, bizarrely, claimed to be family of her landlady, who was Puerto Rican.

Whether or not DeeDee was telling the truth, I didn't care. So long as she got the flat.

Siobhan added one last thing.

"And make sure to keep minutes," she said. "Good candidates who are rejected might want to know why. And if they have a good reason, they can take you to court."

Goodbye in Russian

In less than two weeks we were sitting in the basement – the rusty filing cabinet, as usual, standing sentry nearby – waiting for the first candidate to enter. There were only three of us present: me, Hector and Paloma. Carmen was done with the board, and Liberty had given Hector his proxy to vote on his behalf.

Besides my three candidates there was a fourth, Mohammed's son, Yusuf, whom I'd never seen or met, although I knew he stayed over with his father sometimes. A better quartet of candidates I couldn't have wished for. The evening would be a resounding success. It would be impossible for Hector to screw this up.

The only possible problem was the credit checks the sisters had done. DeeDee had come out badly. Way ahead of her were Katya and Yusuf. The shy paralegal on Four came in last.

Hector knew none of the candidates, even though he must have passed Yusuf many times on the stairs. Paloma knew DeeDee, of course, but the other three were total strangers to her. Katya came down first, and upon seeing her name on the application form Hector called out a foreign greeting.

"*Dos vedanya!*"

He was very pleased with himself, but Katya frowned.

"*Do svidaniya* is Russian for goodbye," she said, correcting him. "I am not Russian. I am Polish. And when we say hello, we say *dzien dobry.*"

Hector took out his comb and stroked three times – side, side, top. It was a bad start to the interview, and he didn't like the rebuff. After that he asked no questions, and neither did Paloma, but I thought nothing of it. They never asked questions anyway.

Wanting the candidates to all shine, I asked as much as I could.

"So how do you like the building?" I put it to Katya.

"I like it a lot."

"How would you act if you were a shareholder?"

"I would contribute as much as possible. I would help in any way I could."

I was struck by how eager each candidate sounded, like they were on show and had to put on their best performance for our ugly old building.

"Do you know any people living here?"

"Yes, I know Carmen on the fourth floor and Esperanza..."

Hector played with his moustache and Paloma looked at her shoes.

As soon as the last candidate, Yusuf, had left the room, Hector spoke up.

"I like that one girl," he said.

Three of the four candidates had been women.

"Which one?" I asked.

"The Dominican."

He meant DeeDee.

"Yes," Paloma said. "I agree."

"She would add nicely to the make-up of the building," Hector added.

"How do you mean 'the make-up of the building'?" I asked.

"She's Hispanic," he said.

I should have been happy. One of my candidates was being chosen, and the old building was about to get a new, responsible owner and start improving. But for some reason – maybe because of where I came from and because of what I'd seen in the old building so far – I had this terrible feeling that things were once again about to go badly.

The words "make-up" and "Hispanic" didn't bode well at all. It was illegal in New York to sell a flat to someone based on their race, but I knew that if I said something about this, Hector and Paloma would see it as racist. I was damned as a white South African if I said something, damned as a resident in the old building if I didn't.

So, instead, I tried to focus on the good that would come of this troublesome scenario – DeeDee would be one of us, and so would one of the other three candidates. The fact that they were American, Polish and African somehow suggested to me a balancing of the scales. The next choice would show that the choice of DeeDee wasn't really racist and that Hector and Paloma were open to other races too.

But that, as I had heard Americans say, was not how the evening was about to go down.

"What about the other apartment?" I asked the others. "Who do you like for that one?"

Hector said nothing.

"We aren't selling it," Paloma said suddenly.

"I thought we were selling both apartments," I said.

"Well, you were wrong," Hector shot back at me.

At that moment, everything fell into place. Hector and Paloma had arranged everything before the meeting: they would sell a flat to DeeDee and only to DeeDee. They had hijacked the evening – and our future. I had done all the legwork to get us to this point. I had got the hallways fixed up and had evicted old man Rafael. I had endured the insults that came with doing both. I had made all the mad last-minute dashes to court on Centre Street. I had found all the applicants to buy the flats. But now the second flat was slipping through my fingers, and with it, I was sure, anything good that could happen to the old building.

"What are you going to do with the second apartment?" I asked.

Hector hadn't thought that far.

"We can rent it," he said finally.

"We have nine apartments being rented illegally," I said, one of many things about the old building Hector still didn't know. "We need owners who live here and care about the place, not renters."

"We are not selling it!" Hector shouted at me. "The Russian can rent the place, but we are not selling it to her."

Paloma shifted uncomfortably in her seat. She was one of the nine owners renting illegally. But that wasn't the only problem. Being related to DeeDee also meant Paloma couldn't vote for her.

The meeting, suddenly on edge, then took the inevitable turn for the worse as the conversation devolved into a surreal burst of accusations and counter accusations.

If only one flat is being sold, I said, *it should be to Katya.* Paloma was very angry, her beautiful face disfigured by that scowl. *You only want white people in the building,* she said. *What? You're crazy.* All the unspoken animosity between us that had built up since the election was suddenly let loose. *Olivia. You sold to Olivia.* She was right, I had sold to Olivia. And look at the disaster that had turned into. *And Brunhilda,* she said. Brunhilda was the white woman who had bought Paddy's place. *No, you're wrong,* I said, *Paddy sold his place to her. That had nothing to do with me.* My denial sounded false, the way it always did when race came up. She was right. I was guilty. I was guilty of being white. *Yes,* she said, *you want to make this a white building. You forget about the Hispanic people who have lived here for a long time.* I jumped in quickly. *But DeeDee was my candidate,* I said, *and she is Hispanic.* I could feel myself losing the argument, grabbing at straws. *You shouldn't even have voted. You don't live here and you are DeeDee's family. Your vote shouldn't count...*

With her prominent scowl and nostrils flared, Paloma had morphed into something horrific. Getting up in a single movement, she gripped her bag and headed for the door. Hector put away his comb and followed. They didn't act in unison, and I still wasn't sure what bound them together besides the sale of the flat to DeeDee, but Hector had done it once again. He had screwed up even the impossible. We had been Hectored.

The room was very quiet after they left, and I sat there for a while, me and the rusty filing cabinet, before closing up the basement. After eight months with this new board, I was still the only one who had keys to all the doors. I had access but absolutely no control over this five-storey juggernaut above me.

Before locking up, I closed the notepad in my lap, grateful for at least one thing: I had been taking down minutes of the meeting. Whatever had been said over the past hour was now written down on paper as a record for anyone who might want to use it.

The departure

By the next morning I had made up my mind to quit. The tenements had taken over my life. Every page of my diary was crammed with duties and reminders. The place was consuming me. Paddy had written in his notes the plea "What's happening?!" to which I would now add, "Get out before it's too late. Before you lose your mind."

The $10,000 I had paid for my flat just wasn't worth the misery, the headaches, the accusations, the gossip, the lies, the sleepless nights, the suspicion, the nightmares. My head was forever crammed with thoughts of the old building. At some point after I had bought, I'd been struck by this fantastic notion that I could one day make some profit out of my flat if things ever improved, but now I thought about how little it was to lose. I would become another bystander, watching as the old building fell to pieces.

The same day that I sent in my resignation letter – not sure why I even bothered with the formality – I went to see my Polish neighbour Katya. With me I took the minutes of the last meeting. The minutes, as Siobhan at the agency had told me, were all-powerful, a record of what had taken place at a board meeting, what had been said and by whom, what was voted on, and how the members had voted and why. It was a record that could be used in a court of law.

I told Katya she was welcome to use the minutes any way she wanted. That same day she paid Hector a visit. I'm not sure how the interlude went exactly – he probably greeted her in Russian – but the visit paid off. Within a few days he had agreed to sell her the second flat, although not without making one final fuck-up of a move only Hector was capable of, which would come back to haunt the old building.

I had been pressing him for a long time to push up the prices of the flats we sold – we couldn't afford to keep it at $10,000 – but he had refused. Until now, that is. As a form of punishment, he made Katya pay twice as much as DeeDee.

CHAPTER 8
HOLIDAY/ VACATION

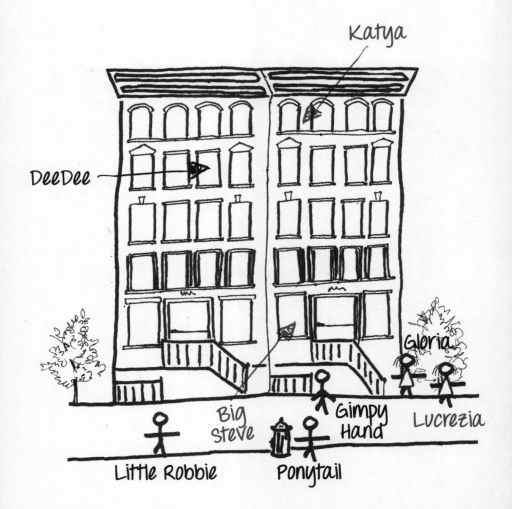

Fishing in the subway

Life grew less bizarre practically the next day. It was, I'd imagine, like being taken off medication after a long time. The world around me quickly came into sharp focus. I started discovering New York again, cycling through Central Park and along the Hudson River, now that it was autumn/fall, the trees ochre/ocher, red and yellow. Africa might have thunderstorms, but New York had spring and autumn.

In the vacant lot next door to the second tenement, I found a kitten and took it home. Then I found another kitten. I also worked more hours copy-editing at various magazines, including *Condé Nast Traveler*. But most importantly, I started writing the book that I had originally come to New York for.

An idea for a book had been bouncing around in my head for some time already, but something was stopping me from writing it – the old building maybe. The idea grew in direct proportion to my visits onto the streets at night to collect things. After I furnished my flat from the pavement, I kept going out after midnight, driven by a mixture of habit, fascination and a desire to find something for free. It was also an escape from the old building.

The treasure hunt for garbage turned into one for collectors, and slowly I started amassing characters to fill my story. A woman collecting bits of computers she put back together again and resold, but not before hacking into the secret lives of people who'd forgotten to erase their hard-drives. A man smitten by buildings that were being demolished and who took home pieces of rubble that were sometimes so big he needed machinery to move them. Another man sifting silt from the sewers to find jewellery lost down stormwater drains and toilets. A homeless person rolling bits of wire onto a contraption on wheels he dragged behind him. A sixty-year-old using a pole onto which he had put chewing gum that he stuck through the street gratings above the subways to try to retrieve coins or rings that had fallen through. A competitor used a fishing rod.

By chance, during this time, I also came across a little-used word New Yorkers had apparently coined in the 1970s to describe things that one person threw away but another found some use for: "mongo". With my obligations at the old building now over, and with no-one else writing about the collectors of mongo, I started putting their story down on paper.

Santo Domingo

At the travel magazine, where I had also started doing some writing, I was asked to go to the Caribbean to do a story.

I had never been to the Caribbean before and it figured in my general knowledge as much as, say, the Seychelles or Mauritius did in an American's. I had heard that South Africans were starting to gravitate to one particular island to crew on yachts. Was it Aruba? Maybe it was one of the Saint places. St John or St Thomas. Was there a St Thomas?

The one country in the Caribbean I knew was Cuba, and that only because it had sent tens of thousands of soldiers to join a war against South Africa in Angola in the 1970s. It had also fought against South Africa in Mozambique. Anyone who had grown up in South Africa at the time was led to believe that Cubans could quite possibly be in league with the devil. And then, when they later sent countless doctors to poor countries across Africa, that was somehow seen as a communist plot to overthrow the continent.

But the island I was sent to was none of the above. It was the Dominican Republic.

As soon as I landed in Santo Domingo, the capital, it felt familiar. The palm-lined corniche, here called a *malecón*, the roads bumpy, the air thick and humid, the architecture a mix of decayed colonial splendour and unfinished cinderblock, the streets and *avenidas* named for revolutionary leaders, and vendors selling sarongs and stacks of paintings that had been in the sun too long of peasants wearing bright colours. There were also the well-meant but often unnecessary warnings not to go out at night because it wasn't safe.

It could have been Maputo or Mombasa.

Even the meagre room I rented in the fishing village of Bayahibe, where I spent a few days just hanging out, had a saggy bed with stained sheets and a hole-filled mosquito net. It could have been the 1-2-3 Hotel in Cape Coast, Ghana, all over again. A rooster outside my window woke me throughout the night and kept crowing on and off until dawn.

I was initially a bit on edge. The only two Dominicans I knew were Liberty and DeeDee, and in that terrible way one has of ascribing the bad qualities of one person to an entire nation, I did just that with the Dominican Republic. Its representative was Liberty. At any moment I expected someone to come up to me and say, Who. The. Fuck. Are. You? What. The. Fuck. Are. You. Doing. In. My. Country? Get. The. Fuck. Out. You're. Not. Welcome.

I couldn't help it, but the old building back in New York was tagging along like an unwanted guest, reminding me of things I wanted to blot out. But after three days of watching village life, eating eggs and beans / *huevos con frijoles* and dorado at a local eatery, the problems in Harlem were lost to the gorgeous sea breeze.

The dwarf

By the time I returned to New York, DeeDee had moved into Orrano's place on Four in the second tenement and Paloma's flat behind mine, where DeeDee had lived, was now vacant.

Katya, meanwhile, hadn't moved. Instead of taking up residence in her new flat, what used to be old man Rafael's place, she stayed put next door to me and continued renting from her Puerto Rican "cousin" in Florida. She used a Polish contractor to renovate the flat she had bought and then promptly rented it out to another Polish woman.

It was illegal, but Katya didn't care. Hector and Paloma had angered her so much – first by rejecting her application to purchase a flat and then, in a final insult only Hector could have engineered, by making her pay double what DeeDee had paid – that it was now her mission to provoke them. She was daring them to challenge her, take her to court, but of course they didn't.

Like a bad meal, Hector's bumbling, half-arsed decisions kept repeating on you. He had turned my peaceable Polish neighbour into a monster. Not only was she the very first owner ever to rent a flat while also owning another, she had also developed an intense hatred for Hector, Paloma and, unfortunately, DeeDee, who, once she had bought her place, saw nothing wrong with Katya being denied one. Hector had not only increased our legal problems, he'd turned two friends into enemies.

Carmen below me, meanwhile, had started getting visits from a dwarf. As I sat at my desk, trying to write about the collectors of New York, I could hear out the front window the dwarf calling Carmen's name from the pavement; her head was flung back so far her nose was to the sky. Usually she approached from the pathway through the projects, swinging her arms in front of her like a speed walker. At her side, more often than not, was her dwarf daughter.

Eva spent less time than normal going to school and more daylight hours on the landing smoking, braiding hair, painting nails. Her boyfriends changed intermittently – they ran the gamut from thin and acned to tall and handsome – and the ashtrays, once they were too full, got dumped onto the tampons several floors down.

As the weather warmed up, Mister Winston, whose faulty alarm in his Chevy still woke everyone at odd hours of the night, set up a deckchair on the pavement, flung open his van doors, and let Earth, Wind & Fire spill onto the street.

Mohammed wasn't around as much because he'd taken a job at a construction site Downtown for a few months. One of the few times I saw him standing next to his car he was inspecting a long gash down the side. He was sure it had been put there by Lucrezia's two boys. For the first time ever, I heard him swear.

"Fucking Salazars."

The picnic table
Whenever I returned to our street late at night after looking for garbage collectors, I noticed two distinct pieces of theatre going on.

Outside the old building a car would be idling, a driver behind the wheel. Someone – young, male, sunglasses – would be entering or, after visiting Big Steve, leaving. Usually he was patting a pocket or holding a small brown paper bag.

Across the street, meanwhile, another car would be idling at the fire hydrant, part of a scenario I had seen countless times from my fifth-floor windows: one car following another, strange men, unattended music pulsating, ebb and flow of conversation, random shouts, sudden inexplicable silences, smell of marijuana or beer, fall of curtain around 3am.

Maybe because I was now focused less on what was happening inside the building, I started noticing what was going on around it. What I took for a random gathering at the fire hydrant was, in fact, as ordered as the traffic in and out of Big Steve's flat. The cars were usually expensive and foreign – Audis, BMWs, Mercedes-Benzes and the occasional Jaguar. They also never came from New York but from somewhere else. The license plates said Delaware, New Jersey, Connecticut, even Florida, a thousand miles away.

On a better-known thoroughfare, the activity might have made sense. But our small street was, in every respect, unmemorable. They might as well have found a needle in a haystack.

Each morning after a particularly bad night, the area directly across from us in the projects always looked like a mini-cyclone had struck. The epicentre was a picnic table, a thoughtless slab of concrete placed on a small pillar of concrete surrounded by four concrete seats. Trash and half-eaten food lay across the ground and the table in diminishing waves, a banquet taken by surprise, its participants having quickly scattered.

The picnic table being right opposite the tenements – centre stage of our private theatre, you could say – every front window looked directly at what was going on there. The participants either didn't know or didn't care about three dozen sets of eyes possibly being trained on them. They conversed, traded, walked back and forth, fought, whistled at any girl who passed by – although mostly only Janice dared to – and urinated on the trees or defecated in the one solitary bush. The picnic table was a combination party place, business zone and public toilet.

The scratched Bushnells

I eventually called Detective Chlumski about the picnic table.

Like Sergeant Steinberg before him, Chlumski from our precinct had suggested that I contact him if I saw anything strange going on around the building. We hadn't spoken for a while and I was sure he had forgotten our old building. But he remembered us.

"I think there is something strange going on outside at night," I said.

I wasn't sure what "strange" meant anymore. What had been strange in the beginning – Carmen, the arbitrary pitch of music from cars that shook the building walls, the garbage in the hallways, the noise-ridden nights, the brutal fights, the blood stains on the pavement – had become commonplace. Even when I heard a rumour that a severed head had been found in a garbage can on our street, I accepted it unthinkingly.

"Is it Big Steve who's making trouble?" Chlumski asked.

"No, it's guys at the picnic table."

The detective admitted that he didn't know as much about the goings-on across the street near the fire hydrant as he did about Big Steve's place.

"Can you see anything now?" he asked. It was dark outside, but still too early for the night-time activity to have started up. "Can you see any drugs?"

"What should I be looking for?" I asked.

"What kind of car can you see out there?"

"It's a BMW, I think. Maybe an Audi."

"Do you have your binoculars?"

"Yes."

After Chlumski's earlier advice to get binoculars, I had actually found a battered pair of antique Bushnells in a box of trinkets tossed out on the pavement.

"Can you see the license plate?" he asked.

There was a scratch across the lens of the Bushnells.

"I can only see it's from Florida, not the number."

The room was in darkness, so no-one from outside could see me. But pointing the Bushnells out the window to watch the street felt as stupid as the conversation with Chlumski.

"It's okay," he said, always reassuring. "You call me whenever you see something."

"I still don't know what I should be looking for," I said.

"You just call. I'll worry about that."

Interlopers

Some nights a new character would stumble onto the picnic table, an interloper. He could arrive stoned or drunk, looking for something, or maybe he had just lost his way. He usually caused a fight, which you could tell, even in your half sleep, from the staccato voices.

A particularly brutal set-to one night was between a man and woman, both drunk. He grabbed her by the hair and pulled her around, she kicked him, and, even when they were in darkness, you could hear the location of their shouts changing. After half an hour it died off.

The next day I phoned a general number for the projects, which, like all the projects in New York, were run by the city, to find out if they had any idea what was going on at their property. I got transferred to someone else. Over the course of several months, I worked through seven different officials, often wondering if each one of them had been promoted or fired or had quit in desperation. Going by their accents and surnames, most of them were also immigrants.

"Call the police," each one said, like a recording.

"But the police are busy doing other things," I said.

Chlumski was already occupied, I imagined, by bigger drug busts. After several more interlopers and several more changes of officials at the projects, I called Chlumski. He said he would send a car to patrol the street occasionally late at night. By the time the patrol car arrived, though, everyone had miraculously left and the picnic table was empty. As soon as the police were gone, they returned.

But sometimes, on that exceptionally rare night, no-one appeared at the picnic table and no interlopers wandered into the projects, Mister Winston's car alarm made not a peep, Janice forsook McDonald's for the night, and all was right with the world. At those moments you could imagine how blissful our street might be.

The trains going along the viaduct whooshed in and out of the tunnel nearby, reminding you that the city was still out there, pulsing but not invading, and the light of a plane coming in to LaGuardia Airport trailed magically across the black sky. A couple walked slowly down the pavement hand in hand. A breeze whispered from the front end of the flat and out the kitchen in the back, and it was so still you could even hear the leaves on the plane trees rustling.

But it never lasted for very long.

Lucrezia's sixth
Several hours after the last car of the night pulled off from the fire hydrant, a matinée version of the night-time theatre commenced. There weren't as many participants, and they used both sides of the street, but they all had one thing in common – they were Big Steve's family, the Salazars.

Lucrezia and Gimpy Hand, all these months, had kept up their daily patrols of the projects, slipping into the well-camouflaged front door, or coming into our building to visit Big Steve or the Old Lady. Lucrezia's two young boys, when they weren't playing in the street, shuttled between the two first-floor flats and, it seemed quite possible, had moved into the old building for good.

Lucrezia's brother, meanwhile, a short, chunky man in his late thirties with a boxer's face and a beard, had started turning up. His position was generally somewhere between our two tenements, where he leaned against the railing, sometimes nudging a pram. It was hard to tell if there was anything inside. Next to Lucrezia and the big-haired Gloria, he was smaller, and his name suited him: Little Robbie.

Gloria began spending Sundays with the Old Lady, something she'd rarely done in the past. When she left late in the afternoon, she always spent at least an hour on the pavement next to her car, talking to people from the corner tenement, her laugh and movements big and insistent. It was as if she and the others were making a point: the street was theirs.

Another of Lucrezia's children also turned up. By my calculation, that made him her sixth, after the two young boys, Big Steve, Gimpy Hand and Dead Eyes. Looking nothing like his siblings, he was about thirty and trim, his light brown hair long and pulled back into a ponytail. Compared to the others, he was actually quite handsome. I didn't think he was a Salazar at all, and suspected he might be an undercover cop whom Chlumski had assigned to our street.

"Nope," the detective told me, "he's not one of ours."

For several weeks Ponytail only came by for an hour or so each time. But his visits grew longer and he stood for extended periods in one particular spot, only changing the way he cocked one knee and then the other. There was a sureness about his movements, occasionally looking right towards the viaduct and then left towards the avenue, all the while saying nothing to anyone.

Not even Gimpy Hand, his own sister, got a word out of him as she walked the Rottweilers straight past him and took a slow circuit around the picnic table. None of the Salazars, in fact, communicated with one another in public. Lucrezia, too, ignored Ponytail. Gloria stood on one side of the street with four or five people gathered around her, while Little Robbie kept his firm grip on the pram in front of the tenements.

As they went about these seemingly mundane activities, anyone watching them would never suspect that they were all from the same family and they were up to something. But they were all members of Big Steve's extended network.

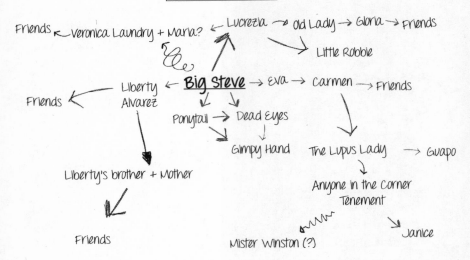

Crimson

Things inside the old building had been going badly for Hector. The boiler broke down right as the coldest month of winter was kicking in, and Guapo the superintendent couldn't be found to open the basement for several days. Then the boiler broke down again. Esperanza took to sweeping her own third-floor hallway.

As a symbol of our mounting problems, the garbage outside had become a beast that grew daily. Guapo had at some stage moved our garbage bins under the front stairs, and Eva, too lazy to walk all the way down, started tossing black bags from the front door. Veronica Laundry did likewise in the second tenement. Almost weekly the pink flash of a sanitation fine could be seen stuck to our front doors.

Above the front doors, at the same time, something very strange happened. Two men in an unmarked truck came by one day and to each lintel they attached a crimson awning bearing words in white print that declared our old building to be PARK MANOR.

Hector had by this stage been president just shy of two years, and this was his first contribution to the building. We now had awnings we didn't need, couldn't afford and which served no purpose other than to give Big Steve and his friends somewhere shady to sit when they gathered on the front stairs. But Hector had finally got his black marble.

The awnings, of course, were meant to make our old building more like the magnificent Italianate edifices on Park Avenue, south of the Split – the real co-ops. But they only served to underscore our differences. Instead of being long and sleek, they were small, squat and bulbous, and the name inscribed on them made no sense. Beneath them, at the same time, more and more garbage cascaded down the stairs daily. Park Manor indeed.

Dirty phone calls

"Why do we have awnings?" Maria asked.

She was sitting in her window next to the front door.

"I don't know," I replied. "But they're a waste of money."

"They are?" she said uncertainly. She seemed to like them.

Esperanza walked out of the building with her Chihuahua Tiny, who barked at a pigeon that took off. White streaks of pigeon shit already streaked the crimson material above our heads.

"Hector, where he?" Esperanza asked me, looking up at the awnings. "Why the sisters they say I owe money?"

Mohammed came out of his tenement, where Herbert Washington was rocking back and forth on his cane.

"Hallway lights are out," Mohammed called out. "Anyone know?"

The questions kept coming my way. Where was Hector? Where was Paloma? Was there anyone in charge? Did Liberty live here anymore? Would we have enough funds for oil this winter? Why was there no hot water? Why was no-one cleaning up? Who was the superintendent? Did we even *have* a superintendent? Why was there so much garbage?

Hector had gone into deeper hibernation than usual, the board seemed to have finally disintegrated, and the sisters were unreachable. Indeed, it seemed like it was each man for himself.

In answer to all their questions, I said the same thing.

"Go read your lease," I said. "It's all in there. Your rights. And you have rights, don't forget that." "If you don't get what you're paying for, you can demand it." "You pay money every month, so you deserve service." "Find the board members. Confront them." "Demand action." "There are ways to fight." "This is how a democracy works."

Before long, needless to say, word reached Hector that I was telling people to rise up against him, to take the law into their own hands. He started leaving dirty messages on my answering machine.

"Hey, asshole!" he shouted. "What's your fucking problem?"

A day later, he called again.

"Hey, asshole, you disrespecting me? You disrespect me, I'm gonna kick your fucking head in. You hear me?"

The third call was much the same.

"Hey, asshole. I'm gonna fucking kill you. You got a problem with that, you call me."

The threats, to be honest, didn't bother me, but I felt bad about antagonising Hector. He was still president, no matter how useless he was, and the animosity needed to end. We needed to talk.

Siobhan at the non-profit agency told me about a mediation board the city had where you could try to settle disputes like this one, so I called and a man explained the procedure that needed to be followed. He would contact Hector and, if Hector said yes, a date would be set for a meeting between us. Hector agreed to a date, but he didn't turn up. Nor did he turn up for two more dates.

"It's voluntary," the mediator informed me. "You can't force him to come. Just keep trying."

I promised I would, even though I honestly couldn't see Hector travelling all the way Downtown for anything but happy hour.

"Do you ever bump into him?" the mediator asked me.

"I haven't lately, but I might. It's a small street with very few buildings on it."

"If you do," he said, "try to have someone else with you who can maybe negotiate. Sometimes these meetings don't go well if the people are on their own."

I didn't see how it was possible to always have someone by my side in case I bumped into Hector, but I said I would try my best.

Sometime after the third unsuccessful attempt to mediate, I saw Hector, my first sighting of him in many months. I was walking down the avenue on the way home when I spied him across the vacant lot that stretched to our tenements, the chain-link fence festooned with plastic bags partly hiding us from each other. With his briefcase in hand, Hector was the only person on the street and was headed in my direction.

Unless I stopped and turned around or crossed the street, we were going to pass each other. Hector had walked past me a dozen times before without recognising me, but I couldn't be sure that would happen again. Maybe it would be best, I thought, if we met and spoke.

At that moment Hector saw me, and he was as quick as a gun. He dropped his briefcase and ran straight at me.

"You faggot!" he screamed. "You fucking faggot! I'm gonna kill you!"

Not being fleet of foot, and possibly not sober, Hector tripped on a piece of broken pavement. He only stumbled, but it took him a few moments to regain his bearings. I used that time to quicken my pace, cross the street, and make my way up the opposite pavement, and then crossed back over to head up to the old building.

From the top of the stairs, standing under one of the new crimson awnings inscribed with the words PARK MANOR, I looked back to see if Hector had followed. The street was empty.

CHAPTER 9
THE COUP

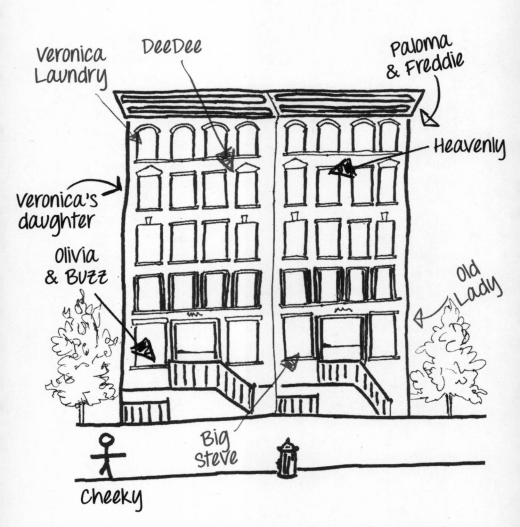

When I caught the subway to Midtown a few weeks later, I felt not unlike a spy on a secret mission. It was crucial that the encounter between me and the person I was meeting not take place at the old building, so it was decided, quickly and surreptitiously, to meet in an atrium at the foot of a skyscraper on Madison Avenue.

People were eating their takeaway lunches at a scattering of tables when I arrived, and in the shadow of a full-size pink plastic palm tree I saw a beautiful young woman dressed in a business suit.

It was Paloma.

She and I hadn't communicated since the evening, more than a year earlier, when we had fought over the sale of the two flats and she had accused me of wanting only white people in the old building. The last time we'd been together in the basement, her face had been torn by scowls and flared nostrils, but now she was smiling warmly, like I was an old friend.

A few nights earlier Paloma had called me unexpectedly, sounding worried.

"Hector is drinking heavily," she said.

"More heavily than usual?" I asked.

It was a bad joke.

"He never answers his phone," she said. "No-one can get hold of him."

"Well, that's Hector for you."

"The others on the board do nothing," she said. "The sisters do nothing. I have to do all the work."

I hadn't seen any evidence of work being done, besides the crimson awnings, but I guess Paloma was doing things in the background. At least she was concerned, which was a start.

She didn't mention our last meeting – the accusations, the insults, the venom, the hate – and that unspoken fact loomed over us like another big pink palm tree in the upscale atrium.

"I'm worried about my apartment and about the building," she carried on. "Hector might do something crazy."

"What do you mean?" I asked.

"He gets so drunk he could burn the building down."

Paloma's flat was directly next to Hector's – in the back – and even though they shared walls in two of their four rooms, they were in different tenements. If Hector burned down anything, it would be his own building first, not ours. But her concern was so real she had decided to finally move back into the old building again to keep an eye on things. She, her son and her husband Freddie would soon be back.

"I will be there next month," she said. "I need to be there to protect my property."

Ominous though it sounded, the possibility of Hector setting fire to the place was only half the problem. The other half was Big Steve, who for some reason was once again trying to claim the first-floor flat as his own. Maybe he too thought Hector might burn the place down, and he wanted to make sure his paperwork was in order before that happened.

Using the same fake documents he had offered before – the four-line letter from Lady Gomez and the letter of reference from G Happy Smith, his aunt Gloria – Big Steve was now adding a little sweetener to the deal: $2,000. Despite having claimed earlier that he'd already paid Lady Gomez for the place, he was apparently offering the board what seemed to be a bribe.

Except there was no board to offer it to. Meetings had long stopped taking place, so Big Steve had resorted to going to each member individually. It was unorthodox and illegal, but no-one cared. He was playing our rule-less version of Monopoly the same way the rest of us were. There were gaps, and he was taking them.

If he could get three members of the board to sign off on the deal, no matter how those signatures had been obtained, the flat would legally be his. So far he had persuaded Liberty and Carmen to sign, but he needed one last person. Unable to get hold of Hector, he had approached Paloma.

"Here," she said.

She reached into her bag and pulled out a fax she had received from, of all people, the sisters Shoshanna and Abbie. A routine credit check on Big Steve – something that should have been done many years ago – had unearthed some unsettling information.

Not only did Big Steve have four banks looking for him, but the words "Federal Bureau of Investigation" were mentioned in two places. He also had used at least five aliases up to that point. Routine credit checks not being that thorough, one could only assume that it had barely scratched the surface of Big Steve's past activities.

The fax made up my mind for me. After a year of watching the old building slide back into chaos, I was ready to jump back into the fray again. The timing also couldn't have been more ideal. The garbage was cascading down the stairs, Guapo the superintendent was absent and Hector holed up in his flat, and the residents were growing restless. Paloma didn't know how to deal with this, but a plan had already started forming in my head.

"There's only one thing to do," I told her. "We have to stage a coup."

Olivia moves in

Several weeks earlier, lots of banging and what sounded like walls collapsing filled the street in front of the second tenement, a chimney of white powder spilling from Olivia's single front window. Almost two years after she had bought her tiny flat, she was doing something with it. What exactly, no-one knew for sure.

She emptied the knee-high lake of garbage inside, gutted the small space, tore out all the walls and ceilings and floors, and filled a skip/dumpster on the street with the debris. All that was left was the original shell, which dated back to 1902.

Suddenly Olivia was there a few days a week. Her flat being on the first floor and facing the street, everyone could see that something was going on.

"She is moving in?" Esperanza asked me one day as we stood on the pavement.

There was a dismissive tone in her voice. She didn't like Olivia. No-one did.

To them Olivia was living, breathing, manicured proof that white people were indeed out to exploit our filthy old building. They weren't sure how, but they knew she was up to something. And they were right. Olivia had bought her place and then left it. Other owners in the building did it too – subletting to illegal tenants, never showing their faces for years at a time – but there was something different about Olivia. They might not have heard her use the word "pigs", but they weren't stupid. They got the message.

"It looks like it," I told Esperanza, but I wasn't convinced.

Olivia came to see me soon afterwards, clasping a pile of home decoration brochures.

"Oh, I love your apartment," she said, the same way she had the first time she'd walked in. "It's adorable."

That time I had believed her, but now I knew better.

"I can't wait to move in," she said breathlessly, her smile broader than I could remember. "This is what I want to do."

She opened the brochures, each of which had dozens of yellow stickers marking different pages. Flipping through them, she pointed out tiles and bathroom fixtures and lighting she wanted to use. They were all very expensive and would have been ideal for a luxury building, not for our broken-down old place. The marble Hector had wanted, Olivia was actually planning to install.

"It's going to be adorable," she said.

Buzz

Olivia's contractor, Buzz, was a big, likable man who worked by himself most of the time. He came from the country town where Olivia had her house. He set up a workbench in the gutted flat and slept on the floor when he came to the city. Soon he had also installed a TV and a makeshift bathroom with an industrial basin.

Buzz, it soon became clear, was also Olivia's boyfriend. Next to Shoshanna and Carmen, it had to be the oddest pairing you could imagine, a fact that became most obvious when they stood next to each other outside. Olivia would be in her Ann Taylor suit and high heels, Buzz in his shorts and torn T-shirt covered in sawdust.

But in all other respects, at least for Olivia, the match was perfect, and you couldn't help thinking – it being Olivia – that she had somehow orchestrated it. She needed a contractor and Buzz, who was going through a divorce, needed a home and a job. She also needed a protector and some kind of connection to our low-income neighbourhood. Buzz was both.

He lingered on the pavement and spent hours talking to Mohammed and Mister Winston, taking up a position our old superintendent Noah had once held. Nothing scared him, and one particular tale of his courage soon became the talk of the street. Sitting in a local eatery one night Buzz had noticed a man come in and point a gun at the cashier. Without a second thought, he picked up a chair and cracked the guy's skull with it. Of Big Steve and the Salazars, needless to say, he had no fear.

Buzz even managed to bring Olivia down from her perch occasionally. When they were in town at the same time, she slept with him on the unfinished floor of her flat. In the mornings, they took their breakfast across the street at the picnic table – in that brief interlude between the night-time cars leaving and Ponytail arriving – which created a bizarre sight: Olivia sipping her coffee in a lake of trash.

Everyone liked Buzz so much – he was a one-man public-relations team for his girlfriend – that the resentment towards Olivia slowly subsided. And that was crucial if the planned coup was to succeed.

How to organise a coup

PREPARE

I don't know why anyone hadn't thought of a coup before. Residents were unhappy; an election was almost a year overdue; a board that had started with five members was technically left with only two, who had long stopped talking to one another. Most of all, the lease made a coup quite simple. Only ten percent of the shareholders needed to demand a special meeting, which added up to a grand total of exactly two people. Without any effort I got ten.

CHOOSE YOUR TEAM

This was the hardest part. Paloma was stuck with me and me with her. We never said it out loud, but we didn't trust each other. The big plastic pink palm tree from our first meeting was in the room with us every time we met, and neither of us mentioned it. Miss Carol, sweet as she was, was deadweight. Mohammed still wasn't interested in any kind of meeting, let alone in standing for a board. Ella May Washington didn't live in the building, which disqualified her. Olivia didn't either – at least not entirely – but at least she seemed one step closer to moving in. I wanted my neighbour, the Pole Katya, but Paloma wanted DeeDee. The four of us probably could have worked, except Katya and DeeDee still hated one another after the botched sale of their flats by Hector. They refused to serve on the same board together, so I had to go with Paloma's choice, DeeDee.

GIVE THEM CHANGE

We needed to break all ties with the past. This election had to be the kind even Mohammed would think about coming to. Everything had to be different: location, mood, proceedings. It had to be removed from the basement, so that Lucrezia and two dozen strangers couldn't wander in off the street looking for some entertainment. There could be no intimidation. There could be no people voting who weren't eligible. Owners needed to know the meeting wouldn't be hijacked by outsiders. So we hired the hall of a nearby Catholic church, and we employed a long-established monitoring group to oversee the evening's event.

ACT QUICKLY

Everything was done as furtively as possible, to avoid giving Big Steve, Liberty, Carmen, Hector, Choose Me Debra and Lucrezia any sign that something was up. The petition was shown selectively to shareholders we could count on. This being a building of networks and rumours, it was only a matter of time before the wrong people found out.

PLAN THE FUTURE

The plan hadn't changed in two years: fire the sisters, fire the superintendent (except now it was Guapo, not Noah), fire the lawyers, join the Trespass programme. Start a new era.

TRY TO FORGET THAT, NO MATTER WHAT, THINGS HAVE A TENDENCY TO GO BADLY

Election No. 1

On the night of the election, quickly called and quickly organised, several people turned up outside the church hall. So did Siobhan from the non-profit agency, a new lawyer I had contacted, and a woman representative from the election-monitoring body.

Change seemed to be in the air – although some things never would. Mohammed still refused to attend and wouldn't even give someone his proxy to vote for him.

As usual, everything started late. At 6.30pm Esperanza came rushing around the corner bearing news. We had, of course, been Hectored once again. Hector had put a handwritten note on the front door of his tenement declaring the election illegal.

"There will be no election tonight," it stated, "due to irregularities."

The only irregularity, of course, was Hector's note. One man had decided for an entire building that it could not meet or vote. It was a coup of his own, but the election monitor said we could do nothing about it. Hector was still president, and he had to be at the election for it to be valid.

When I returned home that night Mohammed was standing next to his car. He cocked his head at me.

"I told you," he said. "It's always the same."

Election No. 2

Another election date was set for two weeks later, and everything had to be done all over again: the venue organised, the election monitor arranged, the lawyer booked – and all of which, thanks to Hector, had to be paid for a second time out of our diminishing funds. Proxies had to be rewritten and enough supporters beseeched a second time to attend so that we would have a quorum.

"Believe me, this time it's going to be different," I said over and over again, words I found it harder to believe each time they left my mouth. "Really."

None of the other three – Olivia, Paloma or DeeDee – knew what to do, even if they had wanted to do it, so I became campaigner, motivator, cheerleader, proxy gatherer, proxy divider. None of the residents knew who DeeDee was, so I had to explain. Eyebrows were raised about Olivia, so I reminded them she was with Buzz.

"I like Buzz," they said, "so I will vote for her."

They had questions about the building.

"Who is on the board now?"

"Why is the hallway so dirty?"

"Is Carmen standing again?"

Several people, DeeDee included, were convinced the election was going to be a failure. She wasn't even sure why we were having one.

"Because this election will be different," I said. "It's all going to be worth fighting for. You will see."

On election night No. 2, I purposely headed to the church

hall later than I normally would have, to see if Hector might write another note cancelling it. When I finally got to the hall I immediately noticed something out of the ordinary. There were new people whom I had never seen before. Unlike the strangers who wandered into our basement off the street, these people nodded at me and some of them even came up and introduced themselves. They were absentee owners – some of the nine people who rented out their flats illegally, never visiting the old building.

"Hello, my name is Martin. I own on the third floor in Paddy's building." He didn't know Paddy Murphy had moved out long ago. "I don't live there now. My cousin lives there."

A woman came up to me.

"Hello, my name is Sara Ramirez. I used to live opposite Carmen. My daughter Heavenly grew up there. I plan to move back to the apartment." She meant the flat the shy paralegal was in. "My cousin lives there."

All of them knew exactly who I was. They had heard that things were happening in the old building, and they had come to see for themselves. I had no idea where any of them fitted into the networks of the tenements. Were they friends with Carmen? Did they like Liberty? What did they think of Hector? Would they vote for them? Would this whole election be in vain?

Inside the church hall, I looked at where the newcomers would choose to sit, with which bloc. But there were no blocs. Ella May Washington and Mrs McGreevy sat together, but Miss Carol was on her own. So was Liberty's brother from Florida, also a newcomer. Choose Me Debra, brandishing a notepad which she clearly intended to use at her first election, took a place next to Katya. Maria sat near one of the new faces, Mrs Ramirez, but far from her friend Veronica Laundry. Carmen wasn't there, but Hector was. Next to Liberty sat a mousy-looking woman I had never seen before, who turned out to be his mother.

Obviously missing: Noah (once again), Mister Singh, Lucrezia, Big Steve, Dead Eyes, all the strangers who had come to our basement at the last election, and the sisters, Shoshanna and Abbie.

The election monitor began by telling people why she was there. Her group was widely respected, having presided over countless school and union elections, and it had a long unblemished record dating back to the time of Teddy Roosevelt.

"Choose me! Choose me!"

Unhappy with the monitor's explanation, Choose Me Debra sprang up and announced that this was all highly undemocratic and she wanted the election postponed until everyone could find out more about... well, she wasn't sure what, but she wanted a postponement. The election monitor tried to talk, but Choose Me Debra interrupted her again.

"Choose me!" she said. "Choose me!"

There was some muttering around the room – Was this correct? Was the election undemocratic? – although only one voice was loud enough to rise above Choose Me Debra's. It was Liberty. He wanted not only a postponement but he wanted the election declared fraudulent. Then he introduced everyone to his mother, reminding us once again what she had done for the building. Ella May Washington rolled her eyes to the ceiling. Words shot over our heads like bullets – "legal", "money", "lawyers", "court", "Hector president", "me", "treasurer", "Paddy Murphy", "stolen money". The word "racist" was there too, but it had by now lost any meaning it ever had in our old building. It was just a word people threw out there to cause dissension while hiding their own agendas.

I saw the election monitor waver, and for a terrifying moment I thought she was going to cave in.

Victory and Coronas

But the coup worked down to the very last detail.

It surprised even me, and I was the one who had orchestrated it. No-one even questioned that there would be a board of not five, but four. And a majority of people voted for DeeDee without knowing her, and for Olivia, who everyone pretty much hated.

In America, this outright win was known as a slam dunk.

With Liberty and Choose Me Debra still shouting that the election was illegal and a swindle, the newly elected board left the church hall together. As we headed to a small Mexican restaurant to celebrate our victory and hold our first meeting, we couldn't hide our excitement, although I knew it wouldn't last. In this Monopoly world of ours, the other side could do anything.

Who "the other side" was I still hadn't figured out, even after three years. But I was convinced there was one – Hector, Liberty, Big Steve, Carmen, Choose Me Debra, and all their friends and hangers-on – and that they were very organised. If we could stage a coup this easily, so could they. That's why we, the new board, needed to move quickly.

At the Mexican restaurant, the four of us ordered Corona beers and then we voted for positions on the board. I hadn't given much thought to who would be president, but I thought the choice was pretty obvious. I was the one who knew the lease, the rusty filing cabinet, Siobhan at the agency, the sisters, the new lawyers, the loopholes, the Trespass programme, the police contacts, the tenants, their names, their relatives, who lived where, who owned what, who was doing what, how to get hold of most of them, how much everything cost, how to find a contractor, and which city agencies could assist us. I had come up with the coup, campaigned for the election, cajoled residents, encouraged them, exhorted them, got their proxies, spread them around. If it wasn't for me, neither Olivia nor DeeDee would be sitting drinking Coronas right now. This was a board I had single-handedly put together. I *was* the old building and it was me.

But Olivia had other ideas. She turned to me, her smile the broadest I'd seen it so far.

"We know you should be president," she said. Paloma winced at the idea that anyone but her should take the post. "But the way things are right now, the tension there is in the building, it would probably be a bad idea if we had a president who is white."

Red lights began to flash, horns blared, sirens went off. There it was again – race – except this time it hadn't been brought up by the Hispanic side but by the white side, Olivia. But I had no doubt that, like all the other times race had come up, it didn't bode well.

"I agree," said DeeDee. "I think Paloma should be president."

Our victory was barely an hour old, the board put together with sticky tape / Scotch Tape and very little hope. I looked around the table and my new partners. Olivia I didn't like. DeeDee, though sweet, was clueless. And Paloma I didn't trust. Nor did I think she knew how to control our old building. But it didn't make sense to jeopardise everything by arguing over who would be president.

Each of us had an equal vote on the board, I told myself, and it was a democracy. Paloma, no matter how bad she turned out to be, could never be as awful as Hector.

So Paloma was voted president, me vice-president, Olivia treasurer and DeeDee secretary.

"What does the secretary do?" DeeDee asked, studying her cellphone.

"You take the minutes."

"Oh, that I can do. That's easy."

She grabbed a serviette/napkin to write on.

Paloma, happy that she was president, said very little from that point on and let me do the talking. I tried not to dwell on the fact that this was what Hector had done.

It was agreed that Paloma and Olivia would go down to the sisters the following day, fire them and collect our paperwork. Paloma would organise a post office box for residents to pay their levy into until we could get a new managing company. Olivia, meanwhile, was given two jobs: find a new manager to replace the sisters and a new superintendent to replace Guapo.

"That I can do," she said, beaming annoyingly.

My job was the defaulters, the deceivers and the deceased. My job was to contact our new lawyer and bring him up to speed on our longstanding legal problems. Together he and I would identify which of at least a dozen offenders should go to court first.

Even though DeeDee wrote none of this down on her serviette, it seemed that we might be able to make this board work. We were on the verge of turning the old building around. I still couldn't believe what we had done. This truly was the start of a new era.

Little did we know, however, that there were two brand-new problems facing us, and both of them were monumental.

The first was Big Steve, who now, besides being a drug dealer, was an owner. One of the reasons Hector had cancelled the first election was so he would have enough time to sign Big Steve's documents and get them authorised.

It was a very dubious sale that any lawyer in his right mind should have questioned. But the lawyer Hector contacted didn't ask a thing, and could possibly have been losing his mind. It was the ever-forgetful Morgenstern, a man who we would never hear from or see again.

The second problem facing us was an even bigger one, and she was seated at our table with a Corona and a carefree toothy smile.

Olivia.

Cheeky

From the following day, things started to unravel quickly.

It took Olivia and Paloma about four hours to get our paperwork from the sisters, who delayed the handover either to make life difficult for us or to remove documents they didn't want us to see. By the time Paloma and Olivia got back to the building, there was an obvious tension between them, but I thought it was because of their tough day.

From the paperwork they brought back, I retrieved our most recent monthly statements, which I needed to give to our new lawyers. For the first time in more than a year I had a chance to see the state of our finances, how much we had in the bank and who owed money. Among the delinquents was a new name – Olivia's. According to the rules of our building, any board member who owed more than two months was disqualified. Olivia, our treasurer, already owed five.

When I called Olivia to find out what was going on and why she hadn't paid, she had already decamped to her country house with Buzz. Keeping guard on the stairs or the pavement outside her flat was Cheeky, a large, doleful man who wore a blue overall and had a shaved head and lips so red they looked artificial.

Cheeky assisted Buzz with the renovation sometimes. When Buzz wasn't around, Cheeky wandered aimlessly along our street and, if he was left alone too long, got anxious that he didn't have a job any more and started drinking. Once, after Olivia fired him for misbehaving, he sat on the front stairs crying. A few days later she relented and gave him back his job.

Like a child, he was truly happiest when they were in town, desolate when they were gone.

Salvatore and Vinnie

After the sisters were fired, we had exactly three weeks to find a replacement. The task was one of two that was given to Olivia, who now was up in the country, where she couldn't do anything. After several calls, I got through to her.

"Oh, the cellphone tower was broken," she said, her latest excuse. "But don't worry, I have a few leads to go on already."

Not entirely convinced, I gave her six or seven names of people I had spoken to two years earlier when, in a moment of madness, I had thought it would be simple to replace the sisters. Most of the agents had sounded good on the phone.

"Perfect," Olivia said, "I will call them."

On the night set aside to interview candidates, however, only one agent turned up. He had been found not by Olivia but by Paloma, whose mother's building he managed way out in Queens. Salvatore wore an expensive suit and a thick gold wrist chain, and he slicked back his hair, as did his assistant, Vinnie.

DeeDee thought Salvatore was handsome and kept making small

talk with him. She was on good form and, only three months after giving birth to her first child, had quickly got back into shape again.

"I like them," she said after a few minutes.

All I could think was glib, oily, shifty-eyed, and inexperienced in running chaotic buildings like ours. But there was no alternative and no time to find one. It was December, businesses were already closing for the holidays – something I'd never thought would happen in New York, the city that never slept – and we needed someone by January.

Olivia noticed the sceptical look on my face and leaned in conspiratorially.

"They'll be fine," she said in a low voice.

Her performances were sometimes so perfect, her excuses so immediate, the lack of remorse so absent, you had to wonder whether maybe she was being sincere. Even when I confronted her about her five-month debt to the building – a few days after finding out – Olivia replied without hesitation and in shock.

"That damn bank!" she said. "It's the bank. They keep doing this to me. I've called them about not putting through my cheques. I will pay immediately."

Now, after failing to come up with a single managing agent for us to interview, she acted as though the omission had nothing to do with her.

Salvatore, flashing a smile now that it was clear the job was his, said his company could take over from the New Year – several weeks away still – so we would be on our own in the meantime. Looking after the affairs of the building with the people around me was a scary notion.

After the two men left, we discussed finding a new superintendent. That was Olivia's second task.

"I have a few people in mind," she said.

Careful to not show too much of her overbite, she coyly brushed the front of her raven-black hair from her forehead. Whenever Olivia said something, Paloma frowned and her nostrils swelled.

"What is Salvatore's partner's name?" DeeDee asked, and then wrote something down in her notepad. She looked at me. "He's cute. I like them."

Drawing doodles

It was my turn to talk about the law.

I explained to the others that there were two very important court cases facing us. Our new lawyers, Rainier & Farber, had agreed that we should tackle no more than two at a time, and we should make sure they were the ones that would deliver the greatest blow.

The first case would be against the Old Lady, Big Steve's grandmother, on the first floor in my tenement.

The second case concerned a flat in the other tenement that was a Gordian knot of debt, deceit and possibly a death. It owed us thousands of dollars already, and no-one had paid rent or a levy for years. The last-known legal resident had been the sister of Veronica Laundry, but she hadn't been seen for years and Veronica's daughter now lived there. The daughter was the one who, I had recently discovered, wore the expensive perfume that was in daily combat with the noxious fumes wafting up the stairwell from Miss Carol's place.

It wasn't clear who owned either flat – the Old Lady's or the one in the second tenement – because the building's paperwork was so patchy. But there were four possibilities: the tenant herself, an absentee landlord no-one could remember, a dead person, or the building itself. And we needed to find out the truth.

DeeDee was worried.

"Can we take an old lady to court? Isn't that illegal?"

DeeDee had forgotten that the Old Lady was Big Steve's grandmother.

"Of course we can," I said. "She doesn't have a lease. There are no papers for her. We have to find out who owns the place."

"Can't we give her a lease?" she asked.

DeeDee went from worry to boredom. The background to the Old Lady's flat had been explained to her countless times already, but she didn't get it or she just didn't care.

"Her grandson is dealing drugs," I reminded her. "There might be drugs in her apartment too. Her apartment, as far as anyone can tell, seems to be owned by a dead man."

"Oh."

DeeDee began drawing doodles in her notepad. Suddenly she realised where the second flat was – on her floor in the second tenement – and that Veronica Laundry's daughter lived there.

"Does that mean we are taking Veronica's daughter to court?" she asked.

"No, we are taking her aunt to court, Veronica's sister. She was the last person to rent the place. But Veronica's daughter will probably be kicked out in the end."

DeeDee was concerned.

"Do we have to do that?" she asked.

"Of course we do. The apartment owes a lot of money. There is no lease. No-one is paying rent."

DeeDee groaned.

"Veronica is baby-sitting for me. She's not going to like that."

She looked at Paloma, waiting for her to step in and help out. Paloma was clearly torn. She didn't know the rules of the building, didn't understand the legal issues, but she was president. She had to make a quick decision. She gave DeeDee a shrug.

"We also need to talk about the Trespass programme," I said.

"What's that?" DeeDee asked.

Once again, I explained about the district attorney's programme, the police being able to enter the building, and the signs that would be placed at the front doors.

"Should I write this down?" DeeDee asked.

Olivia didn't like the fact that the signs, which would be positioned outside but right near her front door, came in only one version: harsh red letters on a cheap white vinyl.

"They're vulgar," she said, apparently forgetting that the warnings were meant to curb criminal activity. "Can't we have our own signs made?"

She suggested gold print on a black background.

"I can organise that," Olivia said. "It won't take me any time at all."

"Yes, that sounds nice," DeeDee added. "Gold and black. That's pretty."

The other rats

At that point Paloma's husband Freddie walked into the basement and stood at the door. Freddie had agreed to assume duty on the cantankerous old boiler until Olivia found a superintendent. It was winter, and with residents ready to rise up if the boiler broke down, we needed to keep a constant eye on it.

Olivia shifted in her chair. She didn't like Freddie – she thought him meddlesome and she believed that he beat his wife – and Freddie didn't like Olivia.

I didn't care for Freddie either – his temper flared as often as his wife's nostrils did – but he and Paloma came as a package. He considered himself as much president of the board as her because his money had bought their flat. He once told me that because he was Dominican he hadn't been allowed to buy the place, but Paloma, a Puerto Rican, had. The person who had made that rule, he said, was Choose Me Debra's mother, the former president Bella, a Puerto Rican. As a result of the slight, Freddie hated Puerto Ricans.

My South African tic, my radar, was of course activated when he told me this. I found his attitude especially odd whenever I remembered that Freddie and Paloma, a Dominican and a Puerto Rican, were married to each other.

"Fucking Puerto Ricans," he'd added for effect when he explained the situation to me the first time, Paloma standing within earshot in the kitchen.

Now, as Freddie peered in at the door of our meeting in the basement, it was clear he had overheard us talking about the Trespass programme.

"Trespass will chase the rats away," he said, speaking in a low conspiratorial voice and pointing up at the low ceiling crisscrossed by its web of pipes. We were seated directly below Big Steve's flat.

DeeDee audibly shut her notepad and stood up.

"I'm going home," she said.

"But we still have a lot to discuss," I said. "We've got a building to fix up."

The other two said nothing. Olivia, who thought DeeDee was sweet, waved at her. Paloma looked at Freddie, seeking some direction from him.

"I told you I can only do forty-five minutes," DeeDee said. "It's already been more than an hour."

The board needed DeeDee more than she needed the board. And she was one of the few people who had actually been prepared to stand in the election.

"What about the minutes?" I asked. "Who will do them?"

Walking out, she thrust her notepad at me.

"You take them."

The battle at 8am

By the following Friday, four days after she was meant to have come up with a new superintendent, Olivia had found no-one. So she appointed the only person she could think of, the person closest at hand, Buzz's assistant, Cheeky.

Noah, Guapo and now Cheeky.

The first chance we'd had in three years to find someone to clean our building, someone of our own choosing, and we were getting a man who openly sobbed on our front steps.

"He's perfect for the job," Olivia said, smiling at me. "He is a hard worker and he knows the building. I can't think of anyone who'd be better."

Olivia didn't have the courage to tell Paloma, so I had to. On my way home that night I stuck my head in at Paloma's front door, which she kept open to let the hot air out when she was cooking. She didn't react to the news because she knew Freddie would. He disliked Cheeky, I thought, because he worked for Olivia, but there was something else.

"I think he's got HIV," Freddie said. "I don't want anyone like that working in this building. What if he cuts himself?"

I was shocked at how unshocked I was by what Freddie had just said. This is what I now came to expect from the old building. Intolerance, anger, hate, prejudice.

At about eight the next morning I heard a terrible sound on my landing, followed by several thuds that made the floor shake. On opening my front door I saw that Freddie had grasped Cheeky by the throat and was choking him. A mop lay on the floor and a bucket had fallen over, its contents pouring down the stairwell. Freddie threw Cheeky clear across the landing, whereupon the poor man hit the wall. He ran down the stairs screaming.

"I don't want that fucking fag up here!" Freddie shouted down after him.

Within five minutes Olivia came bounding up the stairs, out of breath, and started banging on Freddie and Paloma's door. Her hair was dishevelled, and she had no make-up on. She couldn't see me, and I quietly closed my door and went to sit in the far end of my flat, where I could avoid listening to the screaming match that I knew was taking place.

Out on the pavement Cheeky sat with his head on his knees and Buzz stood over him protectively. At one point Buzz looked up and fixed his gaze on two windows on the fifth floor – mine.

Heavenly
Christmas came and went, and an ominous quiet settled upon the old building. The projects across the street came alive again with their festively coloured windows, and a good snowfall left the

windowsills and the picnic table dressed in white.

In January, Salvatore and Vinnie took over running the building and they employed a guy named Billy to be the superintendent. For the first time – after Noah, Guapo and Cheeky – the building had someone who did his job. After three years the hallways got cleaned, Carmen's black bags outside her front door were a thing of the past, and the steam pipes were finally fixed. Billy even wrapped our young trees outside in lights to give our side of the street some good cheer.

Every success, however, seemed to be offset by a new catastrophe. Each one seemed worse than the last, but it was hard to tell because catastrophe had lost all sense of proportion. The latest catastrophe was a twenty-two-year-old named Heavenly.

Heavenly's mother, Mrs Ramirez, who I'd met for the first time at the election, owned the flat where the shy paralegal lived. Mrs Ramirez had promised she would stop renting illegally and move back into her flat as soon as possible. But instead of moving in herself, she moved in Heavenly, who had been living with her outside the city. What had been Mrs Ramirez's nightmare was now ours.

Barely old enough to look after herself, Heavenly already had two children and was pregnant with a third, although there was no man around. She also had two dogs, a pitbull and a mongrel, which she never took out, so the fourth floor, so recently cleared of Carmen's black garbage bags, was filled with Heavenly's children playing and the smell of dog poo and pee. Often Heavenly hung out on the stairs with Eva, whom she'd known growing up in the old building.

Across the fourth-floor air shaft from Heavenly lived DeeDee, who heard the children's screams and got the full brunt of the dogs barking.

"It's your fault," DeeDee accused me one day. "You wanted owners to move back in again. That other girl was quiet." She meant the shy paralegal. "Now she's gone and Heavenly is here.

I can't sleep at night. You did this."

DeeDee was right. Imposing the rules was meant to make things better, the way the renovated hallways were. But instead it brought back Heavenly.

Five million dollars

By February, our new system had hiccuped into its own kind of normality. Residents started paying their levy to Salvatore, and he even paid us an occasional visit, something the sisters had never done. He drove a Lamborghini.

In early March I received a call from someone I'd never heard from before. She was from our insurance company and told me we were being sued. I immediately thought it might be someone who had slid on our frozen stairs and hurt themselves, but Billy kept them pretty free of ice.

No, the insurance agent said. That wasn't it.

The injured party was a five-year-old child who, it seemed, had been severely burnt by a scalding rush of very hot water while he was bathing in one of the flats. Our old boiler, which changed from cold to boiling hot without warning, had finally hurt someone.

The victim was Lucrezia's youngest son, one of the boys who she let play in the street at night, and the incident took place at Big Steve's. Included with the papers the insurance company sent me were several photographs of the boy sitting in a hospital bed with bandages over his one arm. Almost like he was taunting us – although he couldn't have known any better – he was smiling.

The date the boy was burnt, I noticed on the forms, was a day that already stuck out in my head. It was a Saturday, the same Saturday that Freddie had tried to throttle Cheeky, Olivia had stormed into our building and all hell had broken loose in the hallway.

If anyone in the building had been looking for the perfect time to bring down the new board, it was then. We were at a particularly low point, our defences nonexistent. We still had no management agency and no superintendent, and cracks between the four board members were already showing. Everyone in the old building knew that the boiler had a tendency to flare up, but it was on that particular Saturday, of all days, that the boy happened to have his arm under the stream of water on one of the rare moments that the boiler misbehaved.

Coincidence?

Nothing in the old building ever was.

The lawsuit against us was brought not by Big Steve, who was always very careful to keep his name away from the law, but by his brother, the fugitive Dead Eyes. The amount he was claiming: five million dollars.

The gold prospector

I had counted six phases of immigration so far. Trepidation, wonder, recognition, puzzlement, resignation and now loathing.

New York had lost its novelty. No longer the thoughts of E.B. White and F. Scott Fitzgerald and the pinnacles that had filled my head when I first arrived. Maybe the same thing happens in every city you emigrate to. Working at glossy magazines, which weren't as glossy as I'd imagined, and coming home to an old building that was anything but glossy – full of cracks and hopelessness and five-million-dollar lawsuits – made the contrast that much starker. The city I had hoped for versus the city I had got to know.

To stay in love with New York you needed to somehow keep its worst features at bay. Having money helped. With it you could catch taxis and buy theatre tickets and eat at restaurants and afford a flat where you didn't have to worry about anything and remained strangers with your neighbours while doormen created an invisible wall for you and management agencies did the dirty work.

Lacking money, you created an island of your own. The Jews in Williamsburg, the Koreans in Flushing, the Russians in Brighton Beach, the whites on the Upper East Side, the Irish-American construction workers, the Filipino nurses, the Chinese-American children on the buses, the Senegalese on 116th Street, the Colombians, the Haitians, the Dominicans, all of them with their own shops, homes, streets, entire neighbourhoods. There was safety and comfort in numbers, language, history, an old identity.

People out on the street or in the subway did the same. We developed a carapace and took care of ourselves first. We forgot our manners, didn't hold the door for people because they didn't hold it for us, spread our legs wide when seated on public transport to create a leave-me-alone zone, dared anyone to ask us to move over, jumped the queue (or was it a line?) at any opportunity, shut ourselves off from public interaction because good seldom came of it, talked as loudly as possible (to scare off others or to remind ourselves we were alive, I never knew which), screamed, went crazy a bit or, like those collectors I saw muttering to themselves when I went out to comb the streets at night, we went crazy a lot.

I was picking up some of those habits too, not so much a New Yorker as someone stuck in a no-man's land, halfway between immigrant and resident. I was confusing English words with American ones, couldn't remember the exact vocabulary I had used on first arriving here. Was it hood or bonnet? Serviette or napkin? Bill or cheque? Cheque or check? I was pronouncing words the American way to be understood. I chose Fahrenheit first. The voice, tic, kneejerk reaction that had hounded me for so long, noticing the oddities in this new world, was now gone. And I was seeking out the Ivorian on West 8th Street less but becoming more like him, putting on a hard face to the world around me.

"If you hate New York so much," a friend said to me one day, irritated by my complaints about a city that had given me so much, "why don't you leave?"

She was right. If I was to live in New York City I needed to reconcile with the place. It was time to find some roots in America rather than look back to my roots in Africa. It was time to consider a fact that I had long thought immaterial: I actually *had* roots in America. The trouble was, they had been pulled up so long ago, in the nineteenth century, that no-one in our family even talked about them. The roots, such as they were, had been planted in a place called Ohio.

Almost a century before my mother had emigrated from Canada to South Africa to marry my father, her grandfather had sailed across the Atlantic from Ireland to America. His name was Michael Costin Brown, and he was the kind of character who could have crossed the pages of an Allan Quatermain novel. With his signature full beard, sharp features and deep-set piercing blue eyes, he even looked in his later years like H. Rider Haggard.

In 1850, at the time of the potato famine, Mike Brown had left Ireland as a young boy with his mother and sister. Unlike the hundreds of thousands of Irish who stayed in New York and settled in its infamous Five Points slum – many of whom landed up in crowded, disease-ridden tenements – Mike Brown and his family had just enough money to escape. The railroad track being built across America had reached as far west as Cleveland, Ohio, a total of 461 miles – and that's where the three Browns went.

At the age of sixteen, Mike Brown set out on his first adventure. He travelled to New York and from there caught a boat called the *Golden Gate* to Panama and then made his way up to San Francisco, where he stayed for six months before moving north to Portland, Oregon. After working in a hotel, he travelled up to the state of Washington, moving between places with names like Walla Walla and The Dalles, and then trekking upcountry and crossing into British Columbia.

On hearing that gold had been found in the Similkameen Valley, he started prospecting. His fortunes were as erratic as his movements, from the Thompson River to Quesnel, where in the good times he pulled out eight to ten dollars of gold a day. He and two friends had fantastic luck in a creek that they afterwards drew lots to name after themselves. Mike Brown lost out to a man named Bill Dietz – thus it became Williams Creek – and later he would sell his share there for the princely sum of twenty-five hundred dollars.

Again he took to wandering. He bought a pack train in Portland and, with more than three thousand kilograms of provisions, returned to gold country. He opened a store on Williams Creek, and in the great storm of 1862 he lost forty-two horses. Hardship was part of his daily life, and sometimes he was so down on his luck that he went without shoes. But few men prospected and travelled as widely as Mike Brown did.

His knowledge was plain to Sir James Douglas, the former fur trader who became the first governor of British Columbia, when they had a chance encounter out in the wilderness. Upon meeting Brown and talking to him, Douglas changed plans for a major new road that was to be built into the interior, which would become the 480-mile wagon road from Fort Yale to Barkerville in the Cariboo.

On later hearing about gold discoveries at French Creek in the Big Bend country, Mike Brown took himself there, and then went on to Lightning Creek, Germanson Creek and Manson Creek. By 1874 he was in the Cassiar country, in the northwest of British Columbia, where, perhaps exhausted by prospecting, he got involved in a hotel again.

With $9,000 Mike Brown bought some real estate in Victoria on Vancouver Island, where, in 1879, he married my great-grandmother. He was forty years old at that point, the same age I was approaching in New York. He would father eight children and was proprietor for many years of the town's Adelphi Hotel.

In 1897, nearing sixty, Mike Brown went up to Dawson City in the remote Yukon and took over the Melbourne, the only hotel in town. Almost to the day he died, my great-grandfather was a man who kept moving, possibly caught in a no-man's land too – between immigrant, resident, Irishman, Canadian, American – or chased by some ghost, unable to stop wandering.

Island of Tears

Mike Brown and his mother and sister sailed into New York City in 1850. It was four decades before the famous immigration station opened on Ellis Island, and not even its precursor, Castle Garden at the southern tip of Manhattan, had started yet. But Ellis Island symbolised the link to my great-grandfather, so that's where I headed to find my North American roots.

I boarded a ferry with a group of people wearing pale-green rubber strap-on Statue of Liberty crowns that flopped in the breeze as we sailed past the real statue, which stands on Liberty Island. By the sounds of it, the other people had come from all over America – Scandinavians from Minnesota and Slavs from Pennsylvania – to see where their forefathers had entered the country. Maybe there were even Irish people from Ohio. As the ferry got closer to Ellis Island a respectful hush fell over everyone.

Passage on a ship in steerage in the 19th century had cost $25, and the voyage across the Atlantic took three weeks. In the main entrance hall on Ellis Island, piles of suitcases and trunks bore the names Rishka and Schmid, Hughes and Balch. Throughout many of the rooms, recorded voices related the memories of people who had come this way more than a hundred years earlier. Circling the main foyer were the inspection rooms, whether it had been for health or for politics. America was looking for people who could help build it, not live off it or cause trouble. Entry was forbidden to the infirm, paupers, "persons with a loathsome or dangerous contagious disease", epileptics, tuberculars, polygamists and anarchists, many of whom got turned away. That was just one of the reasons this had been known as the Island of Tears.

The confusion of people around me in the main room must have resembled what it had been like before, no-one knowing where to go or whom to ask for help. A display called The Word Tree told you that the Spanish had contributed the word "vamoose", the Dutch "hunky-dory", the Yiddish "schlep". Thousands of pictures showed how people had moved into their Little Italys and Chinatowns, and how they were shown antagonism by earlier settlers and exploited by employers.

Posters of Uncle Sam exhorted immigrants to go to school, learn

English and join the melting pot. Brochures tempted them to catch a train to places further inland like Chisholm, Biwabik and Coleraine, or to sail south to Norfolk or Newport News.

A man excitedly dragged his wife to see a display of the Armenian family Semerdjian. People stared fixedly at the walls covered in faded documents and yellowing birth certificates. Many of them were crying.

Me, I didn't feel anything like them.

Admittedly, Mike Brown hadn't come through Ellis Island and he'd eventually quit America to live in Canada. He had also moved around so much, I'm not sure that he ever considered himself a citizen of one country but someone ever restless.

Then there was the fact that two centuries before Mike Brown left Ireland, Jean Prier du Plessis, my first African ancestor, had moved to the Cape of Good Hope. Maybe my African blood ran deeper, stronger than my Canadian/American blood.

Either way, Ellis Island triggered in me no emotion, no sense of belonging. I had lots in common with the sombre people standing around me – race, language (sort of) and (also sort of) culture – but I had felt more comfortable with a man of a different race, another language and a culture I didn't know anything about who was selling sunglasses on West 8th Street.

A big old fraud was what I'd felt like on entering America more than four years earlier, and now, at this epicentre of immigration showcasing the melting pot and the way everyone had come together to build a great America, the impostor was being exposed more than ever. And the old building in Harlem only made the whole idea of fitting in more unlikely: thirty of us, mostly immigrants, who made up not a melting pot but a group of bickering passengers, our vessel lost at sea.

CHAPTER 10
THINGS GO EVEN WORSE

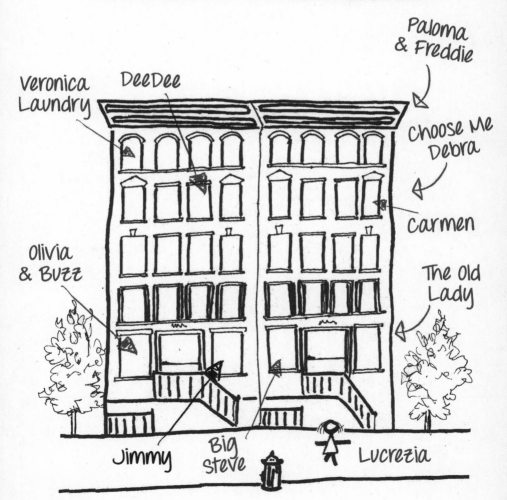

An anchor

As we drifted along – our own little ship of fools going backwards and then sideways, but never forwards – there was an anchor that occasionally held us to the sand.

Of all people, incredibly, he was a lawyer.

Tall and diffident, Morgan had a similar-sounding name to Morgenstern, the forgetful lawyer whose last act had been to help Hector sell the first-floor flat to Big Steve, but otherwise they were poles apart. Morgan also looked more like a young professor than a lawyer. He wore a bow tie and round tortoiseshell glasses, and his hair was cut in a way that let it fall strategically across his forehead. His suit hung well on him, and the near-perfect picture was only slightly marred by the fact that he had always managed to nick himself shaving that morning.

Morgan had begun the two all-important cases for us, The Cases That Were Going To Change Everything, although that statement meant nothing by now. Change so far – the hallways, the sale to Olivia, the replacement of Noah, the sales to DeeDee and Katya, the election – had left us in the same place, bobbing along, going nowhere. Even the newly installed Trespass signs had brought us exactly one visit from a policeman, who didn't even come into the building.

No, change didn't seem to be on the cards for us.

Each day that one of the two all-important cases was scheduled to be heard in court on Centre Street, Morgan insisted I be there. Most of the time I waited in some or other court hallway – for the case to be called, for the defence to arrive, for a change in the number of the court room – while Morgan sat on his phone doing other work.

The hallways were long with dark wooden benches running their length, windows above them giving a view of Downtown, a very different part of Downtown to the one I'd first seen from the offices of *Time Out New York*. It was a starker, less romantic Downtown, one full of blemishes.

Sometimes the bench near me was taken up by an anxious tenant being threatened with eviction. First there was a young woman who swore that her drug-addict boyfriend was the culprit and that he'd stolen the rent money. Then an old artist who had lived in his place for forty years was down on his luck. Finally, a small woman who could barely speak English. The lawyer always cut a deal – he probably knew that the judge would be in the tenant's favour, as I'd been warned was the case – whereupon tears of relief usually followed.

"Why am I here again?" I asked Morgan at one point.

"So you can testify to things that no-one else can," he said. "There is no paperwork for a lot of our evidence, so we need a person who can do it. No-one else knows your building like you."

My knowledge – what I'd read in the rusty filing cabinet, Paddy's two boxes, and the paperwork from the sisters; the information I'd tried to make sense of over the years – would finally be of some value. Under oath, I needed to be able to state things such as, "The woman standing in front of me has never had her name appear on our books." Or: "I have never seen a lease with this person's name on it." Or: "No-one by this name has ever made a direct claim on the dead man's apartment."

It sounded stupid, but Morgan assured me it was crucial.

But no chance to testify came. Nobody from the defence ever appeared: no tenant, no lawyer, no nothing. Our courtroom location got switched again, we waited some more, I watched other dramas from buildings not our own unfold before me, our case got postponed once more, and then, at the end of the day, Morgan and I went our separate ways.

Creeps and slime

Our single most important case was against Big Steve Salazar. Not directly, of course, but he was the person under attack. You would think the fact that the FBI and several banks were on the lookout for Big Steve, not to mention that he'd been known to use at least five aliases, would have made it easier to get rid of him. But none of that seemed to matter. All those allegations sat in a credit check done by a bank, and I had no idea how to turn them into ammunition. I could hardly phone up the FBI and tell them I knew Big Steve's address.

But the drug dealer had one chink in his armour: his grandmother, the Old Lady on the first floor. Get her out of the building and Big Steve would have one-third less the space, one less escape route and a good deal less control over the first floor. And we would be one big step closer to getting rid of him.

The Old Lady was, in fact, not that old. She was maybe sixty, but she looked a lot older. You didn't have two daughters like Lucrezia and Gloria without paying the price. Unlike them, she was quiet and, other than her forays pulling her cart to the supermarket once a week, you hardly ever saw her.

Who owned the Old Lady's flat at the back of the first floor no-one knew. The last owner had been a man named Elis Mateo, but he had been dead for years. The sisters had never bothered to take his name off the monthly roll, so even though the Old Lady was paying for it, Mateo was the ghost haunting it. How the Old Lady got into the building or how long ago, no-one knew. There didn't seem to be any lease or agreement – at least as far as we could tell.

Each time the Old Lady's case was scheduled for a court appearance I felt my stomach pushing into my gullet. I expected at least some of her brood – Gloria, Lucrezia, Ponytail, Little Robbie, if not all of them – to come down the long hallway brandishing a piece of paper that said Mateo had actually sold the flat to them ten years ago, and they were the real owners.

But no-one arrived and no piece of paper was produced. Each time the case was scheduled to be heard Morgan would receive a last-minute call from a lawyer saying that something else had cropped up and we'd have to return to court another day. When a lawyer did arrive in person it was never the same one as the time before.

Once, maybe on the fourth or fifth court date, a man in a dark suit ran down the hallway and breathlessly told Morgan he had been given the case barely an hour earlier and needed time to read up about it. The next time, he was gone and there was a woman in his place.

None of them made much of an impression on Morgan, who, on recognising the name of the lawyer's firm, had a one-word response, usually a word you couldn't imagine him using.

"Creep."

"Sleazeball."

"Slime."

When the Salazars did finally appear, it was two of them, Lucrezia and her brother, Little Robbie, him walking close behind her like a faithful pitbull. Their lawyer, again someone we had never seen before, got there after them. I watched all of this from a safe distance, staying seated on the long hallway bench, always making sure to stay as far away from the Salazars as possible.

Morgan greeted the other lawyer, and not far away from them stood the two Salazars. Clearly agitated about what his lawyer was saying, Little Robbie suddenly lunged at Morgan and grabbed him by his suit jacket. Morgan managed to break free, his neatly combed hair falling into his eyes, his bow tie pulled halfway around his neck. The lawyer restrained Little Robbie and took him to one side, while Morgan composed himself.

Around them in the hallway, no-one had noticed the incident, as if it was all in a day's work at the housing court.

"Dirtbag!" Morgan said as the lawyer walked away with his two new clients.

"Isn't it a good sign that the lawyers keep changing?" I asked. "Doesn't that mean they think the case can't be won?"

Morgan was not what you would call an optimist. Today, after being attacked, he was more doubtful than usual.

"It depends which judge we get," he said. "He could always decide the Old Lady must stay in her place. You can never tell."

Gauntlet

Each day that passed with no outcome in the court case was another day for the Salazars to be unhappy. Lucrezia agitated on the pavement. Gloria doubled her visits to the Old Lady, stayed longer, brought two of her own children, teenage boys, made a bigger commotion when she left. Little Robbie turned up more often. Ponytail put in extra hours at the fence near the picnic table.

Coming home or leaving the old building, which hadn't been a simple manoeuvre for a long time, grew harder than ever. Walking between one or more of the large family, Big Steve maybe on the front stairs with his friends, the residents of the corner tenement on the pavement, with or without Lucrezia in their midst, I could feel the stares and hear the mutters.

Something bad was going to happen, I was sure of it.

"Why don't you move?" a fellow copy editor asked me one day. "Aren't you scared of being killed?"

People said things like that to me a lot during those frightening days, and each time I turned the corner into my street I mentally prepared myself for something to be thrown or shot at me from one of the windows I passed. The way I saw it, the most likely origin would be the corner tenement or a dark unidentified car. Less likely was someone in the projects, but I couldn't be sure.

I told myself that I wasn't alone in this endeavour, that it was all four of us who served on the board. We were in this together.

But who was I kidding? It *was* me. I was the one taking people to court. It was my idea to take them there. I was the one who showed up in the court hallway, with Morgan at my side. Olivia was out at her country house, DeeDee didn't have a clue and Paloma... well, I wasn't sure what she was up to exactly.

No, if there was a bullet out there, it had my name on it.

A conspiracy wrapped up in a lie

Having made it past the gauntlet, I still had Freddie waiting for me. Paloma's husband usually appeared at their open front door when he heard me coming up the stairs. He wasn't a big man and had some flab around his middle, but only a fool would underestimate his power. Ever since I'd seen him strangling Cheeky, a man a lot larger than himself, I was sure Freddie was either a bit crazy or wound tightly enough to snap in a second.

He was also an incubator for conspiracies. On a regular basis he managed to pick up any bad news that happened to be floating around the street. Like lint, fragments of conversations clung to him as he passed parked cars or doors in the hallway. In no time a random snippet had grown into some kind of master plan to overthrow his wife's board, which he saw as his own.

"They are up to something," he told me one day. He was leaning in his doorway.

"Who is?"

His eyes narrowed.

"Them. First floor." His gaze led you to the stairwell. "Fucking Puerto Ricans."

"Who told you?" I asked.

No answer.

"What are they planning?"

"I don't know. But it sounds bad."

"Okay," I said, trying to move away.

"There's a petition," he said, coming closer and talking in a stage whisper.

Several words were loaded for Freddie, and suggested that trouble was imminent. Those words included "petition", "them", "us", "Debra", "Liberty", "lawyers", "court" and "the sisters" (whose names still came up, as if the jinxed old building was some highly desirable object and they were on the sidelines waiting to pounce and take it over again).

"Who has a petition?" I asked.

He shrugged.

"I heard them talking. They are mad that the Old Lady is in court."

He meant the Salazars.

"I know they are," I said. "I see them. I have to go to court once or twice a week."

"The Old Lady has a lease."

In several months no document had been produced in court, so I wondered how Freddie was privy to this piece of vital information that no-one else had.

"Where did you hear that?" I asked.

"They are going to show it in court."

"Who said so?"

"I heard Little Robbie talking."

No matter how daft Freddie's conspiracy theories were, I always left him feeling shattered, only to find more bad news waiting for me in my flat.

It was usually a phone message from Salvatore, the managing agent. He wanted to replace our lawyer, Morgan. The case against the Old Lady had been going on for far too long. We were being charged way too much. Salvatore had his own lawyer, who, he said, was very good and would charge us less and who would have had the Old Lady kicked out a long time ago.

Behind his scheme, I knew, was Paloma. She denied knowing anything about it, but there was no other explanation. There were only two of us on the board doing anything now; if it wasn't me feeding Salvatore information, it had to be her.

And Paloma, as it happened, suddenly had lots of time on her hands to meddle. Shortly after Christmas she had lost her job, her third since moving back into the old building. She always made it sound like she had opted to leave – she didn't like the people in the office or something like that – but it was clear she'd been fired.

With nothing else to focus on, no workplace to go to every day, Paloma thought about the old building. She read the lease over and over, which was good, but she also did things simply for the sake of doing them. She undid work that had already been done, tried to fix things that didn't need fixing, and thought up ways for us to spend money on goods and services we didn't need. We would suddenly have a new oil company or we would be buying Christmas gifts for the people in Salvatore's office or she'd invested in a computer, printer and fax that no-one used and were left unplugged next to the rusty filing cabinet in the basement.

Each time I brought up these subjects, she pled ignorance. It must be Salvatore who did it, she told me. I didn't care too much, so long as she left the legal matters to me. They were vital. If nothing else could save us, the law could.

But then began an inexplicable campaign to replace Morgan with Salvatore's lawyer, undoing months of work that would require us to start the court cases all over again. It was the pointless, shoot-yourself-in-the-foot kind of thing Hector would've done.

"Hey!" Freddie greeted me a few days later, standing in his doorway eating a piece of cheese. "What's going on with the lawyer?" He never used Morgan's name, but just called him "the lawyer". "I hear he's losing the Old Lady's case."

Trying to ignore him, I stuck my head in their kitchen. Paloma, frying some chicken, smiled at me.

"I got another call from Salvatore," I said. "Why does he keep trying to get his own lawyer to do the job?"

She shook her head and remained so straight-faced that I wasn't quite sure if I was imagining things. Maybe Paloma was telling the truth. Maybe it *was* Salvatore.

"We can't change lawyers now," I told her. "The case is going to take time."

"I agree," she said.

"Morgan's doing a good job," I told her.

"I agree. He's doing a good job."

She turned back to the stove, and Freddie came into the kitchen.

"Here," he said, holding out a piece of cheese, "have some."

"No, thanks."

"Have some!" he said again. It was an order. "What's wrong with you? You don't like cheese?" He cut a slice with a sharp knife and shoved both at me. "Here!"

I quickly took his offering and left.

DeeDee does lunch

Communications between Olivia and Paloma ceased the day Freddie tried to throttle Cheeky in the hallway. Previously Olivia had disliked Freddie, but now she hated him and, by extension, his wife. Nor did she any longer make excuses for owing the building money. The assault on her worker, in Olivia's eyes, was a declaration of war. She could openly break the rules, and she didn't care what happened. By this stage she was nine months in the red.

Her renovation dragged on, and Buzz seemed to get nowhere despite banging walls and making lots of chalk-like dust. He also began leaving stuff in the basement under the second tenement, even though he wasn't meant to, storing tools and machinery and wood there, and sometimes even cutting into the building's pipes without telling anyone.

When Freddie found out, he had the lock on the basement changed, whereupon Buzz broke it open. Every time Freddie had a new lock put on, Buzz broke it. Neither side said a word, and our locksmith bill skyrocketed.

Maybe in order to break locks and cut into pipes without being noticed, Buzz started working under the cover of darkness. Since Olivia's flat was located next to the front door – in the same position as Big Steve's, but in the second tenement – we now had surreptitious late-night activity going on through the entrances of both tenements: drugs one side, a delinquent and her boyfriend the other.

The rare occasions that Olivia showed her face during daylight were to lunch with our board secretary, DeeDee. Olivia was infatuated with DeeDee and her boyfriend. They were young and "gorgeous" – in fact, they *were* gorgeous, with movie-star good looks, good taste and great dress sense, things that meant a lot to Olivia – and their flat was, of course, "adorable".

Walking down our street together, the two women were a sight to behold – one alabaster-skinned, the other a Latin beauty – and both were dressed better than anyone in the neighbourhood. They belonged not in a chaotic corner of Harlem with the blowsy Lucrezia and Gimpy Hand but on the refined Upper East Side, and that's where they headed, across the Split, to have lunch.

The alliance didn't sit at all well with workless, home-bound Paloma. Freddie, who was supposed to be DeeDee's cousin, saw conspiracy writ large – Olivia was trying to drive a wedge between DeeDee and Paloma – and for once I think Freddie was right. Then I got dragged into it too, since, in Freddie's eyes, all white people stuck together. It meant only one thing: Olivia, DeeDee and I were ganging up on his wife.

Paloma, as a result, focused more on her obsession – the old building – and spent more time on the phone with Salvatore, did more things on her own without saying anything to me about them, and redoubled her efforts to fire our lawyer, Morgan. I was sure I would wake up one day to find him replaced by someone in a slick suit with gelled hair and an Italian name.

A break in the case

The trips to the court on Centre Street dragged on. I sat alongside Morgan hoping the judge would call our names, but he never did. When a break in the case did finally come, it was, of course, more bad news.

"The Salazars have come up with something," Morgan announced one day.

The some*thing* was, in fact, some*one* – the original owner Elis Mateo's grandson. We had been waiting for the Salazars to dig up a will or a lease, but a friend or a relative who owned the place could be just as bad.

"Let's see what he wants," Morgan said.

Whoever the grandson was I immediately expected the worst. If the Salazars had managed to track him down, that made him as bad as them: a drug dealer, a criminal, maybe even a killer.

"But even if he does claim the apartment," I said to Morgan, trying to be optimistic when everything was telling me to just give up, "it's not the Old Lady who will be living there."

Morgan was not hopeful.

"If the grandson doesn't want to live there," he said, "he could sell the place to the Salazars."

"But they have to get through us – the board – if they want to buy it," I pointed out. "That will never happen."

Morgan knew that the board was in tatters – Paloma scheming to get him fired, Olivia rebelling and DeeDee still unsure why the Old Lady was in court at all – and it was quite possible we wouldn't be the board in a month's time.

"A new board could sell it to the Salazars," Morgan said.

"So you think the grandson will definitely get the apartment?" I asked nervously.

Morgan furrowed his brow. But, then again, he always did.

The soldier

Just in time for the next court date, the grandson came to town. He was from North Carolina, where he served in the army. The first time I saw him – at first I didn't realise it was him, so little did he look like the murderous thug I had been expecting – he was standing outside the building with Lucrezia, who was doing her cigarette-pointing, wiry-hair-bouncing, them-versus-us routine. I could almost hear her.

"Fucking white guy... My family... Mother... Old people... Fucking disgrace..."

The grandson betrayed no emotion, and for some reason that encouraged me.

When I got to Centre Street for the next scheduled hearing – I had lost count of the times I'd been summoned to these hallways – the grandson was there instead of the Salazars. Once again, however, everything took place outside the courtroom, with Morgan and the grandson's lawyer in deep discussion for ten minutes.

As was my custom, I watched Morgan's face for any sign of a smile, a frown, or apprehension, an indication of which way the case was going, but there was nothing. When he finished I went over to him.

"Any luck?" I asked.

"The grandson definitely wants the apartment," he said. "Get ready to fight."

The subject is not drugs

In spite of the grandson's arrival, the tension on our street, which should have eased up, got worse. DeeDee was too scared to walk outside, but not because of Big Steve and the Salazars. It seemed her upstairs neighbour Veronica Laundry had made some serious threats, although they weren't against DeeDee but against me.

"Veronica told me she knows people in The Bloods" – the name sounded like a gang from a movie rather than from our neighbourhood – "and she can get them to kill you."

Our second court case, the one against Veronica Laundry's daughter, had commenced, and Veronica Laundry saw herself as the indirect victim.

"She's ready to call them," DeeDee said. "The Bloods."

More convinced than ever that a bullet might be coming my way, each time I made it through the gauntlet of Salazars and Veronica Laundry and their friends on the pavement, it was only to once again find Freddie blocking his doorway as he ate something.

"The grandson is going to sell to them," he said, eyeing the stairwell.

"How do you know?" I asked. "He has said nothing to us."

"I heard the other one talking."

He meant Ponytail, Lucrezia's handsome son.

Not once had I seen Ponytail talk to anyone, but this didn't bother Freddie. Even though I wanted to get away from him, I needed to talk to Paloma, who was in the kitchen.

"It's getting too tense around here," I said.

"I agree," she said.

I never knew whether or not she did, but I carried on anyway.

"We have to do something to break this cycle," I said.

Instead of battling each other with silence, I suggested, we should talk to Big Steve. He was an owner now, and there was nothing we could do about it. Maybe talking would help.

"Yes, I agree," Paloma replied once more.

What we would talk to him about was the next question. Most subjects were off limits, and their mere mention would end the meeting before it began. We had to avoid drugs and drug dealing, which we had no proof of anyway. We couldn't say anything about the foot traffic into his flat late at night or the police raid led by Sergeant Steinberg. We couldn't mention the five-million-dollar lawsuit. We instead had to focus on the one thing we had in common: the old building.

As dirty a record as Big Steve might have had outside our walls, inside it was as clean as a whistle. He always paid his levy on time – the "model tenant", as the sisters had called him – and he was careful to keep quiet. If we played up that fact, that we were all shareholders and in this together, we could use the old building as our common goal. It wasn't much for us to go on, but it was a start.

"I agree," replied Paloma. "Let's do that."

Freddie said he would act as the go-between, since he sometimes saw Big Steve on the street when they parked their cars. Surprisingly, Big Steve said yes. He promised to attend the meeting, which was arranged for the following week in Paloma's flat.

The ambush

When Big Steve walked through the front door one night a week later, he looked guarded, as if he expected somebody to jump out from somewhere and attack him. The air was heavy with anger, distrust, hate – his for us, mine for Freddie and Paloma, theirs for me – while DeeDee just looked confused. She still had no idea what was going on in the old building, like a character who had wandered into the wrong movie.

For a few minutes we sat in silence. I thought Paloma, as president, would start the meeting, but she didn't. Right then there was a knock at the front door. Freddie opened up, and there stood Olivia and Buzz.

DeeDee, on one of her lunch dates with Olivia, had obviously mentioned that we were meeting with Big Steve. Olivia hadn't been to any meetings since the incident with Cheeky, and was also now almost ten months in debt. She had no idea what we were trying to achieve – a ceasefire with Big Steve – or what we planned to say.

Her face was full of accusation and revulsion. She hated being in Freddie and Paloma's flat, but she was there for a reason. Still gravely insulted by Freddie's assault on her worker and by him locking Buzz out of the basement, she needed an outlet for her anger, and the meeting was as good a venue as any.

Buzz hovered over her like a bodyguard, Freddie over his wife.

Paloma seemed to be doubly intimidated, by Big Steve and Olivia, but before she could say anything Olivia did.

"You have brought drugs into this building," she said to Big Steve like a scolding schoolteacher. "Who do you think you are anyway?"

The two of them sat on opposite sides of the cramped room. It struck me then how little I knew about this large, ruddy-cheeked man. He didn't seem to drink or smoke; he lived quite peaceably in his flat; and he always made sure to pay his levy on time. Olivia, meanwhile, broke any building regulation she wanted, didn't live in her flat, and owed us thousands of dollars. Who, I kept wondering, was actually worse?

"You can't just come in here and break the law," Olivia carried on, leaning forward threateningly. "Shareholders are meant to follow rules. That's what your lease is for. No drugs! We could take you to court. You can lose your apartment because of that."

Whatever slim hope we had of declaring a ceasefire with Big Steve was dashed. Paloma should have stepped in, as president, but she didn't know how. I couldn't say anything for fear of triggering Freddie, who kept a close watch on anyone who might be threatening his wife's authority. DeeDee, in her corner, just looked scared.

Big Steve, meanwhile, had been ambushed. He had been struck at his most vulnerable point: his property, his flat on the first floor. The last time I had tried to do that, he had called in his family and he had quite easily got the board replaced.

"I knew that's why you wanted me up here," he said, standing up. He looked very intimidating all of a sudden. "It's always the same with you people. It's you against us."

Big Steve thought we were acting as one, when it couldn't have been further from the truth. All of us hated Olivia, while Paloma, DeeDee and myself were growing more estranged by the day.

There might be a "them" but there was no "us".

Big Steve walked out, and after a few moments, with not a word being spoken, so did Olivia and Buzz. The rest of us just sat there, listening to their footsteps echoing down the five flights of stairs. We should have heard a door slam shut far below us, but there was nothing.

Choose Me Debra takes charge

Within a few days a piece of white paper went up near the front door.

Pieces of white paper went up near the front door quite often these days – democracy or revolution were in the air, I never knew which one – and it meant that more trouble was brewing.

No-one ever signed the bits of paper, which were all handwritten, brief and often misspelt. They said the board was illegal, the shareholders demanded a meeting, the shareholders would definitely be meeting this Saturday, and so forth – although nothing ever came of any of the threats.

That's because before anyone had time to read the bits of paper, Freddie tore them down. Then our notices got torn down too, even though they dealt with building matters, such as when boiler repairs would be taking place and when the exterminator would be coming to visit flats to spray for ants and cockroaches. It was a childish game of tit-for-tat.

But the latest bit of white paper after the meeting with Big Steve was different. It was typed and well thought out. The signature on the bottom belonged to Choose Me Debra from the fourth floor. It demanded a meeting to discuss building finances and for each shareholder to be given a financial statement for the year.

If only for a moment, I was duly impressed. No-one had ever asked for a financial statement before, which was their right. Choose Me Debra had also gone through all the correct channels to call the meeting, and had even organised an independent: not in the basement but at Siobhan's non-profit agency farther up in Harlem.

This was progress, I guess, democracy on the move. But now that it had come, it didn't make me particularly happy.

That's because the indirect target of the meeting was our treasurer – a role she had in fact never even assumed – Olivia. Her ten-month debt was now common knowledge. Someone on the board had blabbed about it, probably Freddie, who would say anything to get Olivia in trouble, even if it sabotaged his wife's presidency. He reminded me of a child who kept playing with matches even though he got burnt every time.

The problem for us was that once Olivia was publicly exposed at the meeting, she would have to be fired, and the entire board would sink with her. There would have to be another election.

Choose Me Debra's notice didn't mention Olivia by name, but any discussion of the building's finances would have to include the treasurer (Olivia) and any residents in debt (Olivia).

In a sign of how low our spirits had sunk, Paloma, DeeDee and I made our separate ways to the meeting at the non-profit agency office in Harlem and sat far apart from one another. No-one knew whether Olivia would attend.

Choose Me Debra, as the organiser, took a seat up front at a table alongside an agency representative. She looked very official, as if she was born to be at a table in front of shareholders. To one side of them sat our manager Salvatore and his assistant Vinnie, who both looked worried, like they'd done something they shouldn't have.

The people in the room were a cross-section of the good and the bad: Liberty, Miss Carol, Heavenly, Veronica Laundry and Esperanza, but not Ella May Washington, Mrs McGreevy, Carmen or Hector. They seemed more like curious bystanders than concerned owners, waiting for the disaster they knew was going to happen, the downfall of the despised white woman with the big teeth on the first floor. Almost unnoticeable on the far side of the room, Olivia sat in a corner.

"Choose me! Choose me!"

After a short speech, Choose Me Debra demanded that Salvatore immediately hand out copies of the monthly roll, which showed whether each owner was up to date on their payments. Salvatore said this information was only for the board and not for public consumption. Liberty, who also owed money, looked relieved. So did Heavenly, Veronica Laundry and Maria. Choose Me Debra, getting no support on this point, demanded the financial statement, which the accountant handed out.

"We want to know if any money has gone missing," Choose Me Debra said. I'm not sure why she thought there might be money missing, but it sounded like she knew that there was.

Upon hearing the words "money" and "missing", Liberty saw a red flag. He started shouting about Paddy Murphy, fraud, his mother, how she had helped save the building, the length of time he had lived there, and the fact that he was the real treasurer and had been robbed of his post by an illegal election.

Heavenly stood up and began shouting about being unfairly targeted for her children and dogs wandering around the hallway. Veronica Laundry wanted to know why her daughter was in court, and she also wanted the leak in her toilet fixed.

Not even Choose Me Debra could get them to shut up, and I think for the first time she got a taste of what was in store for her as a future ruler of the old building.

"Choose me! Choose me!" she kept calling out in vain.

Olivia had, for the moment, escaped.

As everyone shouted over everyone else, I kept thinking about Mohammed's prediction long ago that our old building would always be the same. A culture of bedlam, distrust and outside interference had been introduced so many years before that there seemed no way of changing it.

Little did I realise, however, that change was upon us.

The vanishing

Our lawyer Morgan had, a few weeks earlier, come up with what sounded like a crazy idea. But we had tried everything else, so it seemed worth a shot. Instead of waiting for the court to decide if Elis Mateo's grandson had a right to the Old Lady's flat, why didn't we just accept that it was his and at the same time offer to buy it from him.

"You never know," Morgan said. "He might just need the money."

"We can do that?" I asked.

It seemed too obvious and simple to work. Could it be that easy?

"Of course we can," Morgan said.

Desperate for a solution, any solution, I told Morgan to go ahead. He could offer the grandson as much as we had in the bank, which was about $30,000. I was ready to spend every last penny we had, so convinced was I that getting rid of the Old Lady would change the building.

"Use all of it, if you have to," I said.

261

"Let's see," Morgan said, solemn as always about our chances.

As it turned out, Morgan offered the grandson not $30,000, not $20,000, not even $10,000. He started the bidding at $3,000, and, quite unbelievably, the grandson took it.

Within twenty-four hours, the Salazars had not only got wind of the news but they had moved the Old Lady out of the building. As was the custom in the tenements, she disappeared in the middle of the night, the same way Lady Gomez had. There was no sign of anything having been moved out of the building.

By the following morning, however, someone else had sneaked in and taken up residence in the first-floor flat: the Old Lady's daughter with the big hairdo, Gloria.

Paranoia

Suddenly the dominoes began to fall, and the first one after the Old Lady was Olivia.

Her debt having been made public, the board had no choice but to officially fire her. Our number now incomplete, anyone could demand an election. And I was sure that someone would. I was by this stage paranoid – full of fear, doubt, suspicion, delusion, anxiety, distrust and a panicked sense of urgency. I was convinced there was an enemy, the still ill-defined, possibly nonexistent Other Side, just waiting in the wings to take over and drag the old building down again.

The way I saw it, the board would quickly be overthrown. Big Steve and Liberty and Hector and Choose Me Debra and Carmen and Eva would be the new rulers. Lucrezia and Little Robbie and Ponytail would take over the pavement permanently. The Old Lady's flat would somehow find its way back to the Old Lady – her daughter Gloria was obviously squatting there until this could be achieved – and we would be back to where we'd started.

No, it would be far worse.

The solution was obvious: we had to get rid of the Old Lady's flat as soon as possible. There was also a second flat we could sell, one in the other tenement from which Morgan had just got a delinquent renter evicted. The paperwork had taken months to go through the courts, but now the flat was ours. If we sold both flats, I told myself, got two new owners, two good owners who would be on our side, who would be...

Suddenly I had a terrible thought. Hadn't I been in this exact same place before?

Two flats. Two flats that I'd gone to court to get possession of.

A hopeless, ineffectual board.

A president I didn't trust and who had grown increasingly isolated.

A belief that our salvation lay in two new owners, Katya and DeeDee.

It had all happened before, and it had gone badly.

"We need to sell those two apartments as soon as we can," I told Paloma.

"I agree," she said.

Did she agree? Maybe. Had she agreed too fast? What could that mean? What is going on in her head? Am I hearing voices?

Kar-ma! Hey, Kar-ma!

Did Paloma smile when she agreed?

They have a petition.

A smile from Paloma was good.

Choose me! Choose me!

Maybe a smile wasn't good.

It's not safe to keep the documents there.

Black marble. I want black marble.

But what will happen after Paloma's door is closed? Will Freddie change her mind?

He's with Olivia. They're white.

The Bloods will kill you.

Can I trust her? Yes, no, maybe.

Parp-parp-parp, weeeeeeeeee, awe-eee-awe-eee-awe.

You want a white building.

Who was that I saw going into Paloma's flat? Was it one of them? Or one of us? Are we together? No, yes, it depends.

I'm going to kick your fucking head in.

Who was Freddie talking to on the street? What are they doing behind my back?

Fucking racist.

"We need to sell those apartments," Paloma said. "I agree."

DeeDee, who had cut all ties with Olivia and was once again friends with Paloma, agreed with everything Paloma said. So Paloma agreed with me, and DeeDee agreed with Paloma: we would sell the two flats without delay.

Morgan the lawyer said he could complete the paperwork as soon as we had our buyers in place. What would normally have taken months in New York Morgan would speed through in a matter of days. He knew the urgency. Paloma could change her mind at any moment, an election could be called, he could be fired.

There was only one problem: Gloria. Now that the Old Lady's daughter, Lucrezia's sister, Big Steve's aunt, was squatting in the first-floor flat, no-one would be able to view it. At least one buyer would have to put down his money without seeing what he was paying for.

Buyer No. 1

Within days a very keen buyer had turned up, and it was someone who couldn't have been more perfect for our lawless building: a New York City policeman.

When I first heard the news, I couldn't stop smiling. Fortune was finally on our side. It seemed like the most brilliant solution to all our problems, and it was one I'd never even considered. I had thought of getting help from the police but never of selling to them. We would bring the law not only into our old building but to within centimetres of Big Steve's drug den.

Both flats that were for sale happened to lie on either side of Big Steve, so I immediately had visions of the new owner using listening devices and mini-cameras to keep track of the goings-on at Big Steve's place. Yes, that's how our drug dealer on the first floor would be taken down in the end, with high-tech gizmos from the flat next-door.

It was genius.

The policeman wasn't anyone I knew – not Detective Chlumski or Sergeant Steinberg – but someone Paloma had found. During those days and nights that she had spent obsessing about the building, concocting plans, fixing things that didn't need fixing, Paloma and Freddie had started making contacts in the police force. Not content with the cops I had told her about, ones who knew the building, the Salazars, the street, Paloma had sought out her own cops and had kept her acquaintance with them a secret.

Why she had done that, I didn't know, and at this point I was beyond trying to figure out her motivation. I was just glad she had found us a cop. The fact that the policeman was, in fact, a policewoman somehow made the plan even more brilliant. A female cop would be even less tolerant of drug-dealing going on next-door to her, and Big Steve would be bust in no time.

I felt guilty for having doubted Paloma. Why had I been so worried? Why had I got paranoid? It had all been for nothing. Yes, she had turned out to be alright in the end.

But then, at the last minute, the female cop, who I never met, changed her mind. Not even the price, way below market value, could tempt her. Our flats were too small, our building too dirty, or something like that. At least that's what Paloma said.

She announced this very bad news only a few hours before we had arranged to meet the other potential buyers, and there would be no time to find another cop. My heart sank for the thousandth time. In this city of unlimited possibilities, every chance that we were offered to fix up the old building was snatched away from us.

"But," Paloma added quickly, "I have found another cop who is interested. His name is Jimmy."

Instead of being happy I was suspicious. The questions started again. How many cops did Paloma have up her sleeve that she could quickly find a second buyer? Had there ever been a female cop? Maybe Jimmy was the cop she'd had in mind from the start but didn't think it was safe to tell me. And why was that? What would I do with the information? Did she think I'd find my own cop? Would her cop be better than mine? The questions wouldn't stop.

Indeed, Paloma had known about Jimmy long enough already to have taken him on a tour of the old building. He had even decided which flat he wanted: the one in the second tenement that lay directly across the air shaft from Big Steve.

That meant the Old Lady's place was still up for grabs, the flat that could not be viewed. We still had to find someone who would be crazy enough to buy it sight unseen.

"Asshole"

I phoned as many people as I could who might want to buy a cheap flat. Their responses were the same I'd got when I moved into the old building.

"You've got projects across the street," they said.

I somehow managed to coax five people to come to the interview, although I knew that only one of them would be prepared to buy a flat sight unseen: the shy paralegal who had once lived opposite Carmen, in the flat now occupied by Heavenly. She knew the building, the problems, had applied to buy a flat before, and realised how unbeatable the price was.

We arranged to meet the candidates at a small restaurant on the Upper East Side that DeeDee had sometimes gone to with Olivia. It was far enough from our building that no-one would accidentally stumble upon us and cotton on to what we were doing.

Everything about the sales felt wrong, our actions secretive, hurried, unprofessional. This wasn't how you sold property, but I convinced myself, as I always had, that it was all for the good of the building.

I nervously kept looking out the window to Madison Avenue, expecting someone like Lucrezia to appear outside, staring at us accusingly. But the passers-by were mostly well coiffed and well turned out, and Lucrezia in her plain smock would have stuck out like a sore thumb.

Besides my five candidates, there was only one more. He had been found by Paloma, and as soon as he walked into the restaurant I knew the battle for the old building had really been lost. It was Freddie's brother. I had met him once or twice before, and he seemed nice enough, but his connection to Freddie didn't bode well. Having him in the building would also create another network, of which we already had enough.

I could see how things would go tonight: Paloma would vote for Freddie's brother, and DeeDee would vote the way Paloma voted.

For a very brief moment I thought of bringing up the fact that Paloma wasn't allowed to vote for her brother-in-law, but the last time I'd done that – with the sale of a flat to DeeDee – it had turned out badly. Plus, the shy paralegal was white and Freddie's brother was Dominican. Someone would bring up race, and the night would get even worse.

So I didn't bring up the subject.

It was now down to the final two candidates – the shy paralegal and Freddie's brother – the only ones prepared to buy the Old Lady's flat without setting foot in it. None of us said anything, not wanting to show our hands, until DeeDee spoke.

"She's white," she said, meaning the shy paralegal. "Every time a white person buys in the building, there is a problem."

A woman at the next booth looked over at us. Like everyone else in the restaurant except the waiters, she was white, although DeeDee didn't seem to notice.

"Olivia and Katya. Look at the trouble they caused," she said. Both women had been her friends at some point, but not anymore. "And you are the one who sold them apartments."

DeeDee was right. Both women were white and both had let

me down terribly. Even though it was Paloma and Hector who had sold to Katya, I somehow felt responsible for what had gone wrong. Olivia, Brunhilda and Katya had all proved true those long-held fears about white people: we were entitled, broke rules and would do anything to get a cheap flat. (Brunhilda, who had bought Paddy Murphy's flat, had just sold, the fastest-ever turnaround of a flat in our building.)

Yes, each one of them had screwed over the old building. If you wanted to judge the residents by their race, white people hadn't been particularly upstanding or worthy.

So there it was. The Old Lady's flat was slipping through my fingers after five months in court, walking the gauntlet, listening to conspiracy theories, enduring the conniving of Paloma and Freddie, never mind all the years of Hector that went before them. It was all for nothing. Paloma got the cop of her choosing in one flat, her brother-in-law in another.

"I like Freddie's brother," DeeDee said. She waited a moment before adding something no-one expected. "But you know, Paloma, you aren't allowed to vote for him."

Paloma struggled to control her shock. Here sat DeeDee – who barely knew the residents in the old building or the lease – bringing up the very same rule I had tried to use on Paloma when DeeDee was the candidate. What I couldn't get away with, DeeDee could.

"But that white girl," DeeDee repeated, turning back to me, "she could turn out to be just like Olivia."

DeeDee smiled, savouring her moment of power. She had Paloma and me in the palm of her hand. She could go either way. Shy white girl? Freddie's brother? Her vote would be the deciding one, and she knew it.

She smiled at me.

"You are an asshole," she said.

By this stage in the old building, I'd lost count of the times I had been called an asshole, a racist, insulted, accused, threatened – but this time I didn't care. I knew that DeeDee was about to do something I had repeatedly failed to do no matter how hard I had tried. She was going to change the course of the old building forever.

Van daz dick

The shy paralegal left the restaurant smiling a short while later, the Old Lady's flat now hers. Paloma, meanwhile, looked like she had been hit by a bus. How could DeeDee have turned on her like this? How was she going to tell Freddie that his brother had lost the flat, and that his very own "cousin" had been the reason? Freddie was not going to be happy.

At that moment the second new owner, Jimmy the cop, walked in.

He was tall and boyishly good-looking, if it weren't for eyes that always looked puffy from too many late nights. His surname was Hungarian or Czech, and even thought he didn't exactly have an accent, every now and then his words harked back to another country. "If" became *eev*, "have" *haff*, "but" *bud*, and his favourite expression was "you guys".

"I just wanna tell you guys I think you are van daz dick," he said.

He kept looking at me, like he needed to convince me he was worthy of buying the place, even though we were already committed to selling it to him. We had no alternative cop waiting in the wings. He *had* to be a new owner, our inside guy, our own personal lawman. It was Jimmy or nothing.

"I will do everything to help you guys," he went on. "You name it, I'll do it. You just wait. Eev there's anything you need, you just ask. I wanna be there for you guys, I wanna make the building a better place. I haff heard all about what you're doing" – again, he turned to me – "and I think it's so great. Van daz dick. I'm gonna get those drug dealers out. I been on the force ten years, and let me tell you the only way to get scum out is by force. You started it" – there it was: the look at me once more – "now I'm gonna finish it.

You guys picked me and you won't be sorry."

I was already sorry, because something about Jimmy made me feel uneasy. His talk was too fast, too smooth, and he said too much. Could our old building's losing streak also include the policeman we had just found to buy a flat? That wasn't possible.

"Bud I gotta tell you guys something," he said. Here it comes, I thought. "And you guys are gonna haff to trust me on this one."

Because of some weird, convoluted police regulation, Jimmy said, he wasn't actually allowed to own property in the same precinct where he worked. So what he wanted to do – "Eev you guys don't mind" – was to put the flat in his nephew's name and then to transfer it to his own name later on.

"I'm gonna do that as soon as I can," he promised. "I'm gonna get sent to another precinct any time now. It's gonna be soon. Believe me."

There was no time to check on whether such a regulation existed, and even if it didn't we were stuck. Leaving the restaurant that night I kept wondering whether Jimmy had intended all along to buy the flat not for himself but for his nephew. Was it possible he had no intention of moving in?

A bad movie

And move in Jimmy never did.

He claimed the flat was a wreck, which was true – the delinquent renter had even removed the toilet when he'd left – and it needed to be renovated, which Jimmy promised to do as soon as he had the money. The lease, meanwhile, stayed in his nephew's name.

"Don't you worry," Jimmy said. "I will renovate real soon and I will get the lease in my name."

"But what about our deal?" I asked. "The whole point was you were going to move into the building to bust Big Steve."

Jimmy was one step ahead of me.

"I know," he said. "But in the meantime, you are my eyes, man. You can see what's going on in the building. I gotta haff someone inside." He repeated himself. "You are my eyes."

Jimmy talked like that, like he was in a movie, and much of his behaviour added touches of mystery and suspense to a scenario that didn't seem to call for them. He made abrupt phone calls where he was careful to never say too much. He kept changing his phone number. He disappeared for weeks at a time, unreachable, only to return with no explanation but sounding like he'd been on a clandestine mission. When he was around, he set up meetings quickly and in odd locations. And at least once I saw him wearing a disguise.

Going out one evening, I passed a man standing at Paloma's front door. His jacket bore the logo of a pizza chain and he held a large pizza box. He was tall and wore a baseball cap, but he kept his face from me as I passed by. Jimmy called me the next day and told me that the pizza delivery guy had been him.

"You recognise me?" he asked.

"No," I said, "but why were you dressed like that?"

"Just zniffing around the building," he said, sounding pleased with himself. "You see? I'm there for you."

I never saw Jimmy with Chlumski, the drug detective in our area, even though he claimed to be in the same precinct. In fact, I always saw Jimmy on his own, wearing civilian clothes, and I sometimes thought he was simply a lone cop who had taken a special interest in our old building because he – or someone in his family – now owned property there.

When he returned from his top-secret missions he would call me sounding a bit breathless. I filled him in on the most recent late-night activity at the picnic table and the fire hydrant across the street or through our front door.

"Where are you right now?" he asked.

"I'm at home," I said.

"Meet me down at the drugstore in five minutes," he said and hung up.

I headed to the pharmacy a few streets away, wondering why

Jimmy couldn't say what he had to say on the phone. Were we being recorded?

When I got to the store I couldn't see him, so I wandered down the aisles. Near the back, between the shelves for detergent and toilet paper, I heard a voice.

"Psssst! Psssst!"

I turned and saw Jimmy, dressed in a jacket but no tie. He motioned me to the next aisle, the furthest from the entrance.

"We haff information on Big Steve," he said.

"Great. That's great news."

He looked around cautiously.

"There could be a bust soon."

He couldn't give me any details and, quite honestly, he could have told me this brief piece of information over the phone. Then he instructed me to wait a while in the back of the store and give him enough time to get out before anyone could see us together.

Domino three

On a sunny day a few weeks later – Jimmy had gone missing again and his number had changed – the next domino fell. After the Old Lady and Olivia, it was domino three.

Without any warning, two men with a jackhammer pulled up at the fire hydrant one morning and went into the grounds of the projects. They spent several hours smashing the little concrete picnic table to pieces, and then the four concrete seats. By midday there was just a mound of earth left behind.

It took only a few nights for the word to spread, but along with the picnic table the late-night activity disappeared: the cars from out of state, the men in luminous shirts, the thudding music, the interlopers. In the nearby playground, too, the benches were almost empty after ten at night. The darkness outside was filled only with the *kertuck-a-katuck* of trains in and out of the city – and occasionally Mister Winston's car alarm, still broken after four years. The brand-new quiet was bizarre.

The red car
The fourth and final domino to fall was by far the biggest:
the Salazars.

The eviction of the Old Lady had thrown the family into
disarray. Whereas in the past they had been very careful to cover
their tracks, act as lone operators, and pass each other in public
without saying a word, now they became reckless. Big Steve's sister
was the first.

Gimpy Hand had remained fairly consistent in her behaviour
the last six months, walking the Rottweilers from Big Steve's flat
every day, making her regular visits into the bowels of the projects,
dragging her one foot behind her, the bent right wrist leading
the way.

In May, the birds coming to joyous life outside at the start of
spring, I sat in my window enjoying the good weather. A train
from the north rolled down the tracks and into the tunnel south of
us, and a breeze blew through the length of my flat. The planets
were starting to align for our old building.

Right then a red two-door car pulled up at the fire hydrant
below me. I had given up long ago on using the binoculars to see
anything on the street, although this time I didn't even need them.
From where I sat I had a bird's-eye view right into the car because
its sunroof was wide open. Two young men sat up front, and one
in the back.

Their movements were erratic, like they were expecting
something to happen. They kept looking around towards the
viaduct, and the one in the back leaned forward repeatedly. Several
more trains motored up and down the tracks.

After fifteen minutes Gimpy Hand came limping past the
corner tenement, tossing her hair-curtain in front of her. She went
straight to the red car, looked into the front window and said a
few words to the driver. Through the open sunroof I saw her take
a fistful of dollar bills and then go into the projects. Five minutes
later she returned and handed the driver a brown paper bag.

273

It was the first time ever that I could call Chlumski and tell him I had actually seen something going on downstairs. I couldn't reach him, but it didn't matter. I knew that something on our street had changed.

Two days later, in the same place where the red car had been parked, a fight broke out. Gimpy Hand was there again but she stood to one side, near the mound where the picnic table had been. In the full light of day the fighters were easy to identify: Lucrezia Salazar and her brother, Little Robbie.

The reason for the fight wasn't clear, but they carried on for some time. Lucrezia did most of the screaming, her hands flapping, and the two of them crisscrossed the playground and the pathways of the projects, first her following him, prodding his shoulder, and then him behind her.

The Salazars, who had gone to such extremes to avoid communicating with one another in public, weren't just talking, they were shouting. It now became obvious to anyone that they were related. For the first time things were going badly for them.

By the end of the week Lucrezia's sister with the big hairdo, Gloria, had stopped squatting in the Old Lady's flat. She didn't have to leave – she could have kept us tied up in court for months – but, inexplicably, she did. And like her mother, she moved under the cover of night.

The following day we found the front door to the Old Lady's flat unlocked, and for the very first time the shy paralegal got to see what she had paid for. All the furniture had been removed, but the scooters belonging to Lucrezia's boys and lots of kitchen trash had been left behind. In several places on the walls where pictures had once hung there were fist-sized holes that must have been used for hiding things. I imagined Dead Eyes running from Sergeant Steinberg, stashing something away, and escaping through this flat and out the back window into the yard.

A few weeks later, Dead Eyes himself, who no-one had seen since he turned up at our first election long ago, was arrested.

Kaleidoscope

Now that the summer had begun in earnest and most of the outside noises – except Mister Winston's faulty alarm – were gone, I took to sleeping with my windows wide open. Out of habit maybe, I was startled awake one night, although instead of sounds there were lights, bright red ones that flickered off the walls of the projects.

Looking out my window, I saw a kaleidoscope of law-enforcement vehicles – blue-and-white police cars, unmarked black cars like Sergeant Steinberg's, and a red-and-white-striped ambulance from the fire department – all jammed near the viaduct blocking our street. A lone late-night train came out of the tunnel and made its ghostly way up the tracks.

By the looks of it, the vehicles had been there for some time already. Residents of the corner tenement were standing outside their building, most of them in their pyjamas. Mister Winston, the lady with white hair, the woman with the sour face who gave the finger to the police every chance she got, some holding the hands of young children. They watched as a stretcher was brought out of their building and taken to the ambulance. On it lay someone covered in a sheet, an oxygen mask hiding the person's face.

The next morning a few police cars were still parked outside. Cordoned off with yellow tape was a Jaguar that was parked at an angle, like someone had only had enough time to pull in halfway before escaping. A trail of blood ran from the driver's side, along the pavement and up the stairs of the corner tenement.

The Jaguar belonged to Lucrezia's son Ponytail. The young man who had stood sentry across the street from us had been shot in New Jersey, across the Hudson River, in a drug deal gone bad. Because Ponytail already had a police record in New Jersey, he didn't want to be caught there. Despite being wounded, he had driven across the river, to Manhattan, and sought refuge in a place where he felt safe – the corner tenement.

The godmother

After Ponytail's arrest, you would think anyone dealing drugs would be careful to stay away from the corner building. But Guapo, our old superintendent who had been appointed by Hector, was not. And he was the next person to go down.

Once again, the action took place in the dead of night, but this time it didn't wake me. Jimmy the cop called the next day to tell me what had happened. He never seemed to be directly involved, but he always knew the details.

"Guapo's been caught," he told me. "He sold cocaine to an undercover cop."

The speed with which things were happening was almost dizzying – Gimpy Hand dealing drugs in the open, Ponytail and Dead Eyes and Guapo arrested, a public battle between Lucrezia and her brother, the Old Lady gone, Gloria gone.

But that wasn't all.

"There was someone else in the apartment with Guapo," Jimmy said.

Even though I hadn't seen her around for a long time, I thought it might be Carmen's friend the lupus lady, Guapo's daughter. Or maybe it was Janice with the cackling laugh from the rat building. They all seemed to be connected somehow.

"Lucrezia," Jimmy said suddenly. "We got Lucrezia."

In all the years of things going badly in our old building, Lucrezia's arrest was the one scene that I really wished I could have witnessed. I tried to picture her being led away by the police, her hands unable to fly around in protest because they were in handcuffs, her Medusa-like hair pointing in all directions furiously, shouting "racist!", "you!", "us!" the same way she had the very first time I saw her on the pavement.

"There is more," Jimmy went on. "Zeems she is a much bigger fish than we thought she was. Zeems like she was a godfather – or a godmother – in the neighbourhood."

So, I had been wrong all the time. Big Steve hadn't been the leader, after all. It was Lucrezia, racing so industriously up and down the avenue and into the projects, constantly doing something, on her way somewhere, the leader of the petition, the person grandstanding outside, the voice of rebellion. I thought she had been on the side of the underdog, trying to save old man Rafael, when she'd really been trying to save her own drug business. And our old building had been much more important to her than I had ever imagined.

"She also gave us a name," Jimmy said.

"What do you mean?" I asked.

Lucrezia had cut a deal with the police. They would be more lenient with her if she gave them the name of another dealer.

"And you won't believe who that person is," Jimmy said.

Streetlights

The old building, despite the justice that was being meted out in bits and pieces to the Salazars, was still in a chaos all of its own.

The election I had feared never happened – either Choose Me Debra couldn't get it together or The Other Side was a figment of my imagination – but more skirmishes took place. Olivia, who now owed more than a year's levy, was being taken to court by us. Paloma and Freddie continued to scheme with Salvatore the manager and then deny it. The new superintendent Billy started to slack off. The insurance company kept phoning me about Dead Eyes' lawsuit. And Heavenly's dog bit someone in the hallway.

But somehow, and ever so slowly, things also seemed to be getting better. Eva no longer smoked on the stairs. The garbage was gone. Our bank account was healthy. Our trees were two years old and growing stronger by the day. Even the neighbourhood around us was shifting in a new direction. Streetlights were being repaired for the first time in years, more yellow taxis dared to come north of the Split, and it had been announced that this December we would get our first Christmas trees with lights like the rest of Park Avenue.

Change of some kind was on its way.

A ride with Jimmy

Jimmy, who I hadn't heard from for a while, called me out of the blue.

"Where are you?" he asked.

Jimmy always asked me this, as if he expected everyone to move around as much as he did.

"I'm at home," I said.

"Check out your window!"

"Which window?"

"The front one."

I went to the window, one of the pair that had led me to this flat in the first place, the windows I had looked out so many times over the past four years. But tonight I could see nothing outside, hear nothing. The after-dark visitors were gone. The picnic table was gone. Lucrezia Salazar was gone.

"What am I looking for?" I asked Jimmy.

"Me. Can you see me?"

"Where are you?"

"Look at the building past the projects."

The building in the distance had a few lights on in its windows.

"Are you inside?" I asked.

"No, on top."

"I can't see anything. It's too dark."

"Here. I haff a flashlight. I'm going to wave. Can you see me?"

A speck of light moved jerkily in the distance.

"What are you doing up there?" I asked.

"I'm looking into your building," he said.

"Into Big Steve's place?" I asked. Since Big Steve's windows were always covered in black plastic, I wasn't sure what Jimmy could see.

"No, not there," he said. "I'm looking into Carmen's place."

The fall of the Queen

I had probably suspected for a long time that something illegal was going on at Carmen's place, but I was never quite sure. I knew from the sisters, Shoshanna and Abbie, that she changed her phone number more regularly than seemed necessary. She spoke with few people – not once in four years did I ever see her publicly acknowledge Lucrezia or Big Steve – and her visitors were limited, mostly the lupus lady and the dwarf, who both shouted for her from the pavement. And like Big Steve, Carmen had made sure to always pay her levy on time.

Ever since the coup, though, Carmen had become conspicuously quiet. She hadn't attended the election or the meeting Choose Me Debra had called. Indeed, she and Choose Me Debra no longer met on the landing for their night-time chats. The dwarf still pitched up weekly, but the Tuesday shopping sprees grew more discreet; no more loose high heels clacking down the stairs, no more screaming, no more doors slamming, no more "Fuck, ma!"

With things in the neighbourhood heating up, Carmen was trying not to be noticed, for hers was the name that Lucrezia had divulged to the police.

As soon as Jimmy told me this, I found myself paying special attention to things at Carmen's. Coming home from an early copy-editing shift one day, in the mid-afternoon, I saw a woman in dark glasses get out of a livery vehicle and walk into the tenement while the car waited. I had never seen her before, and she looked like someone who didn't belong in our old building. She took the stairs slowly, letting me pass her, and as I was about to close my front door I heard her knock at Carmen's.

I edged closer to the stairwell to sneak a look at the woman. I couldn't see her or Carmen's door, but I could hear, a few minutes later, the stranger leaving. Then I saw her. Still wearing her sunglasses, she walked slowly down the stairs, got into the waiting livery vehicle, and off they drove. She was still holding the small brown paper packet she had got at Carmen's.

White powder

"Hey, it's me." Jimmy's voice on the phone was urgent. "Meet me around the corner, two blocks down. Five minutes!"

By now I was used to the vague orders. I hung up the phone and went straight down to wait in the middle of the block, watching passers-by and wondering what character Jimmy might be dressed as this time. A black car pulled up next to me, someone I didn't know driving. Jimmy, sitting in the passenger seat, leaned across.

"Get in!" he barked.

I jumped in the back seat and the car took a quick turn into a street moving west and across the railway line. A train rolled under us and shook the road. Jimmy turned to face me.

"I've got good news," he said.

"Yes?"

As the car waited for the traffic light to change, Jimmy made his revelation.

"An undercover cop bought cocaine from Carmen and Eva. They are going down."

Ponytail, Dead Eyes, Guapo, Lucrezia, and now Carmen and Eva. I had been after Big Steve, and he was the only one left standing.

"The raid is tomorrow," he said. "At four in the morning. You will hear us. It ain't gonna be priddy."

At eleven the following night, five hours early, pandemonium broke out on the fourth floor. Banging echoed from the hallway downstairs and up through my front door as well as up the air shaft. Someone was trying to break into Carmen's place.

I opened my front door to see what was going on, only to be confronted by a policeman with his gun drawn.

"Get the fuck back inside!" he shouted. "And stay there!"

Outside on the street, a dozen police cars had pulled up, but there were no lights flashing, nothing to give away their arrival. The voices below my floor started, but they weren't the gay screams, the murderous screams, the irritated screams that I had become used to over the years – "Baby, fucking shoes won't go on!" "Fuck, ma!" – they were screams of terror. Sometimes I could make out Carmen or Eva or the little boy, but there were other voices too. Carmen's parents were visiting from out of town.

The door finally gave way.

Added to the screams were a series of bangs, scrapes, thumps.

I tried to imagine what was going on in Carmen's flat – the voices I had got to know so well through the stereo coming through the floor and the windows – and part of me felt sad. I couldn't explain it, but no matter what Carmen had done, I felt sorry for her.

I don't know how much time passed, but finally Carmen and her family were taken away. The banging in her flat continued, so loud it sounded like they were tearing cupboards out of the walls looking for something. With the last sporadic noises coming from under my bed, I fell into a fitful sleep.

Early the next morning, I went outside. The hallway floors from Carmen's flat all the way down the stairs to the front door and out onto the pavement were coated with white powder. I imagined for a moment that it was cocaine the police had found, but it was only cake flour, the last garbage trail from Carmen's flat that would ever be left behind.

Within a few days of the arrests, Big Steve disappeared. He fled in the middle of the night, the same way the Old Lady and Gloria had. By the next day, someone else had moved into his flat. She was a sweet girl who claimed she was a Mormon and Big Steve's sister, which would have made her Lucrezia's seventh child.

She was also the last of the Salazar clan to ever turn up at the old building.

AFTERWORD

Many lesser battles followed over the next few years. Noah the old superintendent has never spoken to me again. Hector the former board president was knocked down by a car after wandering into the road drunk, and has since moved away. Miss Carol had a heart attack.

The sweet Ella May Washington died and, because she lived in the projects and did not fit into any of the networks spreading news in the old building, I only found out a few months later.

Mohammed died too. My fellow African who had refused to vote in any election or attend any meetings lay undiscovered in his flat for three days. It was only when he didn't come out to park his car that Mister Winston got worried; he climbed the fire escape and broke into Mohammed's flat, where he found the body.

Paloma kept fooling people with her pretty smile, until no-one trusted her anymore, which to her husband Freddie was the ultimate conspiracy.

Choose Me Debra on the fourth floor turned out to be not such a bad egg, after all.

Dead Eyes's five-million-dollar lawsuit never got anywhere, and the Salazars were paid a few thousand dollars by the insurance company to go away. Lucrezia is still around, but no longer walks near our street. Little Robbie we never saw again, although he did appear on television one night. Completely by chance I caught a news item about a teenager who had been fatally shot in a drug deal gone wrong. I heard the surname, the mother's name, and suddenly I realised it was the child of Lucrezia's big-hairdo sister Gloria, G Happy Smith, the head of the substance-abuse group who had vouched for Big Steve and squatted in the flat on the first floor for a few months. Her son had sometimes stood outside the old building with her when they came to see the Old Lady. After the shooting, Little Robbie was the family member interviewed on television, and he kept saying this was a mistake, that they had killed the wrong person and his family had never dealt drugs. He was still talking when I turned off the television.

Olivia was eventually evicted, owing as much money as poor old man Rafael once had. At the final meeting she ever attended Olivia made an appearance that no-one there will ever forget. Convinced she was being victimised, she began throwing her hands in the air, screaming and swearing – at me, at our lawyer Morgan, at anyone – and suddenly she was transformed into the person she most despised, Lucrezia. All of us sat there in our funny little basement transfixed: the train wreck we had all expected to see at Choose Me Debra's meeting had finally taken place.

I have never been able to figure out what was behind Olivia's bizarre mix of empty promises, easy lies, bigotry and undeserved entitlement. But of all the residents in the old building who taught me some nasty truths about human nature, no-one was more effective than the white woman with the toothy smile. Happily, I've never come across Olivia again.

Jimmy the cop continued to disappear for months at a time on his "secret" missions and never moved into his flat. He renovated it for a small fortune and let his nephew live there until he sold it several years later. To this day I'm not sure if Jimmy ever had a role in the disappearance of Big Steve and the fall of Lucrezia and Carmen. I'm not even sure any of them found out he was a cop.

Nor do I care. Most importantly, the drug dealers are gone, and the old building today is quiet and clean. The last flat to be put on the market fetched over three thousand percent more than I paid for mine: $320,000 (or, going by the most recent dollar: rand exchange rate, R3.5 million). My piece of Musgrave Road, in other words, has now become Strand Street, and the Monopoly game has turned out thirty winners.

The residents today are more diverse than ever: Puerto Rican, Dominican, African-American, Indian, South African, Chinese, Russian, Polish, Korean, New Zealander, Colombian, Irish – a building of immigrants, you could say. The old building, meanwhile, is a pleasant enough place to live. The board has regular meetings, our bank account is healthy, our superintendent from Turkey keeps the place clean, our managing agent responds to calls, people go to meetings (even Mister Singh), and residents – except, of course, for Maria and Veronica Laundry – pay their levies. And the street outside is, for the most part, peaceful. (This is New York City, after all.)

I still consider myself an immigrant, an itinerant, ready to hop on the next plane back to Africa, convinced that I should have left New York as soon as I fulfilled my dream of getting a book published here. That book turned out to be the one that came from my late-night trips onto the streets looking for collectors. I called it *Mongo: Adventures In Trash*. But something stops me leaving, and I sometimes wonder if it's not the old building.

The two tenements sucked me into a local drama that I never expected and which, at the time, I thought was quite exceptional. But it wasn't. I have since learnt that ours was just one drama out of millions playing out in apartment buildings across New York, and probably in every apartment building in every city in the world. Each one has its own liars, thieves, saints, gossips and little old men named Rafael, and each one guards its own secrets.

Sometimes, bizarrely, I miss the old world. I wake up in the dead of night and hear the stillness. I don't miss the thudding cars shaking our walls, but something feels amiss about the absence of voices and sounds coming up the air shaft. I think of Carmen clicketying down the stairs on Tuesdays, Eva plaiting a boy's hair, old man Rafael's nephew collecting soda cans by night. And I can't help smiling just a little at the memory of Lucrezia's fire-and-brimstone sermons on the pavement. Looking back on that world, it seems wonderfully colourful, but that might be my memory.

Without them the street and the old building have become, dare I say it, bland.

But that was the choice, in the end. We could live in chaos with never a dull moment, or we could live in an order that was peaceful and predictable. Part of me wants both but knows that's not possible. And so our once-graffitied hallways, now newly decorated, bring to mind less each day the unexpected world that I first found here.

ACKNOWLEDGEMENTS

There is a hero in *Flat/White*, and that would be the doorman at the St Regis, the man who asked me if I wanted to buy my flat, Paddy Murphy. (His name, like most names in the book, has been changed for obvious reasons.) Paddy always did the right thing and tried to make the old building better, although few people ever gave him credit for it. Instead he was insulted and despised. So, wherever he is today, I say thank you, Paddy, for opening up the door to a strange world.

Ella May Washington, before she died, was a good woman, and tall, bow-tied Morgan was a good lawyer, and both earned my deep-felt gratitude through the bad years.

Catherine Stock gave me a huge helping hand when I first arrived in New York, and long afterwards, and I can never properly repay her for what she did for me. Claire Dippel at Janklow & Nesbit has encouraged me over and over again to write what I believe in, even when she hasn't needed to and especially when others told me to give up. I can't tell her how much that has meant.

Andrew Alpern gave up precious time to show me around Park Avenue and explain at length the history of its gorgeous apartment buildings, the other side of the New York coin to our old tenements, and how strangers living together in one building was once scorned upon and called unthinkable.

Thanks, finally, to Tim Richman for being open to reading the story of an old building thousands of kilometres away, and for letting others read it too.

THE BUILDING - 2014